Yoga inVision 9

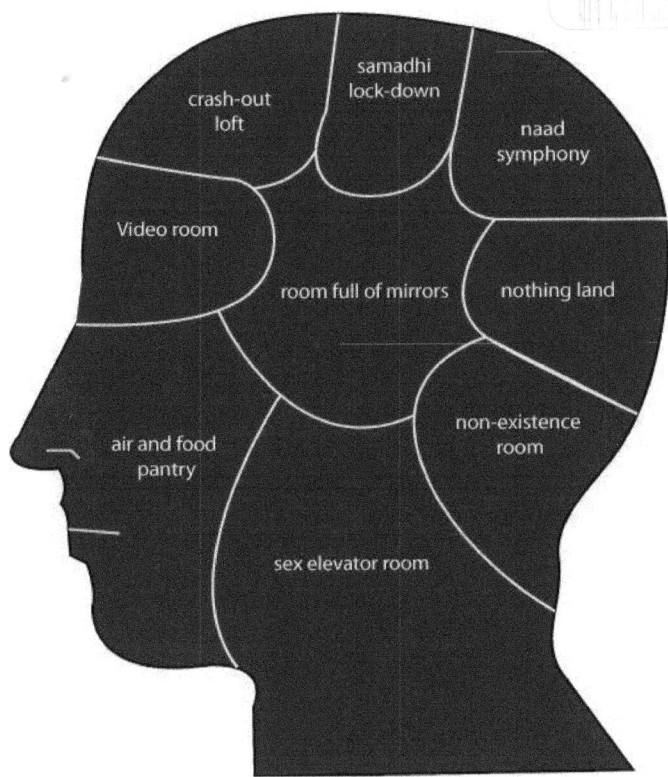

samadhi
lock-down

crash-out
loft

naad
symphony

Video room

room full of mirrors

nothing land

non-existence
room

air and food
pantry

sex elevator room

Michael Beloved

Shiva Art: Sir Paul Castagna
Illustrations: Author
Correspondence:
Michael Beloved
19311 SW 30th Street
Miramar FL 33029
USA
Email: axisnexus@gmail.com
              michaelbelovedbooks@gmail.com

Paperback ISBN: 9781942887249
eBook ISBN: 9781942887256
LCCN: 2019919807

Table of Contents

INTRODUCTION

This is the ninth of the Yoga inVision series. It relates experiences and practices done from September to October, 2011. These give beginners ideas of the physical, psychological and spiritual experiences one may have when doing asana postures, pranayama breath-infusion and *pratyahar* sensual energy withdrawal. Beyond that is higher yoga, which Patañjali named the *samyama* procedures. He defined *samyama* as a combination of *dharana* deliberate focus, *dhyana* spontaneous focus and *samadhi* continuous spontaneous focus. During practice, these progress one into the other. If one is expert at *pratyahar* sensual energy withdrawal, one may graduate to *dharana* which is deliberate focus of the attention to a higher concentration force or person. As soon as one masters *dharana* one may slip into *dhyana* which is an effortless focus on a higher concentration force or person. Once you practice *dhyana*, *samadhi* happens as the continuous effortless focus on a higher concentration force or person.

Many persons on a spiritual path feel that they can construct a process as they advance. This idea denotes failure. After all, if the supernatural and spiritual environment, is not already there, no one can create it now. It is either there or it is not. For instance, if one intends to moves to a different country, then of course one will fail if the country intended does not exist. It has to be there prior. Similarly, what you aim for as spiritual life, must be there already, or one will find that the aspiration is incorrect. This is why I speak of a concentration force or person. I could have said concentration person or divine person, or God. I did not because I do not know how anyone's spiritual path will develop.

One may leave an island in the safest boat and still the vessel may sink. One should keep one's mind open and be willing to work with fate. In spiritual development, there is providence too. What one desires to have one may not achieve. What one wishes to see may never appear.

These *Yoga inVision* journals show how sporadic my course of yoga was. This is after years of practice. It gives some idea of what to expect. Once you get through the lower yoga practice, you will see advancement in a more stable way but it may be incremental, accruing little by little, with bright flashes here and there.

Part 1

Buddha's Practice Overview

During breath infusion practice, this morning, a Buddha Deity from South Korea contacted me by a transmission of his subtle form into my body. His subtle form was all light, a light-gold color inside, sheer light and nothing else. His discussion was this.

The ascetics should use whatever method is effective and should not be idle in locating and implementing procedures. For instance, I went to India to find methods. I got some. I continued on my own. It is not that I rejected the methods found in India. I used those methods and moved from where I was, advanced on and on. When I got to the end of those methods, I struck out further on my own.

When you explore an isolated region, you may begin from a city by a means of transportation. When you get to the end of the route for that conveyance, you get directions from persons who are familiar with the area. Someone will say, 'Go here. Then go there.' At last you will reach the end of civilization. You contact aborigines. You will ask them for directions. Some old geezer may know the place. Or someone may have heard of it but never went there. He will tell you what he knows. He may take you to the edge of a territory. He may give warnings. You continue on your own.

I was on my own. For most seekers, self-discovery will turn into shambles, into abject failure. They need direction from others but only in what these others honestly and consistently practiced. No one should be so attached to a method that when a better system is available, he or she rejects it. Seek productive methods. Gage them by the way you progress and by the increased psychic perception, they yield.

Third Eye /Intellect Comparison

Since I did the agnisara subtle abdomen elimination practice of Swami Rama, meditation after breath infusion was different this morning. It usually resulted in third eye opening but this morning during the infusion in the lower part of the body there was a special clarity. Thoughts which came from others or which lingered in the psyche from before, were forced down into the body to the area which was infused. They were dissipated by the infused force.

Agnisara is a subtle abdomen elimination procedure. It begins with infusion from the navel down, through a tube which is about two inches in diameter and which travels from the navel down the center of the body at a slant through the pubic floor. When that is first done and when that tube is cleared of grayish energy, there is a

navel

down tube

switch to another part inside the subtle body. The yogi does not try to control or dictate this switch. It happens automatically. Breath infusion causes switches in the subtle body.

Because of efficient breath infusion, the physical eyes turned up into the head as soon as I sat to meditate. This meant that no effort was made to do this. The eyes were pulled by a mystic force which was generated by the infusion. One can sit to meditate and then force the eyes up but this is not that practice. This is when the eyes moved of their own accord. One notices that this was done. One observes the pulling force.

When this happens automatically it means that the energy which coursed through the optic nerves was retracted. This is a pratyahar attention retraction practice. In the *Meditation Pictorial* book, there is a third eye blast practice. In that one can practice to pull the eyes but the objective is to discover the optic nerves and realize that they are a primary cause of leakage of psychic energy out of the psyche.

One should find the optic nerves, the energy which courses out of the psyche through them and retract that energy. When the eyes move up spontaneously, it means that the energy through the optic nerves reversed by itself. The yogi no longer has to exert for that practice.

This is a glory day for a yogi when the effort for *pratyahar* sensual energy restraint is successful. The energy which tracks out of the psyche through the optic nerves is a large leakage of psychic power. If by doing the breath infusion practice that leakage stops, the yogi achieves the fifth stage of yoga, which is *pratyahar*.

The next discipline is the sixth stage which is dharana linkage (not mergence, not oneness) of the attention of the yogi to a higher concentration environment or extra-dimensional place or person. This begins with the dismissal of third eye focus. The reason why third eye focus is dismissed at this stage even though it is a very advanced and desired practice before this is:

The yogi focuses on the intellect which is a psychic organ, a globule. This is called buddhi in Sanskrit. In chapter two of the *Bhagavad Gita,* buddhi yoga, yogic control of the intellect, is discussed.

The third eye has importance but it is nothing in comparison to this intellect which is a psychic organ in the head of the subtle body. We normally think that it is our ability to analyze and understand but that function is done by a psychic organ.

This adjunct is troublesome but it is the gateway to supernatural perception from this level of existence. It is known by its location. Initially one should be confident of how I describe it because one cannot see it. Initially one knows it by taking note of the location of thoughts and images which appear in the mind. Wherever those impressions arise, that is its location.

When the energy pouring from the eyes spontaneously retract, one should note that as a signal of approval that one shifted to an advanced level.

One should locate the attention energy which comes out of the sense of identity which surrounds the coreSelf. This attention energy will be like a ray of light or like a flickering ray. This should be used to make contact with the intellect which is like a crystal ball which one focuses. The ray of attention is directed into the intellect.

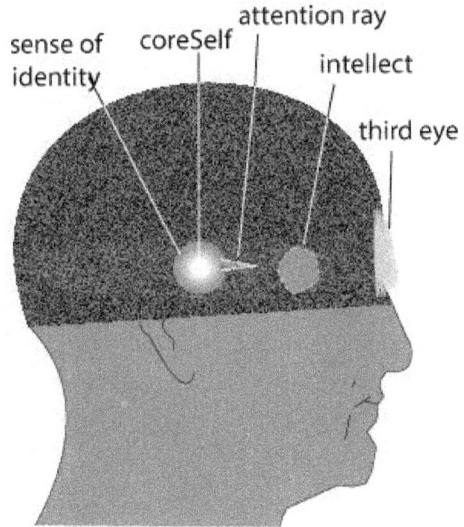

sense of identity   coreSelf   attention ray   intellect   third eye

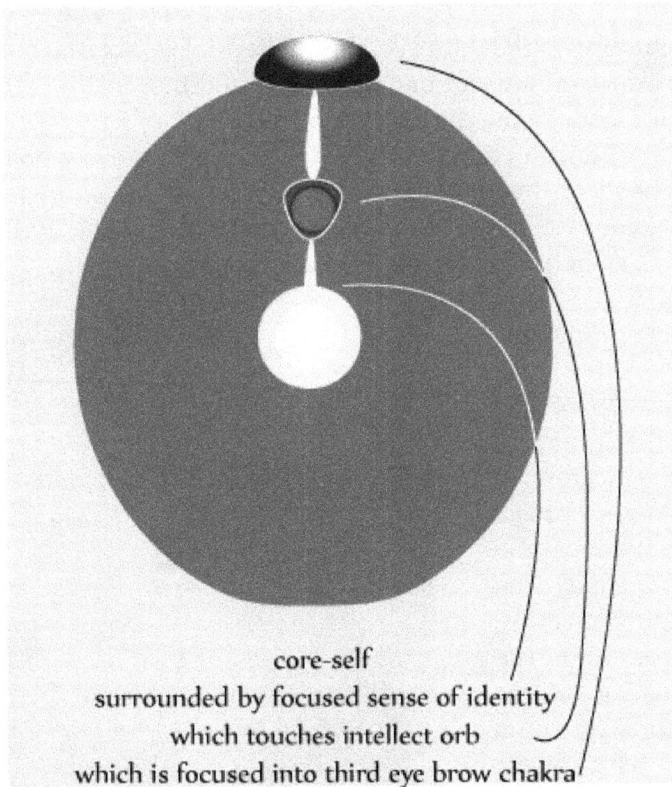

core-self
surrounded by focused sense of identity
which touches intellect orb
which is focused into third eye brow chakra

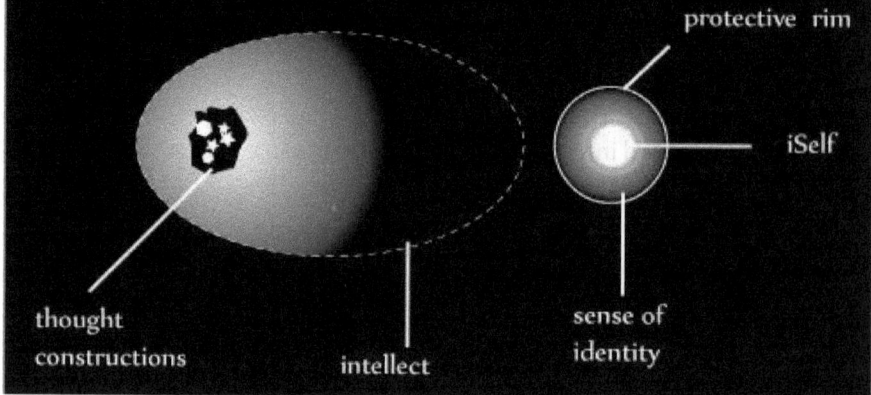

iSelf and sense of identity escaped from influence of intellect. Thought constructions shrink due to lack of energy supply from sense of identity.
Sense of identity centralized on iSelf and with protective rim, after abandoning entertainment show of intellect.

protective rim

iSelf

thought constructions

intellect

sense of identity

In comparison to the third eye, the intellect is like a crystal ball while the third eye is like window which one peers through. One looks into the intellect but one peers through the third eye.

Another distinction between these is that the third eye is on the surface of the forehead of the subtle body in between the eyebrows, while the intellect is about half way between the coreSelf and the surface of the forehead. Location is important in distinguishing the psychic apparatus

Appearance of the third eye chakra may be similar to the diagram. In the example it is not like a window because the energy is opaque. One cannot see through it. The black center is the window opening but it is too small to allow vision through it. Its darkness prevents clarity.

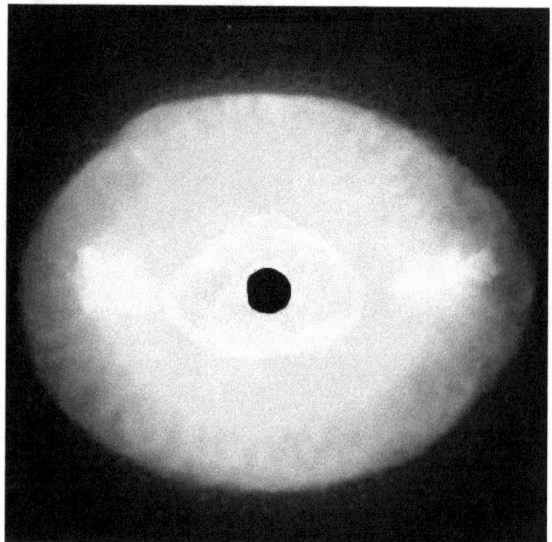

This is the third eye chakra which is a bit different to the third eye as a window through which to view other dimensions. In its feature as a window the black center will open as a clear space. One will see through it either close-up or from far away.

The intellect cannot be seen like that because its vibration is too high to be perceived in that way. One can see it in a lower frequently vibration when one day dreams.

Practice this instruction below regularly in meditation and one will see it:

Sit quietly, either in a dimly lit or dark room or in a forested area where no human made noises are heard. Think of something that happened long ago. Try to visualize the incident.

Some of this visualization will be imaginary but some of it will be actual memory. In some experiences suddenly you will find yourself peering into the mind so that the experiences occur as a factual replay.

The perception instrument which does this visioning is the intellect. You will see the scene from a certain mental distance, with a laser focus and in a clear translucent area. That area is the imagination faculty of the intellect.

Another way to see this intellect is that it is located between the coreSelf and the object being pursued. It is also located where the thinking and imagination takes place in the mind, except that there it does not show to the self. Instead of seeing it the self sees what it displays.

Thought Control

When following the Patanjali meditation method, thought control is vital. He instructed that thoughts be banished along with image constructions and imaginative activity of the mind. The tool in the mind which constructs thoughts is the same psychic gadget which creates visualizations and imagination. If it stops this activity for a time, it develops into accurate supernatural perception, something that is a must for those yogis who are desirous of going to higher environments, into a spiritual place which is free from the reverses which are experienced in an ever changing temporarily-configured world.

There are many methods of thought control but most of these are haphazard processes which do partial regulation of the psychic tool which constructs thoughts. The achievement is to perceive the instrument which produces thoughts.

The common experience is that the mind produces thoughts and ideas. However, in my experience, one psychic organ, the intellect, produces the ideation.

It is important to understand how thoughts are produced. Chasing thoughts in the mind endlessly, trying to control them day after day in meditation, is the primitive and very ineffectual way of thought control. One should find the thought producing psychic mechanism and deal with thought control in that way.

My Depressed Featureless Silent Mind

This morning, meditation after breath infusion was ideal, in the sense that there were no thoughts produced by the intellect. That psychic instrument was silent. Where it was located, there was an upward pushing force which forced the physical eyes upwards and which on the psychic side, felt like a constant gush of supernatural wind moving upwards, blowing everything upward.

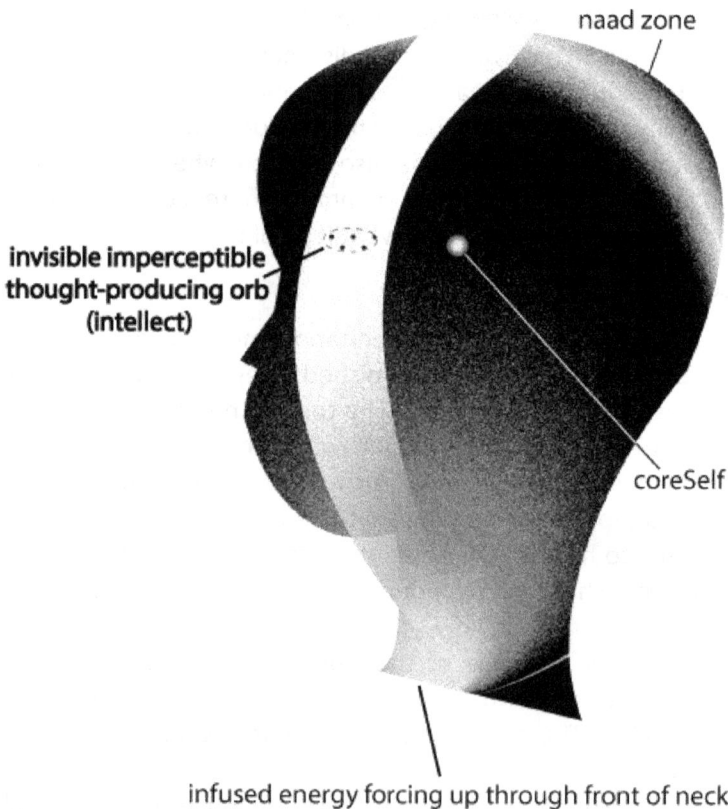

naad zone

invisible imperceptible
thought-producing orb
(intellect)

coreSelf

infused energy forcing up through front of neck

After ten minutes of this, the space in the frontal part of the head no longer had that psychic gush of wind, which was the infused breath energy rising. Instead everything was silent. I moved into naad sound while keeping in touch with this silence in the front.

Usually the frontal part of the brain obstructs meditation practice. That part of the brain is involved in nuisance thoughts and image construction which distracts the meditator. In this practice, due to the breath infusion, the frontal part became cooperative. I could use it along with naad sound in the back.

Patanjali required that the meditator remain in that *no thought* condition for some time. A student may have difficulty with this *no thought* situation because this state may be boring. To get away from the boredom one should listen to naad and should discipline the mind, causing it to give up its hunting habits which conditions it to physical and mental excitement.

Boredom means that when the mind is silent, it assumes a low quality tasteless depressed state, which is disliked by the self and which causes the self to hunt for excitements. The excitements enliven and entertain the child-like self. This becomes a habit where the person hates to be alone.

To break the boredom, the person craves newness and variation. This is due to the low quality of a silent mind. The breath infusion practice rids the self of this low quality tasteless mental and emotional condition.

Avoiding Astral Horrors After Death (October 2011)

Possession by others is common in the astral world, especially when a person assumes a ghost subtle body hereafter. I may not recall the story very well but when I was in High School there was a school friend who took pleasure in hitting others in a hurting way. He had a muscular body which many other boys did not have. He struck others in spots that were tender and painful. Then he would smile.

Sometimes teachers punished him but many times he did it when teachers were absent or inattentive. Recently within the last three months I got premonitions about death, I was with this person in the astral world. I have not seen him in over forty-five years in this body, either physically or astrally. Still I was with him in a place which is an adjacent astral realm to the place where we grew up in South America. He attempted to hit in tender parts, even in the astral world.

One can see hell hereafter. Hell is not merely a state of mind. There are hellish locations in the astral dimensions. As in this world we have prisons and we can imprison ourselves mentally by destructive lifestyles and thinking patterns, the same holds true for the astral realms.

There is a story which is in many of the Puranas from India, about Ajamil (uh-jaa-mel). He grew up in a religious family which had a good reputation. Somehow, he got involved with a prostitute. She introduced him to sexual pleasure. That gave him happiness. The woman bore children for him but his relatives shun him because he degraded the family.

Later, on his death bed, when he was to leave the physical body, his sensual perception shifted to the astral side. He saw apparitions. He saw ghost police who were armed to hurt subtle bodies. They tied him by the neck and yanked his subtle body to displace it from the physical one. Being scared, Ajamil called his son, whom he had named after the God, Narayana.

The point is that when it is time to die, if I get disoriented and if I see psychic things which are not to my liking and which are threatening, I will call my living relative(s). In fact, one major way of escaping from having to deal with resentments and inconvenient claims in the afterlife is to take shelter in the body of a living relative.

Even if I do not believe in reincarnation, I will after death, instinctively take refuge in my child or children or in anyone who is dear to me or is fond of me. Through that energy I may get the next body.

Rebirth as Compensation

Elders in the family have every right to influence the youngsters to beget children. Commitment to care for progeny is the only method by which the family can extend itself into the future. If a family does not beget children, that family becomes extinct.

Since I was serviced by elders who cared for my infant body, it is reasonable to expect that they will need compensation. Of course, good people in this world are supposed to do things selflessly.

When one needs the next body, many previous selfless acts may be reimbursed when one bargains with would-be parents to acquire an embryo.

My next mother, who may be my current grand-daughter may avoid pregnancy altogether. Suppose she wants to keep her body fit for the life of a celebrity? Or supposed she wants to be successful as an fulltime entrepreneur?

What should I do? Wait until she is 45 years of age when her career developed?

What is reasonable?

A human body is not free. As soon as one gets it, one is obligated. One takes a loan in the form of the services which are performed by the parents, medical professionals and educators. If an ancestor, who supported the body in infancy, passes away, what right does that person have to demand an embryo and the caring services for its infancy?

What is Beyond control

There is much unfairness in the human societies. Everywhere one goes one can observe this. What can be done about it? If I can correct something I do so but if I cannot I do not lose sleep over it. This is not indifference but it is rather, knowing my time and place and recognizing that the cosmic energy is in charge, not me.

It does not matter if what happens is right or wrong, what is important is if it is my duty to be involved. If it is not, it is not my concern. For instance, right now there are farmers in the Amazon jungle who spray pesticides which kill millions of ants, ruining their little civilizations. What should I do about it? There are planets in space which are impacted violently by comets. Should I go into space and stop this?

But there is a greater concern which perhaps we overlook. That is why these things happen in the first place. What force, person or thing permits this? Why is there disease in the first place? What power imposes undesirable things?

Why will the earth be drawn into the sun sometime in the future with everything being burnt and nothing being left not even ashes?

Blaring Naad

This morning not one of my yoga gurus was present astrally during exercises. When the teacher is absent, the student should continue the practice.

I worked on the agnisara abdomen infusion. During the session, there was a shift from the navel-down tube to a tube which runs along the spinal cord on the outside of the spinal cord inside the body. This tube begins under the brain in the neck and goes all the way down. At first, I tried to infuse it from its top but I could not locate the top of it. Then I tried to infuse it from where the lowest part of the neck is but that failed as well.

I continued the rapid breathing. A passage opened in this tube like a slot. This was in the tube behind the chest area. The infused energy went into the tube at that point and then it went down. I infused this and flushed it from that area downwards.

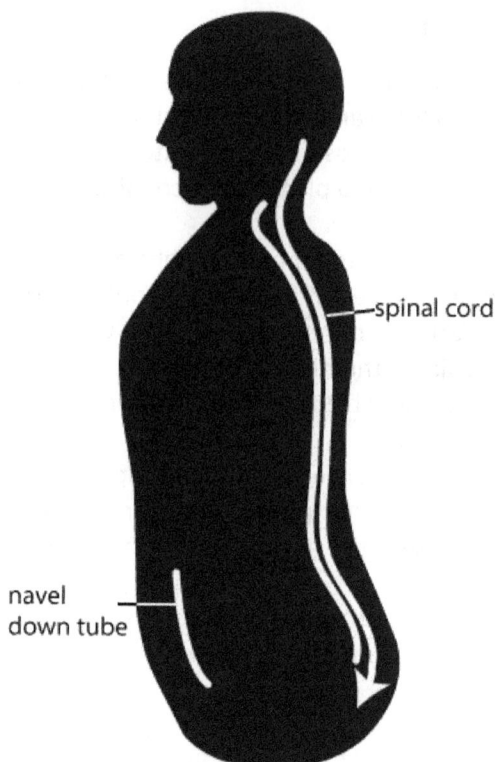

spinal cord

navel
down tube

When I sat to meditate, naad sound blared. There was a particular expression from naad going to the outside rather than its usually focus into the psyche. From where the right ear is, naad blared to the outside of the subtle head. It had a sharp treble frequency as its primary expression. It had many treble sounds added to that like little pieces of glass falling and making a sound when they hit a marble floor. I could be on the inside of the psyche and hear the sound on the outside and then go on the outside and feel its blast force outwards.

After this I decided to do a compliance-with-Patanjali meditation which is being in the silence and having no interest in the thoughts-image-idea apparatus. Because of the infused energy which caused the eyes to move upward and caused a pushing force to push up on the frontal part of the head, the thought-producing apparatus disappeared. This caused it to curb back around the top of the head.

Sitting in the head as the coreSelf, I realized that the infusion caused a pratyahar practice all of its own. In this the energy from the front of the head came backwards with great force, like flowing through a funnel which was flared towards the front and which ended at the coreSelf. That energy came backwards, like multiple trains suddenly reversing and travelling into the central terminal in a city at rapid speed and then vanishing into nothingness This was experienced for fifteen minutes.

This practice helps considerably to cause the yogi to become detached from sensation in the physical world and in the lower astral places. The craving for sensation is a force to contend with. Unless it is curbed the yogi faces failure.

Swami Rama's Moral Breach

One way to be in an ashram if you are not in one, is to be consistent in the practice of postures, breath infusement and meditation.

Association with great yogis comes through consistent practice. This morning during practice, I had a visit from Swami Rama. He showed the top of the agnisara abdomen passage which is from the bottom of the brain above the neck descending through the body on the inside part of the body running parallel to the spine. Yesterday I looked for the top but could not locate it because the psychic visibility where it began was nil.

He showed that there is no set top to it, hence I could not discover one. There is a region on the top. It is a round cloud of energy. As one goes down into it one sees nothing because the energy is like a mist. Suddenly, one finds oneself in a tube.

Besides this, Swami Rama wanted to make some points about criticism which was leveled to him when he used a body. He was accused of having sex with some female students and of begetting a child with one student. Without discussing details of these charges, he said this:

For a yogi there are three departments

- *degree of proficiency*
- *isolated lifestyle*
- *social interactions*

People usually lump these together because they do not see distinctions. However, these are distinct accounts. To learn yoga, one may have to go to an ascetic whose social interactions are in shambles or even are immoral. There is a story in the Mahabharata *about the ascetic who sold meat. A brahmin was instructed by a woman to go to this meat-selling ascetic for teachings. That is in the* Vyadha Gita.

If someone wants to learn advanced yoga, he must get techniques from someone who is proficient because one cannot learn everything from books or even by discovery. Much can be discovered and much can be learnt from books, for example from the Bhagavad Gita *of Lord Krishna or from the* Hatha Yoga Pradipika *of Swatmarama. Still, one will find that certain aspects must be learned from one who is proficient.*

Suppose that person is a butcher, debauchee or murderer, what should one do? Will one refuse to go to the teacher? There were legal cases, in which the government sends one of their agents to a criminal, a well-known murdered who was on death row, to get information to save the country from military attacks.

Even though a person's behavior is immoral, even if it is wicked and inexcusable, still sometimes if that person is proficient, one must take instructions from him. But of course, this should be done with care since a student should not adopt the immoral teacher's behavior.

A sannyasi should not have association with females. It is prohibited in the Vedic system. Still, as a sannyasi, I was circumstantially involved with females and so I am casualty. The rule says that a sannyasis should not associate in private with his mother or sister even, what to speak of a female to whom he is sexually attracted.

The old traditions which worked in the old societies fall apart when they are applied in the modern situations. Without the protection of society itself, anyone who takes the monk position and who lives in a society that does not isolate men from women, will more than likely breach his celibate vows.

Naad Focus

When I sat to meditate, naad sound was heard loudly and distinctly within a few minutes. The sound blared inside the subtle head from an emittance point where the right ear is located. A message from Swami Rama which entered the subtle head. It read:

Do naad alone this morning. Hours need be spent in naad to acclimatize the self to be without the sensations which it is accustomed to. The self is an addict to those sensations. During the stage of withdrawal, the treatment is naad sound. Hours must be spent listening to naad to break the addiction.

During this time with naad, I peeked forward. There was a sweep of light passing at the third eye brow chakra space. I immediately returned and stayed in naad as instructed. No attention was invested in the frontal part of the head.

Sort the Adjuncts

When light is outside the psyche it is comes from a chit akash atmosphere or from the supernatural level of the causal plane. Chit akash means sky of consciousness according to how Swami Muktananda translated it. Sky of consciousness is the entire existence of the spiritual world but the particular zone of it the yogi penetrates is the one that yogi gains access to. When the yogi sees that light, he may or may not know where it originated. Initially it is not important that he knows the origin. The important thing is to study the dynamics of how to make contact repeatedly.

If the yogi sees a bright light in the short distance inside the head of the subtle body, that is not from the chit akasha. That would be from either the intellect or from the sense of identity psychic organ. These two organs may be seen objectively as tiny sparkling lights.

However sometimes when these lights are seen, suddenly they act like a perception tool, like a magician looking into and through a crystal ball into another world which could be the chit akash or elsewhere.

When the yogi sees the light outside of the psyche, and when that light seems to want to strike the coreSelf with a force beam, usually that it is from the causal plane. It will strike either the intellect, the sense of identity or the coreSelf. The yogi may not know which of those components is struck. This is because the yogi may not be advanced enough to sort the adjuncts. Student yogis are usually in the mind-set that everything in the head of the subtle body is one, as one mind. They fail to distinguish the psychic organs and the core. That is not a fault of the yogi but it does prevent the yogi for further clarity.

Sun Environment

Some dreams are a mixture of astral reality and mind-created fantasy. It is important to observe how the mind interacts with the astral energy to create objects on the astral planes. One should know how the astral world responds to or resist one's creative notions.

A student should study this and become objective in dreams. One should awaken in the dream itself so that one realizes that one is in an astral place and the place is responsive to one's conscious and subconscious desires and motivations.

When I lived in Denver sometime around 1973-1974, I astral-projected daily at noon. I would lie on my back on a lawn so that the sun was in line with my brow chakra and then I would astral-project within fifteen minutes for the most. Sometimes I would transit from this planet to the sun.

If I referenced to the earth, I would be earth bound. I could recall when I lived on the sun in a body which instead of being made out of solid and liquid materials, was made of light energy. Imagine a place in which there is an environment which is made of light frequency with varying colors, even the vegetation and the buildings.

To go beyond the earth, the yogi must release himself or be released from the earth reference. So long as that is there, one's experiences will be limited to physicality.

Kundalini Neglect

During exercises this morning, Swami Rama appeared for a few minutes. He wanted me to focus on the sacral bone. This is the bone structure which is in the buttocks.

This place is usually hidden by the kundalini lifeForce system but when the yogi gets kundalini pulled into the head, he can infuse the rest of the psyche with fresh subtle energy. The real value in pulling up kundalini is that the yogi sees that what he took for granted was amiss. The normal configuration in the psyche is for the self to be lazy like a crippled king who can do nothing for himself and who is dependent on servants.

If that king dismisses the servants what will happen? He would be helpless. He could do nothing for himself? When the yogi pulls up kundalini, it is left for the yogi to infuse energy into the psyche. The yogi realizes that the kundalini lifeForce was a bungling incompetent all along. While the self, as king was laid back doing nothing but enjoying the benefits of its servants, like the kundalini lifeForce, intellect, sense of identity, senses and the memory. Some functions were not performed, especially by kundalini.

Instead of servicing the entire body aggressively the kundalini neglected certain parts. But this is discovered only after the self serves itself. It finds many energy-deficient areas in the psyche.

Swami Rama instructed that I work on the sacral bone. Then he faded away astrally. I focused on infusing that area. It was so dark and so de-energized that I realized that kundalini did not energize it.

Kundalini's main interest in an adult body is sex and social power. It puts it energies into manufacturing sex hormones and in doing whatever is necessary to maintain and promote the status. It is not interested in anything else. It neglects any and all parts of the psyche which are not directly related

to sex and status. Many of us live our entire lives with kundalini dominating for sex access and status pursuit.

After the exercises I sat to meditate. Swami Rama already convinced me that if one works on any energy deficient area of the psyche which is below the neck, that increased infusion energy would result in an advanced condition of mind when one sits for meditation.

When I first sat, naad blared loudly outside the right ear. I noted that but I got a message imprint which Swami Rama left in my psyche. It read:

Naad should be seen as nutrition for the self. It is a replacement for sensation. Let the self feed on naad and become saturated with it.

Monk who Married in the Astral

Last night in the astral world, I was with a sannyasi monk who was a member of a religious sect when he had his last body. We were in that sect at the same time some years ago but he compromised his principles in order to get a high position in the society.

These societies profess high standards but on the inside among the leaders there may be a tussle for power. If one wants to be senior, one must display certain principles, put on combat boots and fight for power over the institution and its followers.

As he is deceased and he knows that the guarantees of the institution did not work for him, and that he is in the astral world rather than at the zone of the deity of the sect, in the astral he organized himself in a religious way.

The first thing he wanted was to get married and have children. He told me that it was something he always wanted but that in the society, marriage was discouraged for those who wanted seniority.

He showed a woman to whom he would soon be married in the astral world. Even though it is rare in the astral world to see child bodies, this lady was accompanied by two children.

He wanted a ceremony and wanted me to participate. I told him that I was not interested, but I would do whatever I could to assist him.

After this another monk from the same sect who is still alive on the physical side and who manages a large temple for the sect, arrived. This monk discussed some issues. As he did so, I took the opportunity to disappeared.

A little while after, I found myself with the deceased monk again except this time he was in a Christian church. He was the pastor of the church. It was a large place, there were to have a marriage ceremony. He wanted me to clean the place. I began doing that.

After the place was cleaned, he came with followers. They had the ceremony. The woman was officially his wife. He got approval because in many Christian sects, marriage is a plus for seniority as compared to the sannyasa celibate monk status of the Vedic system.

After this we went into a room which was his room in the Church building. Immediately he began to explain that the walls of the room should be anchored in case there would be a tornado.

In the astral world there are tornados but their power is so tremendous that anchoring anything is a waste of time. I did not say anything about this to the monk. The other interesting thing is that because as a Christian he could fulfill family desire and also be approved as a religious authority, he transferred from an Indian religious system to the Christian one.

When one sees these lifestyles in the astral world, one is left to wonder about the dire illusions we are afflicted with in the subtle and physical circumstances.

Visit from Deity Earth (Oct 24 2011)

During breath infusion practice this morning, I got a visit from one of parallel forms of the earth goddess, who is known in the Vedic pantheon of deities as Bhumi Devi. The particular form of this deity was one wearing a flowing western type robe and not an Indian sari.

This deity appeared for about fifteen seconds and then vanished into thin air. As soon as this deity appeared, her left hand stretched out and in it there were golden grains of sand. These began flowing through her fingers and dropping away. When she first appeared, she said, "This is your share. This is your merit."

In a flash she was gone, disappeared into thin air.

It is interesting because whatever it was that she had in her hands, did not stop flowing through her fingers and vanishing into thin air from the time she appeared to the time she disappeared. If it was mine in fact, I was in no position to collect it as it fell through her fingers.

Whatever merit I have at this time, is gone anyway. That is the idea. Nature gives the merit or gives the opportunity for the performance of acts which result in merit. The same nature takes it away. It is done within a time frame which one cannot control.

Around the year of 1976, when I was in Roosevelt Minnesota, I saw the Primal Deity from whom this earth deity emanates. Since then I had not seen this deity or any of her parallel divine forms. At the time in Minnesota, I was with Sir Paul. Due to his deep interest in art, I did oil paintings. I did a large painting of that Primal Deity but I no longer have it. I recalled this because of what happened this morning.

When I saw the deity before, the galaxy seems to be shrunk to about the size to fit into the palm of her hand. All beings were within her purview. Her body was cosmic. In a book named *Mistress of Mistresses*, E.R. Eddison portrayed the deity as Fiorinda.

The cosmic power of this person Fiorinda is beyond anything a human being could imagine.

Beverford / National Karma (October 25th 2011)

During the night, I met Arthur Beverford. We were in an astral realm that was without disturbance, where the atmosphere was like the deep blue sky, littered with stars on a full moon night.

He wanted to discuss his focus on martial arts and the failure to make yoga his primary practice. In retrospect, he considered his life in his last body and said this:

Each generation carries a certain burden, call it karma or whatever. Mostly it is not personal karma because there is national karma. I was in the generation just after World War 2. We had to do certain things which seemed to be the priority. It was because of Hitler, Mussolini, Stalin and those persons who were undesirable rulers. Due to that we became occupied with defense. I traced it to that. This is the reason why yoga was not my primary practice. I should have developed the pranayama practices more.

I cannot blame Rishi for not stressing it. Even if he did I would not have regarded it with too much importance. The West was obsessed with survival, with war, with acquiring resources, with developing its civilization.

The same thing happens today with digital media. Regardless of its spiritual uselessness, youths in school will be forced to regard that as a priority.

O well, these things happen!

Association Affects Meditation (October 2011)

Bad association affects the next meditation session. Yesterday I attended a religious ritual. This was conducted by a priest who is fluent in Sanskrit.

When I did infusion breath, vibrations from the people who attended the ceremony, their thoughts which were directed to me and just the general atmosphere of the place, was in my mind. By mind, I also mean the intellect organ which creates and projects thoughts.

I spend at least twenty minutes, dealing with these ideas. At first, I shifted it from the head into the lower trunk. In one posture subtle energy went through the kneecap. I pulled the thoughts there.

Near the end of practice, I directly infused the intellect and that did it. The intellect changed. It no longer constructed thoughts nor illustrated vivid memories of thought and images.

A student yogi should study the mind chamber, identify the psychic components in it, and gradually gain control of the interactions of these organs in the mind.

Association with others is a main cause for irregular practice. There is a saying that one should be like the lotus leaf. If water falls on it, the water glides away. The leaves have a slippery surface which is resistance to wetness.

The idea is that a yogi should live in the hassle of a large city and not be affected. But this is so much of an untruth, that it is amazing that anyone ever said it. The truth is that unless one mastered *samadhi* practice, one cannot be that resistant to the circumstances.

To my view it is best to avoid association which will cause one's mind to digress into its impulsive and spiritually-destructive pursuits. Instead of staying with spiritual-depressing associations, it is best to live in isolation and astutely practice.

Sensation-Craving Psyche

During the night I was harassed by some persons from the island of Trinidad. When I checked to see how their subtle bodies reached mine, I saw that it was due to atmospheric astral energy, which provided a pathway from the astral side of the island to where I was located in the Southern United States.

There were six people in particular. Their main interest was to learn yoga and discuss meditation practice. When I rose to do breath infusion, they did whatever I did, to the extent of even superimposing their astral forms into mine frequently to get an inside look at what I did in the subtle body.

Yoga practice is more than physical actions. It is also psychic movements which cannot be seen physically. Due to being on the astral side these persons observed what I did within the psyche during the various postures which were combined with breath infusion.

Essentially, my exercise session was ruined. This happens when one teaches others, where to assist them one must divert attention to their practice.

When I sat to meditate, I reached naad sound and used it as a source for sensations. This prevented the intellect and the senses from pursuing sensations elsewhere.

The psychological part of the psyche is addicted to sensations. The need for gratification and experience through the avenues of sensations drives the psyche to do even self-destructive actions. To curb this one may focus on naad. The existential mouth of the psyche which craves the taste of various sensations, may be force-fed the naad sound. Eventually when the psyche appreciates naad, the self would be released from the sensation-craving tendency.

Kundalini Sex Adaptability

During practice this morning I related to four persons on the astral side. Two were astral students, people who are deceased but who come to do practice in the morning. Two others were from Guyana. These were shown yoga postures and breath infusion some years ago but had only a superficial interest.

Part of the time, I spent helping these people while doing my postures with breath infusion. As a result, my practice was confused with their practice which is very novice.

At one point during the session I realized that kundalini is adaptive to either a male or female configuration. Some students questioned before about the origin of the sexes, as to what determines if a body is male or female and as to if the spirit in the body is male, female or neuter.

Kundalini is adaptive. It may adapt to any sexual orientation. Sometimes when doing practice, with somebody of a different gender, one may find that one's kundalini force assumes the postures of the other gender. This is subjective proof that kundalini may adjust to another configuration. It does not answer the question as to the gender of the self. That is a different topic. Right now, everything is done by kundalini, more or less. The sexual identity of a self is irrelevant. Until we can bring kundalini to order, gender orientation cannot be accurately determined.

During practice, a friend came with the teacher, Iyengar. I did a special posture at the time, a Patanjali posture. My friend asked the guru about it and wanted to know if such postures could be combined with pranayama practice. Iyengar said they certainly can. He said that any posture can be combined with specific appropriate breath infusions. After that with his usual broad smile, they left.

When I sat to meditate, some ideas and energies from those four persons were present. That caused diversions from meditation for about fifteen minutes. After that everything calmed.

A yogi may be physically isolated but psychically bombarded, in which case, the meditation fails. For isolation to be complete, it has to be physical and psychic.

After the diversions were lifted, there was a flash connection to the cosmic intellect. This lasted for four seconds. Then there was a third eye flash opening. Naad sound streamed but the diversions were effective in causing me not to focus on it.

In yoga practice, there is always the possibility of being attacked by the effect-energies of past relationships. When these penetrate, they may come into the psyche of the yogi with such force as to end the meditation practice.

Special Breath Infusion Posture Inspired by Patanjali:

The practice of moving down into the body is part of kriya practice. This is done daily during the postures and breath infusion, but it is also done during meditation. The idea is to get to understand how the inside of the psyche is constructed, and to locate the psychic organs. Generally, we call the psyche, the subtle or astral body.

Chitakash is a combination of chit and akasha, which means higher consciousness or transcendence realm.

Hridayakasha is hridaya and akash, which is chest area and realm or the realm of the chest area of the subtle body. In some applications hridayakasha means the causal body which is in the subtle form but which is interspaced in its chest region.

Hridayakasha usually refers to the area above the navel. The navel is a special zone which segregates the other top parts of the body from the lower part below the navel including even the toes.

The subtle body is like the physical form, except that the subtle one comprises air and light energy (light like in sunlight).

Astral Students

With the help of science, we know that in the atmosphere there are trillions of frequencies. In fact, with our cellphones we can understand that human beings generate billions of special frequencies which they inprint with data, which travels through the air, enters a digital gadget and is represented in sensible way.

The subtle body has different frequencies which it can synchronize into. When someone exits the physical body and assumes the self objectively in the subtle or dream form, what really takes place is that the person's attention is displaced out of the physical system into the astral one. The astral one is synchronized into a specific energy range of the subtle world.

In the physical world one physical body cannot become interspaced into another physical form. In the subtle existence you can have thousands of bodies superimposed or interspaced into another. On occasion when I do yoga practice, a teacher may enter my subtle form. This happens because his body is in a slightly different frequency.

This morning as I did exercises, a few students who are on the astral side only, because they are deceased, superimposed their astral bodies into mine and imitated the postures and breath infusion which I did.

Before these students came which was about five minutes after I began the session, I was aware of another person who was there with me for the purpose of chatting. This other person was exposed to yoga before and still uses a physical body, but he is not serious about the practice.

This one has a physical body which lives in South America. After the two students who are deceased arrived in their subtle forms, the most advanced one asked if they should go away. That person said, "Since you have a guest, we will return tomorrow."

I replied, "No, practice whatever I do."

That person said, ": But we do not want to do practice in the presence of your visitor."

I replied, "You are thinking that this other person can see and hear you but that is not happening. Look careful. You will see that this other person has no idea that you are here. This other person cannot hear the words which I speak to you. Unless I direct the words into the other dimension this person cannot hear the conversation."

After this those two persons who are deceased followed the practice. The other one, who was never serious about yoga, was restricted to a particular astral level of existence which does not allow multiple perceptions.

Radio Song in Yogi's Subtle Head

During breath infusion, a tube in the subtle body which is in the font middle of the body under the skin, became evident. These tubes may be dormant, not being used, and they may not appear because in particular phases of the subtle body, they do not exist. The magnetic field which is created by the spinning action of metal and wires may not exist until the mechanism is turned at a certain speed. Similarly, there are parts of the subtle body which do not occur until one does a certain amount of practice.

The discovery of various parts of the subtle body gives the yogi an opportunity to energize and elevate certain parts of the subtle form, so that there is more transfer of attention to higher levels of existence, and more extraction of interest from the physical plane.

This tube which became evident was from below the navel to the genitals. It was grey-white in color about the diameter of ⅜ of an inch. There was nothing in the tube, but as the infusion was done it became more solid on that subtle level.

After sometime infusing it, the attention shifted to the chest where the same tube passed and then to the throat where the same tube was linked to the underside of the tongue. This tube runs from the base of the tongue to the genitals.

During the morning session, this tube became evident again. I focused on it. While on the previous afternoon I was aware of sections of it, like from the navel to the genitals, then its passage through the front center of the chest, and then from the base of the tongue to the chest, the entire tube was evident this morning.

When I sat to meditate there was thought disturbance. Luckily, these were from people who were present astrally and who wanted to discuss circumstances which had little to do with yoga. I did not have to track thoughts to their remote sources because the sources were present astrally. I shifted attention to naad sound and took refuge in naad.

One person who was present, is already deceased. This one sang a Nat King Cole song. This was a song I heard on radios when I was an infant. The person, who was an elder, still sang that song from years gone by just as if it was played as a popular song on a radio today. This singing melody was in my mind because this person was present in my mind. I shifted to naad sound and that ceased the radio song immediately.

Yogi Goes Back 2000 years (November 2011)

It was about 2000 years ago that the Romans first crossed from the European mainland to conquer Britain. This action still affects the world. Last night I was summoned to a group of people in Ireland who were still trying to get rid of the Roman influence which came from Europe so long ago. Some of these people were into Celtic religions and cults. One woman who knew me in the astral world told the group that I was a mystic and that I could help them to go back into the past and track the Roman influence. They felt that the present British Royal family is part of a blood line from Roman times. They want the royal family dissolved.

Their request of me was to go back to the time when the Romans first planned to cross the English Channel. This was easy to do because everyone at that astral meeting was psychic and mystic. In some way or the other, each dabbled in the occult. I said to them,

> "If this is what you want to look at, let us return and see. We went back into time. There was this Roman male in a house with a Roman female and a child. The Roman male was dressed like a Roman nobleman with a short skirt-like fabric for pants, a shawl across his shoulder and a paper scroll across his arm. He showed how the invasion should occur."

As soon as we got there and they saw that, I left and went away. In the astral distance, I could hear them arguing about the man as to who he was, so that they could identify his name in modern history books.

When we got there in that past time span, some 2000 years ago, we saw everyone there but no one could see us. Everything was acted in three dimensions but we were in a fourth dimension. We could not be perceived and we could not interfere or influence anything.

As the Roman man explained himself showing things on the scroll which he laid out, we could not hear his words but we could see his mouth moving. It was like watching a silent movie.

Everything that we do is recorded in nature on several levels. Our forms are also recorded. There is a three-dimensional recording capability which the subtle energies have. These keep everything in intact just as it happened before.

There is a mystic skill which is the ability to go into the past and then view forward into the future from that past even if that future occurred somewhere else. These are abilities of the subtle body when it is on certain levels of existence. It is not so much a personal mystic power but it is a power of any subtle body on a certain level.

Let us assume that we want to know what a certain sun being would do before he does it. We go to the sun. We get ourselves into a nuclear body and enter into the sun at the point at which that sun being will be in exactly five minutes. He is not there yet. We have five minutes to set up and be ready to observe his actions. We move back into the time of the sun, five minutes. In other words, we retrogress five minutes. At that point we remain there and look. We have a total of ten minutes to wait for the sun being to act, because we transited five minutes from the moment we arrived there. We wish to observe his arrival which is five minutes into the future from when we got there.

As soon as we stopped backing, we began to move forward on the time conveyor so that in ten minutes we will be in the presence of that sun being.

Because we retrogressed five minutes, we can set up the observation, just like when a photographer on this planet sets up his camera outside of a building to capture the movement of someone leaving through a certain entrance at a certain time.

In the Roman experience, I took those persons back to before the point in history they wanted to see. Rapidly things began to happen which led to the interesting moment. Things kept happening. Nothing stopped, the actions rolled like on a movie set when the producer gives the order for a drama to be acted.

Remember however, and always keep this in mind, this happened because of the psychic technology with which the subtle body is enabled on certain levels. It did not happen because of a development of mind. It happened because the subtle body has that ability on that level, just as say a calf has the ability to walk on four legs soon after it is born. The body of the calf has that ability, while a human body even though it is a superior form overall, cannot walk on its feet immediately after birth.

Part 2

Yogi Runs from Pleasure and Reproduction (November 2011)

The main infusion areas this morning were the thighs, which assumed a white-hot color in the subtle body. The subjugation of the thighs is part of sexual energy conversion practice. Sexual energy is necessary for reproduction but when an entity realizes that reproduction is linked to pleasure acquirement the sexual energy is diverted for pleasure purposes.

Pleasure becomes a vice when the entity decides that it should be procured with no respect to the responsibility for progeny. When nature first introduces sexual pleasure, it does so with the intention of luring the entity to reproduce but the entity soon finds a way to outsmart nature by frustrating the reproductive feature and taking the pleasure. This however develops as a vice which causes the entity to owe nature for the energy enjoyed. Nature then reacts by setting up complex nearly-unsolvable destinies in the person's future.

Realizing that nature's pleasure system can only be separated from its reproductive functions with dire consequences, the yogi aspires for celibate lifestyle. It is not a religion. It is sheer mathematics, because when one figures, one realizes that one loses in the effort to cull pleasure from the reproduction process. Nature is the one which does the tally. The entity is not the accounting agent. Nature tallies in its own interest.

Meeting Deceased People (November 2011)

Last night there were two primary visitors, an aunt who is now deceased for about a year and Arthur Beverford. Years ago, this aunt took a surgery which disfigured her face. She lived for many years in that disfigured body. Finally, about a year now, her subtle body was compelled to leave the physical system. Now she is in the astral world in an adjacent dimension hovering, in preparation for taking the next body.

Her interest was the health of her subtle form. She expressed surprise at the effects of yoga practice on my subtle body. Now that her gross body is done for, her only recourse is the subtle form. Before she had no interest in it because she lived by Christian belief which does not consider the condition of the subtle body.

Once the physical body is done, people who developed an interest in taking care of that form are left with a caring interest only and with another body which they paid no attention to during the physical lifetime. They become interested in maintaining that other form, especially if the deity of their religion did not appear to help them when they left the physical system for good.

I was with Arthur Beverford in the Philippines. I do not know how I got there. I realized that I was in a room with him where he reviewed some details of his life. His subtle body resembled his old physical form but it was in good health on the subtle side. Suddenly he began doing yoga stretches. He showed a bottle of vitamin pills which had the Centrum label. Even in the astral world people take vitamin supplements. That is crazy when one considers it in the terms of the operation of the subtle body as compared to the physical one.

Beverford was very good at the asana postures but he did not practice pranayama much. He is still with that asana expertise only. He considered how his physical body became terminally ill.

Soon after this my alarm rang. I arose at 3.45 am and did breath infusion. During the practice Beverford was there and so was my deceased aunt. As I did the exercises my aunt looked on with great interest. She thought, "You were a strange boy." She recalled when I had an infant body and she assisted caring for me.

Usually when one makes contact with deceased astral beings, it is made mentally in an impersonal way. This causes one to feel that perhaps these persons if they do exist, do so without forms. But one should always hold reservations about no-form conditions because what is no-form is frequently no ability to define the form. The viewer's lack of sense perception is no reason to declare everything unseen as formlessness.

Usually when we get contact with deceased people, we get that contact as a mere thought. In other words, the person is present but we only detect the person's thoughts when it enters the subtle head and is then translated into thinking. We then identify that thinking as thoughts of our own but actually these are foreign ideas.

Naad is Boring?

During meditation this morning, the main focus was naad. This focus is vital. The psyche aggressively procures sensations hence to tell someone to be satisfied with naad, is an instruction which many students ignore. Yet, I repeat this. Kirpal Singh stressed it. For meditation one will eventually have to relax, stop sensual hunting and settle on naad focus.

Naad was blaring silently as if it emitted little sound. It did so on the inside of the psyche with very little of its sound being expressed outside. Time and again I checked the frontal area of the subtle head. I noticed that it was devoid of thoughts, images and ideas.

When I sat to meditate, there was an infusion force coming from the throat. It pushed the chin and eyes upward. After five minutes I shifted from naad focus. Gradually I relaxed the chin downwards but the eyes remained upward. I retreated into naad and left the eyes up with the chin down. The physical muscles which held the neck were pressured by the psychic force generated in the infusion. It became necessary to relax those muscles.

Naad is the sensation replacement. One must have a certain amount of sensation, just as one must have a certain amount of food. The mind should become habituated to naad so that naad is the sensation which it craves.

Naad may be boring but it is the key element in higher yoga. It is the ultimate mantra. It is the unspoken Om.

For the development of supernatural vision, one must practice naad focus. Regrettably I cannot say that if one meditates on naad, for this or that many hours, one will get success. It is not like that. Each person has a different quota which is required. Still the sooner one can practice, the better.

CoreSelf Jumps to Its Default Position (November 2011)

During exercises this morning, I had a visitor: Swami Muktananda. His remark concerned the thighs where he said that the secret to conquering sex drive is to completely remove the lusty energies from the thighs. He made a criticism of my meditation practice, saying that it was not extended.

For at least 10 years or more I tried to come to terms with this requirement but there is a preventative energy which restricts the time allotted to meditation. However, a yogi should persist with the intention of meeting the standards. Every step of the way through this human lifetime, one is faced with obligations and energies which are prohibitive of spiritual advancement. Some energies cancel the desire for progress but even so one should practice. In time, the negative feature will slacken. Then, because one practiced consistently one can take the advantage. Each student must log hours of practice. The only way to meet the requirement is to practice. When I sat to meditate naad was immediately evident on the right side near the ear. It was inside the psyche as if it did not have an existence anywhere else.

Usually for naad one can trace an entry point into the psyche but in this case, there was no detectable port. When one finds an entry point, one can go through it to the other side which is outside one's psyche. In other words, the coreSelf can leave the psyche by passing through that vortex into the chit akasha sky of consciousness, leaving behind the other component of consciousness of the psyche like the intellect, kundalini and memory storage.

In this meditation though naad entered the psyche with no perceptible entry point, it was in the psyche like a virus which penetrated the body.

There were very few thoughts arising in the frontal part of the head. When these arose, they did so in slow motion, instead of rapidly as they usually do. Periodically, abandoning naad, the coreSelf would jump to its default position in the center of the subtle head. When this occured, I shifted back to naad focus abandoning the default location.

The core has this addiction to receiving information from the intellect and receiving feedback from the kundalini life force. It needs to be in its default location to connect with the psychic equipment, thus it always jumps back to the default location to connect with the adjuncts.

A yogi should forego this appetite for information and sensual feedback. The intellect and the kundalini get scratchy and itchy when the core is out of their reach. This causes the core to feel a need to communicate with them but a yogi must resist these urges.

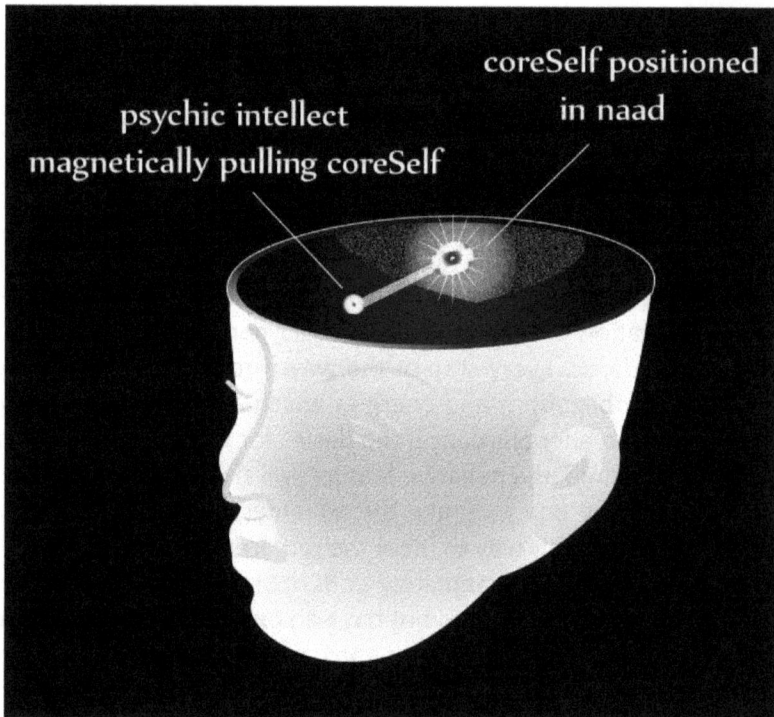

coreSelf positioned in naad

psychic intellect magnetically pulling coreSelf

Yogi Yeilds to Kundalini (November 2011)

For the afternoon session I had a visitor, Muktananda. The sudden urge to do an afternoon session came from him. He deposited energy in my psyche which nullified some other energy which blocked the afternoon session. This may be considered a case of having to take help from a yoga guru.

If one is unable to transcend negative influences, one may take energy from a yoga guru who is resistant to such forces. That may be enough to cause one to overcome the retardative force.

Swami Muktananda wanted me to record this:

Eventually one comes to realize that one fights a losing battle against kundalini which is present in one's body as the lifeForce. In a losing battle even if one is courageous, one will continue fighting if one does not understand the odds. Once the fighter ascertains that the odds are against him and that there is no advantage, he becomes discouraged from fighting. He raises a white flag.

In yoga there is no such thing as committing suicide to avoid capture by the enemy because the yogi is confronted with the fact that he will survive the body. Killing the body is no solution because even then nature will be present on the subtle side of existence, and then again, the yogi will face the enemy.

The yogi yields temporarily because a hero cannot surrender to the enemy. The yogi pretends to surrender but in the back of his mind, he conspires to escape. He is captured by the enemy after yielding but still he thinks of a way out.

And what is that way out?

It is the realization that to escape capture one must go into another dimension where this nature has no influence. That place is the chit akash.

The psyche of the yogi should be altered in such a way that it is no longer responsive to the sensation which it once craved in physical existence. A thorough overhaul is required. Who should do it for the yogi? Should God? Should it be a yoga guru?

Infusing Sunlight Energy into Subtle Body (November 2011)

Swami Muktananda directed me in a posture for removing all dark subtle energy from the back thigh-buttocks area. This is done while the back of body faces the sun. The yogi pulls sunlight into the subtle body. This is done by doing breath infusion with attention on that area.

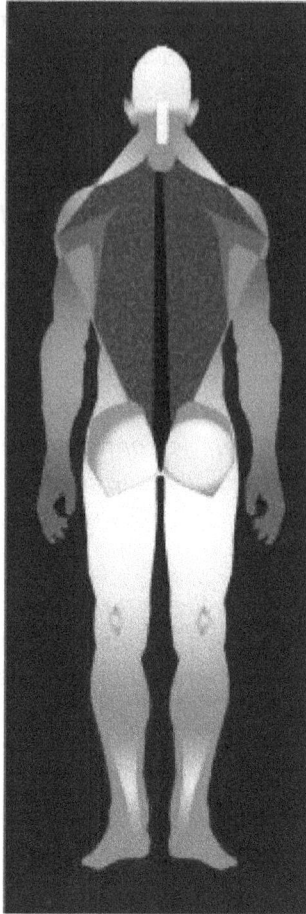

Children in the Astral World

Last night I found myself with a friend from South America. This person is a carpenter by trade. He showed a carpentry workshop and some buildings.

He had this idea that I should be in South America. He desired to make a house which I could live in with my children. The whole thing was crazy but I could not say anything because in his case, that is the sum total of his existence.

I no longer have minor children. Still in the astral world, he thought that I will be with children. Having children is the high feature of his idea of how a person should live but if we did that the children would never be adults. Life would be stalled with us as the center of existence as parents.

One gets a physical body. One becomes focused on whatever one does for a livelihood. The subtle body adapts that as the ultimate objective irrespective to the fact that such ideas are irrelevant in the long range.

We should get the subtle body out of this attitude by conscious astral projection and by clarity in dreams to discern the difference between physical and subtle existence.

I did breath infusion just after 4 am. That is the right time to do practice. Because of negative forces which enter the psyche and dictate that to rise that early is unreasonable, one is reluctant to do that. These negatives forces encourage one to rise early if one has to fly in an aircraft to go to another city to get money, but for the purpose of developing psychic perception and disciplining the psyche, these forces are reluctant. They force the ascetic to sleep through the night.

During breath infusion I realized that Swami Muktananda left an instruction in my psyche. It read:

Eliminate all dark areas. Create little kundalinis in such areas. Infuse those regions fully. Search everywhere. Banish all mists.

One way to understand this is to review sexual pleasure experience. Imagine if the human body had the potential for sexual arousal in every part of it but with the intensity everywhere as it has in the genitals.

We know that sexual arousal happens in all parts of the body but not with the same intensity. In the genitals the intensity of the greatest.

The kundalini life force has its greatest most impressive expression in the spine and brain of the physical form and the corresponding areas of the subtle body. That is the natural system. By directed breath infusion that kundalini system can be invoked in other parts of the body, in psychically-dark and unknown regions like in the toes, knee-cap, thighs, shoulders and fingers.

Just as when we are materialistic, we get crazy about the physical body, so an ascetic should be sensitive about the condition of the subtle form so that it is saturated with high-dimension energy and has no area where there is low frequency astral force.

Remove Ideation (November 2011)

When I sat to meditate there was some infused energy where the intellect is located. This location is important. One failure that I have had in teaching meditation and psychic perception is to convince students that there is a psychic organ which operates analysis and mental illustration.

I proposed that students not be alarmed by my statements of the psychic organs in the subtle head. Instead they should regard the place in the mind where images, thoughts and ideas are created, as a location where there is a psychic organ which cannot be seen, an invisible organ.

Begin with that idea. Follow my proposal which is that this location is capable of giving visual psychic perception. It is a mental crystal ball in which you can see into other dimensions.

Patanjali is important because in his second sutra he laid down the rule for developing this psychic perception which is to put an end to the normal operations of the intellect. His idea is that during meditation the yogi must by some means suspend the mental operations. When this happens for a while a supernatural perception may occur.

If for three weeks you put a fertile egg in a warm place, the contents of the egg will convert into a chick. To incubate the psychic perception of the intellect organ one must suspend its involuntary operations for a time.

The problem with this instruction is that students get bored waiting for the intellect to give higher perception. They become discouraged and abandon the practice. Some students fight with the thoughts which this organ manufactures. Others observe the thoughts. Others are entertained by them. For some others, this is their only area in life, where by creating mental images they can play God on themselves. Thus, to shut this down is to rob them of self-created fantasies in the mind.

When I first sat to meditate, the frontal part was devoid of ideation. This is an objective of doing pranayama breath infusion. If the breath infusion session was successful one will notice that the mind is no longer involved in creating thoughts. That function reduces or disappears altogether.

After noticing that I checked for naad in the back of the subtle head. I stationed the self in that and then looked forward. In the fontal part of the head there were shimmer gold-brown lights intermingling with black space. There were many forms passing. These were like transparencies. They were translucent. I remained anchored in naad.

There was a time during this meditation when I checked the back of the physical body. I supported it. If the back is collapsed, some of one's attention goes there. That upsets the meditation. Be sure that the spine is positioned so that it requires no attention during the session.

When one does asana postures, one should note the aches and pains while enduring them with patience. When meditating one should not splinter attention away by sitting in a way which requires attention which should be invested instead in the components of consciousness of the subtle body.

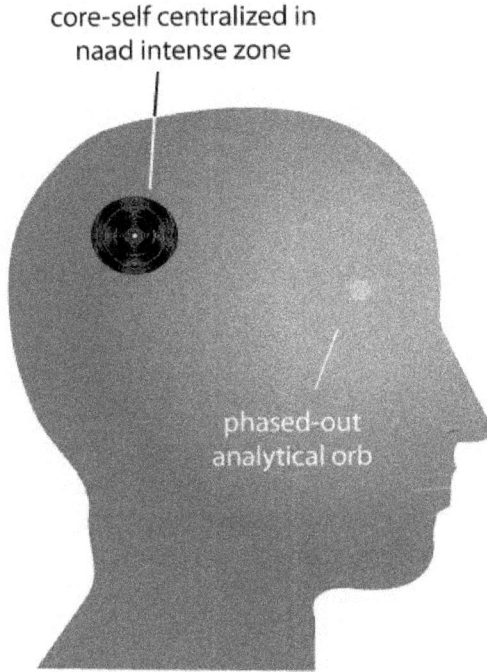

core-self centralized in
naad intense zone

phased-out
analytical orb

Game of Life

In the situation of the *Bhagavad Gita* discourse, life is a game. Each person is fixed or pressed into a certain role, the way a baker presses dough into a pastry press. Sometimes there is not sufficient dough. The shape desired is manifested in part only. Sometimes there is too much dough. The shape is achieved but some dough is forced from the press. That is like when one is given an opportunity but when one assumes the role, circumstances deny one the control.

The dough may be perfect in terms of the ingredients selected by the baker, but when the baker puts the dough into the oven, the dough may be afraid of the heat. At that time under pressure of the heat, the dough may swell until the heat takes complete control of its development and the swelling ceases.

Many males run through adolescence with a huff and puff with much happiness and giddiness but when they are confronted with the responsibility for progeny, they develop cold feet and try to run in the opposite direction. This is like when the dough is so afraid of the heat and is so stressed over it, that it rises over the pan and tries to run out of the oven. Of course, the heat on the outside of the pan, the social pressure, does not allow it to escape from the cooker. In fact, any of the dough which climbs over the edge of the pan is burnt by heat of the fire.

All persons who were ascetics in their past lives, and who sensed that something is amiss in the material world, may try to escape from social responsibilities. Thus, whenever we get a new body, we frequently try to escape from family life. Of course, nature does not allow it. Nature places a levy on everyone who has a physical body. It demands some minimum participation. Thus, it becomes necessary to find a teacher who can show us how to function socially and still make spiritual progress. Arjuna found such a teacher in Krishna.

Attaining a Yoga Siddha Form (November 2011)

During the afternoon session I worked on the energy flush-way at the bottom of the trunk. This is the equivalent of the anal pouch or rectum. In the subtle body there is no long winding alimentary track or upper intestines. The subtle body is not concerned with digesting solid matter but with using energy which is made from light (like in sunlight). Usually the Sanskrit term for this energy is *prana* (praa-nuh).

This flush-way should be of a bright color. It should not be dark in the subtle body. By breath infusion one can clear this flush way so that it promptly expels energy which was used by the subtle body and which should be expelled from it. Again, this type of expulsion is not like evacuating waste from the physical body.

I worked on two corresponding areas in the upper back. These are like two plates of energy. Usually this energy is dark but a yogi can infuse it with breath. If the infusion is sufficient, this area will change from a dark cloud of heavy subtle energy to a whitish light-weight energy.

In this way, a yogi can do his work in attaining a yoga siddha form. There is no point in getting too crazy about maintain the physical body because no matter what one does, one will lose it within at least 120 years of its life. The subtle body lasts for the duration of the galaxy. Thus, it is worth the effort to keep it in the best shape.

If one's subtle body is not automatically kept in a high vibration, it becomes necessary to strive with pranayama practice to push the subtle body to higher planes.

A yogi will notice that with an increase in breath infusion, the physical body appears to be healthier. For instance, when breath infusion is done with focus on the rectum, a yogi may notice that there is more prompt evacuation. Seeing this, a yogi who is not properly grounded in transcendence may get the idea that yoga is for improving physical health. This will result in more focus on the physical body resulting in a materialistic yogi who has a misunderstanding.

Even though one may notice that there are physical health benefits to yoga, one should not be distracted but should keep the focus on the enduring subtle form and not be concerned with the short-lived physical system, which will develop a terminal illness no matter how healthy it may be.

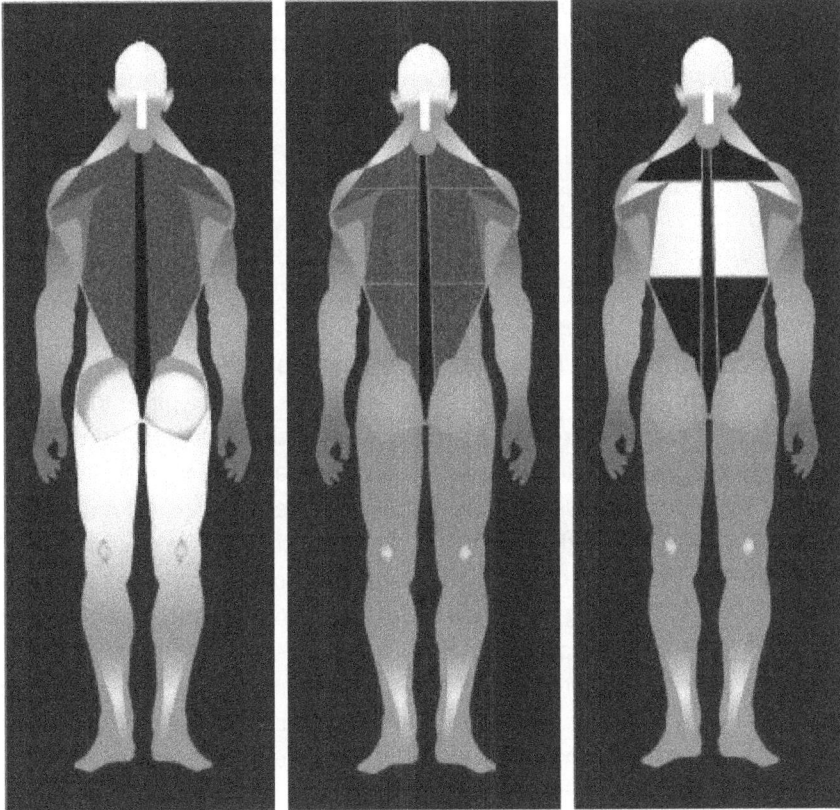

Yogi King Becomes the Servant (November 2011)

There should be a development in meditation, where the self finds that it has the power to squelch thoughts, images and ideas which arise in the mind. The normal condition is to be entertained by the mental and emotional constructions. With the mind automatically doing so many emotional and mental tasks, the self relaxes and is entertained by the mind, like a king in a luxurious palace.

The problem with this arrangement is that eventually the king will become crippled and incapable of even feeding himself. He has to realize that, and slowly but surely, wrestle control away from the servants. But then that means he must do menial tasks.

This morning during breath infusion, I was bothered by some persons who are related to my body. Some relatives appeared on the astral side during the night. They were there during the morning session of exercises which was about 4 am.

One person was my deceased father, a person who was negligent to his first wife and children. Up till now he does not understand what happened regarding how irresponsible he was. Some entities are born with little sense of duty. They live their lives and pass on in the same way without a change in behavior.

During the breath infusion I managed to change dimensions making it difficult for these relatives to reach me. They wanted to talk about how my father would get his next body and also about how we would come back into this world when our living bodies would have no life.

I did a full session of breath infusion but I was unable to produce any little kundalinis. Still, the psyche was cleared of heavy subtle energies. The air was cold, near freezing, but I was dressed appropriately. When I sat to meditate, the first thing I did was to support the lower spine. Immediately after I heard naad but there was an inspiration in the psyche to remain in the front part of the subtle head. This was due to the fact that the intellect ceased its chattering and imaging concerns and was present as if it did not exist.

There were no thoughts because of the successful breath infusion. The coreSelf moved from its default position and stood in the position of the intellect, just as if the king had fired his Prime Minister and took the tasks of the minister under direct control.

The king was happy to find out that even though he was handicapped because of years of being a lazy man, at least in one task he did not need a servant. He must train himself to responsibly assume the duties done by so many servants in the psyche.

The fourth stage of yoga which is pranayama effectively brings the shutdown with the infusement of the subtle body and the shifting of the intellect into a higher mode of operation where it loses interest in the lower planes of consciousness.

The intellect craves sensation. It plots how to acquire that. However, it loses that interest as soon as it is removed from the level where that intrigue functions.

Pranayama is not the only method for achieving cessation of the vrittis which is the creative play of the emotions and rational energy on the lower planes. It is just that pranayama is for those who follow Patanjali's ashtanga yoga syllabus.

Pranayama has the special feature of upsetting kundalini and separating kundalini from its primal animal instincts while other methods do not attack kundalini but lull it to sleep or into dormancy and then cause it to suspend its operations for a time.

I do not care what method a student uses, provided it is effective and has a cumulative resistance effect to the resumption of lower behaviors on lower planes of consciousness.

In kundalini yoga, the coccygeus muscle is a valid focus point and has to do with the base chakra. This is called *muladhara* which means root (moola) anchor (adhaara). Perineum has to do with the second chakra *(svadhishthana)* which has to do with the sex chakra. In the final analysis in uprooting kundalini and getting rid of its nuisance instincts, one must conquer the root chakra not the sex one.

In breath infusion one should first conquer the navel chakra and then the sex one. Then one can attack the root chakra. This is because to conquer kundalini one must conquer its food intake. It eats in two ways, through taking air and through taking food. In both cases, the passage of food goes through the navel area and then it is converted into hormones and then kundalini consumes that. It so happens that it gives the sex chakra the most nutritious part of food, just like when a man has a wife, he may always have his wife take choice pastries first.

Kundalini is not a stupid force. It is the instinct intelligence which we use. It knows that it has to survive. For that it must rely on the sex chakra and even though that is the second chakra as one goes up the spine, it is actually the opposite as one goes down the front of the body. In other words, as the nutrients go down the front side of the body, the gut etc., it has to pass the pubic area before it reaches the base chakra on the spine. This is why the perineum is important.

Kundalini cannot be conquered if one does not destroy the assistance it is gets from the perineum. It is like if you want to invade an enemy. If he is protected by an assistant you should deal with the assistant first.

In any case, coccygeus muscle is important in the conquest of kundalini. In the animal species, the tail is important. It is the extension of that same coccygeus muscle. The animal must use the tail more often than the genital but when it enters the human form there is a flip. It finds that it is attracted more to the genitals. The need for a tail is reduced.

Kundalini has no intentions of leasing one ounce of its control of the psyche to the coreSelf. The core is called *atma* in Sanskrit. Sometimes to stress that it is an individual unit, the terms *jiva-atma* is used, since *jiva* is a singular something. Kundalini will never of its own accord work for the release of any individual self from these transmigrations. Anyone who thinks that kundalini will work in his interest is a fool.

It is not a matter of arguing over it. It is not even a matter of what method is used. The point is to conquer kundalini and to take from it control over the operations of the components of the psyche. For sure, we went through this mundane evolutionary cycle by the grace and instinctive intelligence of kundalini. Some ancient yogis, call it the *Great Potency (MahaShakti).* Still, to be free of this creature existence business, one must conquer it.

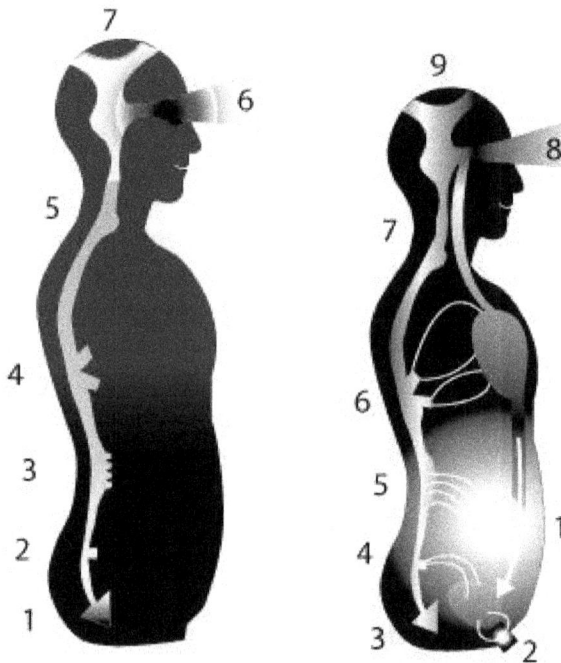

In the two diagrams notice the order of the numbers. Usually a student feels that his concern is with the first, less complicated diagram but the second diagram tells more of the truth, with the expressions of the navel chakra and sex chakra interrupting the effort to deal with the base chakra. It is like the navel and sex chakras have two locations, one on the spine and the other in the trunk of the body.

Male Yogi doing Female Practice (November 2011)

I awoke after 4am. I was with persons who stayed in an ashram in Scandinavia. This was an ashram of Swami Muktananda who is now deceased and who many people doubt was a worthy yoga guru. At the ashram, a lady arrived who used a Scandinavian body.

There were other ladies who used Scandinavian bodies. This was on the astral side of the ashram. Muktananda has ashrams in the Scandinavian countries, like Sweden, Finland and Norway.

At the astral ashram I did not see the Swami. I spoke to three Scandinavian ladies. One just arrived at the ashram. I gave her instructions on how to stay there and in which room she would be domiciled.

Soon after I rose to do exercises. Swami Muktananda appeared with the same lady whom I instructed at the ashram. It was then that I realized that it was his ashram. Now I was on the physical side but with astral perception. The swami and the lady were on the astral side only.

As I did postures, he showed her what happened in the subtle body, where the infused energy went and what it did. The lady was struck with wonder, expressing that she had no idea that yoga was anything but a physical practice.

He had me show her a *yoni* cleansing exercise which is done by yoginis. *Yoni* is a Sanskrit word for female genital organ. In this exercise, the person focuses on the genital organ on the subtle side of existence (in the subtle body) and works with breath infusion to remove the lusty attitude of that zone. This involves moving the energy which is usually sheltered in the organ and changing that energy into a higher infused force.

The genital organ is naturally the chief servant of passion but it can be reformed from that and can be made to serve the mode of goodness and clarity. However, that change occurs only under the pressure of yogic mystic procedures.

Even though my body is male, I can sometimes assume postures which are for yoginis. This is because primevally, even the male bodies were adapted from the forms of both male and female deities. The potential for these bodies is that they can assume either polarity as male or female.

For that matter these bodies have more female potential than male. Assumption of postures which are particular to the female form is easy. The lady was wonder struck when she saw what the breath infusion did in the subtle body. Even though she did postures in her physical form for many years and had perfected many of the asana poses, she never imagined anything like that.

Now she knows that yoga is not a practice for physical health and beauty. A question may arise as to whether this person would remember that astral encounter when she returns to the physical side after that astral projection. The answer:

Who knows? Who cares?

It is the Swami's disciple. That is his worry.

After I did the infusion having to do with the trunk of the body, I switched to finalize the practice with infusion of the intellect. The Swami wanted the lady to take note of that. Since the intellect is so subtle even to subtle perception in the subtle body, the lady could not see the infusion's effect on the intellect.

The Swami explained what happened to the intellect. Then because the lady had some doubts about his practice as compared to mine, he said this,

Yes, no one sees me doing these practices. I mastered these in my youth. I do not need to practice that now. Do not worry about my practice. Focus on what you need at this stage. Because you may be at another stage you cannot always do what a guru does. I brought you to him, because he is at a stage of practice you can learn something from. Each yogi is at a different stage of progression. One learns best from the one who uses the method which would cause one to progress currently.

After that the Swami went away and the lady too. She left with a look of wonder.

Yogi Shot through by Arrow in Past Life (November 2011)

Meditation this morning had to do with going back in time. I was a prince in India a long time ago, when we used arrows, bows, and sword for weapons. During meditation this morning I went back to a part of that life when I was killed during a battle. *I was killed* means when that body was killed, and the subtle body permanently separated from it.

When I did the breath infusion, I finished the last ten minutes doing infusion into the head. Because Swami Muktananda was present, I tuned in to his instruction since he wanted postures which would be beneficial to the lady who was in attendance with him on the astral side.

At first, he directed me to infuse the lower back of the head, then the frontal part where the intellect is located. To understand where this is, just think of the place in the head where thinking, imaging and ideas take place. The infusion was done at that mental location. After that mental place is infused it changes its function, so that it no longer continues with thinking and imaging in the usual way.

When I sat to meditate, I relocated the coreSelf to the location where the thinking and imaging usually takes place. Usually one cannot do this, because the coreSelf is kept at a specific distance from this place by a force field. Due to this force field, the self is hypnotized by and is attentive to the intellect thought-producing psychic mechanism. The coreSelf has a default position in the psyche, it is not all-pervasive. What pervades is subtle energy. When the self synchronizes with that it feels all-pervasive.

With breath infusion, one can shatter these force fields and free the self so that it is no longer anchored to a default position. As soon as I was shifted to the intellect's location, I switched to a past life where I was in a battle. I was a prince in India. It was on a battlefield. Most of the warriors around me were dead or fatally wounded. I was alone without body guards. I rode a horse but due to the carnage the animal was skittish. There was no place where the horse could place its hoof without stepping on a body of a dying or dead warrior.

One of the opposing warriors aimed an arrow at my body. It shot through the stomach region of my body. It was a horrible death. I did not feel the pain of it, but the anguish was present as a loss of energy, a blank space in time.

I remembered my thoughts at that time which were that the opposing soldiers were not supposed to use arrows in close combat. They were supposed to use swords. The rules of combat were that arrows were only used at long range but some opposing soldiers violated the standard. This is how they won that battle. Arrows were used then mostly like the way snipers are used today in battle. My last thoughts in that wounded body concerned how those warriors broke the rules.

Arrows are now replaced by bullets. Instead of a sharp point with a shaft, we now have a hot piece of metal which rapidly penetrates and kills the body. Just as arrows would stick in the body or an arrow may go through the body, the bullet is an improvement over the arrow with the same intention of fatally piercing the body.

Lucid Dreaming / Astral Projection Compared

Astral projection can convert into lucid dreaming and visa versa. Some experiences come about spontaneously without desire and without trying to control or visualize them.

Many experiences just happen or one finds the self in an astral projection after it began and one realizes it for what it is. In other words, imagine if I regularly sleepwalked. My partner usually tells me how I got up, went to the toilet, got the car keys, went again to the toilet and then again got the car keys. Started the car, and went to bed.

I am never aware of this even though it happened factually to the extent that my partner can show it on a video which was recorded. Why did I not know of it? If I am so much in charge of what happens on the subconscious side and on the dream side, why do I sleep walk?

Once while doing this, I caught myself in the act of starting the car. I tried to realize how I left the bed and went to the car without knowing what I did.

In the same way we usually find ourselves astrally projected or involved in a lucid dreaming. It is not that in most cases it is deliberately done. The first thing to realize is that astral projection happens every time the physical system sleeps. There are three factors involved:

- physical body
- astral or subtle body
- imagination

In the physical world, imagination is the act of mentally creating ideas and images. It is related to reality but it is not reality. In the astral world imagination can be reality however. In the astral world something I imagine can be real. In the physical world if I dream that I have a book in my hand and there is no physical action to pick up a book, there is nothing I can do with that imagined book but in the subtle world depending on the level, that dream book can become a real book in my hand.

In the subtle world imagination can become reality. In the physical world we do not have to deal with that because the imagination provides less bewilderment, because physical substance does not yield to our wishes that easily. If I imagine a device, I have to either hire someone to manufacture it or I must buy it from someone who imagined and then manufactured it. But in the astral world my imagined product may instantly become a reality. It depends on how the astral energy responds to my desire.

In astral projection the subtle body is displaced from the physical one, so that one is in the astral body and one is not simultaneously in the physical form. When this happens, one is in an astral world or subtle level of existence, in the hereafter.

In lucid dreaming the astral body remains in the physical body and one is more aware of the astral form but one is slightly aware of the physical body. In other words, the astral body is not fully displaced from the physical system but one's attention is more in sync with the astral one and it is no longer fully in sync with the physical one.

It is a difference of full or partial displacement of the astral form. In the case of lucid dreaming the astral and physical systems share the same space, they remain interspaced in each other. But in the astral projection the astral one moves out of and away from the physical one.

The difference is that in lucid dreaming the subtle body is still interspaced in the physical body while in astral projection the subtle body is displaced out of the physical one.

To be clear, imagine that I am in a house. I pick up a cell phone and call you. I was in the house and I made contact with someone who is outside the house. That is like lucid dreaming where you are still in the physical body but your subtle perception is so acute that you can contact someone in the subtle world.

On the next day I am outside the house, out in the garden. I again call you. That is like an astral projection, where one leaves the house or physical body, one goes outside of it and makes contact with someone in the subtle world.

This type of experience gives evidence that there is a subtle body which will exist beyond death of the physical one. This is part of self-realization, where one gets direct evidence of the self as a subtle body. One knows for sure that when the physical body is finished, one will go on living nevertheless.

There are many experiences with the subtle body when it affords the user no vision. However, one should not be worried. Kittens are born with closed eyelids. This continues for them for some days.

It is natural to be in the subtle body and not to have vision. That should be no worry. Eventually vision will happen spontaneously. One should not get excited if one finds the self without vision.

Once someone has an astral projection, he can discuss it sensibly because he is no longer just a person with physical perception. The next step is to tour the subtle world to see where one will be once the physical body dies. Where will one go? Will it be a heaven or hell?

Even if the subtle body still has contact with the physical one, a displacement of the subtle body out of the physical is an astral projection. You can be here and there simultaneously. So long as the astral body is displaced from the physical system even if it is displaced slightly, it is an astral projection.

Both in astral projection and in lucid dreaming one may have some awareness of the physical one. In lucid dreaming there is always a residual awareness but in astral projection there may be some awareness or there may be none.

Sometimes one may astral project into an adjacent dimension where souls linger for rebirth. They live as their ghost bodies. One may be stuck in this type of astral world because one did not cultivate the spiritual disciplines which results in going to a higher zone.

One may be invited to reside in an astral parallel world by someone to whom one feels sexually attracted. It happens that one may transit to a strange place and may be stuck there for hundreds of years without remembering one's social identity in the last body on earth.

If this happened on an LSD trip or while taking narcotics, one may lose the physical body permanently. Relatives and friends on this side would think that one overdosed on drugs.

Yogi Learns from Two Vicious Businessmen

The night was quiet and mostly uneventful which is really great for a yogi. It is a very good result of practice if one finds that during the night one does not have much social involvement with people whose primary interest is not yoga practice.

I did breath infusion just after 4 am. At first no one was present astrally but then Swami Muktananda appeared as an astral body. I focused in the trunk of my body, infusing energy into the thighs, when he appeared. He made this remark:

Those who are unable to keep the attention in the psyche during asanas and pranayama practice are never able to reach the heights of Patanjali yoga. Subsequently they go about speaking of things which they have no knowledge of. Baba used to whack us if at any time during practice, our attention stayed outside of the psyche. In the subtle body, you would get this stinging whack on your back. You realized that your attention strayed. It is nice that you keep the attention inside even though no one inflicts pain on you for violating that.

By Baba he meant Siddha Swami Nityananda.

During breath infusion, the air was cold but I persisted. Presently my circumstance does not allow me to practice the breath infusion indoors. Sometimes circumstances are not ideal but a yogi should not allow that to deter practice nor distract one from the real issue which is to utilize any opportunity. For breath infusion one should never use polluted indoor air. There should be ventilation so that fresh air reaches the nostrils.

If one lives in the Northern Hemisphere, one should when the weather is cold, do the breath infusion indoors with windows opened partially so as to warm the fresh air but if that is not practical, then one should practice anyway. I dress in warm clothing and go outdoors. People make many sacrifices and go through much hardship and austerity for materialistic aims. There is no reason why a yogi cannot take their example and apply their persistence to spiritual practice. There is much to learn from dedicated persistent materialistic people.

Yesterday I was with a few businessmen. They went to a wholesaler to purchase items for retail sale. It was interesting how they badgered and whittled the wholesaler on prices. They were persistent. They stripped the man to the bare bones to get the cheapest prices so that on the retail side they made the highest profits.

There was no shame on their part. It was all about the profit. As far as they were concerned the wholesaler should make no gains from the purchase. He should give it to them at the price at which he bought it or less even. They were vicious like efficient predators, like hyenas and lions, which strip everything to the bone and crack the bone and take the marrow within it if that is necessary.

There is something to learn from these people about how efficient to be in spiritual practice. Regarding their lack of conscience and total efficiency, these people are great gurus to a yogi. After they completed the transaction, I interview the two men about it. I asked if there was some satisfaction in getting the best prices from the wholesaler.

They explained that there was and that if they did not do that, the whole thing would be spoilt for them. "We must get the price down to the bare bones," they said, "then we are satisfied. The pleasure is in getting the best prices so that we can make the highest possible profit."

I was struck with wonder because I do not see life in that way. These men had some circuits which were missing in my psyche. But still it was an important lesson how to deal with life and get from it what one requires for fulfillment. If these materialistic persons can do this, why should the yogi sit back and get nothing out of spiritual practice.

Intellect Zap

When I sat to meditate there was this upward force from the trunk of the body into the neck and then through the top back of the head. It was so strong that it pulled the energy which usually courses through the optic nerves backwards.

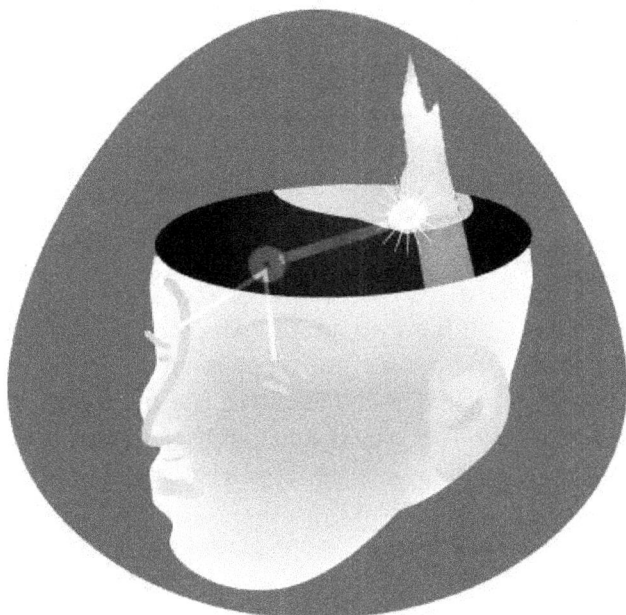

As it is, there is an energy which leaves the coreSelf and travels through the sense of identity, intellect, optic nerves and through the eyes into the world to procure color and shape sensation. This energy must be withdrawn into the psyche for the completion of the pratyahar sensual energy withdrawal, the fourth stage of ashtanga yoga. In this case this energy did a reversal and of its own accord, flowed back into the psyche. It was drawn by the kundalini upsurge which passed through the back top of the head.

This experience is verification that the kundalini commands the senses and the sensual energies. It makes those forces serve it. Since kundalini lost interest in sensations which came through the physical body and even the senses of the subtle body, these energies followed the kundalini like obedient servants of a dead pharaoh who are told that they should enter the room of his sarcophagus for voluntary entombment.

I watched as this optic energy obediently pulled itself back into the psyche. Some years ago, I pioneered a practice for retracting this energy. I published this practice in the first chapter of the *Meditation Pictorial* book. Without mastering that practice, one cannot master the fifth step of yoga, pratyahar sensual energy withdrawal.

Here, without doing that practice, due to the breath infusion's impact on kundalini, the most stubborn of the sensual energies, the most impulsive which is the visual energy, retracted on its own.

There is a part of the *Upanishads* where there was a tussle between the various senses and the life force. It was an argument about which was the most essential. One sense after another challenged the psyche and stated that if it left, everything would shut down but when the life force threatened to leave, all the sense hushed and became scared, because the system would be disabled without the life force.

After noticing that the sensual energy was retracted merely by the action of the infused kundalini, I went forward in the frontal part of the head. There were no thoughts. The place was like a ghost town. It was vacant like when a man who had a large family gets up one morning and finds that his wife and children abandoned him.

I decided to make a test. I thought of something, just to see if the intellect would operate. It barely operated. The thought did not continue as thoughts usually do. There was no supplementary memory. It showed whatever little I thought of then it was blank, like the silence after that last click from a dead battery. This is evidence that the intellect can shut down to such an extent that even if it is given energy from the coreSelf, it still will not operate.

After this I stayed in the frontal blank place and meditated but suddenly there was this flash at the left edge of the left eyebrow. There was subtle heat in the flash. It lasted for four seconds. This was the cosmic intellect hitting my limited individual intellect. It did not last long but it was impressive. Just then Swami Muktananda returned. He made this remark.

That should happen for a longer period of time. The restriction of the attention within the psyche causes that. The individual adjuncts should be reconnected with their cosmic sources.

Only some thoughts occur directly from the intellect. Other ideas enter the psyche from other persons, from other psyches. These enter the psyche and go to the intellect for translation and display to the coreSelf. These entry-thoughts were created by other intellects in other bodies of other persons.

In the case of entered-thoughts, these were not created initially by the yogi but by others. These were transmitted as subtle signals which penetrated the psyche of the yogi. Once they penetrate, they go immediately to the intellect and cause it (force it, in fact) to translate and display inside the mind. This may take place even without the coreSelf realizing what happened.

But it is an important question as to if the coreSelf can create thoughts on its own without using the intellect. That would be like asking the pilot of an aircraft to move through the air at 500 mph without using an aircraft. Can his body endure that? Of course, the answer in the case of the pilot is no. He cannot. He must take help from the machine if he wants to move at that speed.

The coreSelf cannot directly construct thoughts but it can issue an expression from itself which may cause the subtle energy to manifest thoughts even when the intellect is disabled. A similar thing can be realized by those who pulled kundalini out of the spine. They can cause the formation of little kundalinis in the subtle body without having the main kundalini in operation.

If you run an electric current though a coil of wires, as in the case of a motor, that current will cause the core part of the machine to spin. Now if you take the same current and you run it through a wire that is laid out haphazardly, you will not see the spinning effect. The intellect is like the motor-core which spins when the coreSelf or when even other core-selves or their psyche, send out a particular type of expressive energy.

Sometimes, an infant controls its mother? How is that? Sometimes it seems that the mother does exactly what the infant desires, as if the mother's body is remotely controlled by the infant's willpower?

The individual adjuncts are the sensual instruments (four in number), the kundalini life force, the memory chamber(s), the intellect and the sense of identity.

These together with a coreSelf make for a psyche or content of consciousness. The mind is the head of the subtle body but the entire subtle form, is an individual psyche.

Part 3

Yogi in a Pitch-Black Night (November 2011)

Exercises yesterday afternoon were squashed because of being with a businessman. It does happen that even the most astute yogi neglects practice. Instead of doing exercises in the afternoon sometime between 4 pm and 6 pm, at least before sunset, to infuse sun energy, at that time I was on a ladder figuring how to replace fluorescent lights in a business location. Because my mind was overwhelmed by the energy of the businessman I forgot the practice.

Finally, at about 9 pm, I did exercises. That is better than not doing it on any given day. It is better to do it late, even to do it partially than to not do it. A partial effort contributes to the habit.

In the morning just after 4 am I got back on schedule. I practiced breath infusion. It was a fair session. When I sat to meditate, the frontal part of the head was in silence but a few slow-moving thoughts flashed across the mind as if they were afraid of being suppressed. It was like when a thief sneaks through a house with the intention of not being discovered.

After some time, the third eye had shimmering golden images of persons in another dimension. This was like if you were in a pitch-black night and then suddenly nearby there were shimmering golden objects which you could not touch.

Swami Muktananda came for a split second. He left a message which read:

Be open to that cosmic energy. Invite it to penetrate.

This was in reference to the cosmic intellect. From within the psyche, a yogi may change the quality of energy which surrounds the coreSelf. That change could be made in the direction of making the psyche penetrable by a ray from the cosmic intellect.

It is not easy to do this because first of all the yogi cannot identity the level where the cosmic energy is located. He may not know how to alter the psyche to make it compatible to that plane of consciousness. Guess work or fooling around in the mind, even imagined states, does nothing to affect this. One should have frequent contacts with the higher planes and then over time one may have the insight required to judge how to affect the psyche to make it conducive for penetration of energy from higher planes.

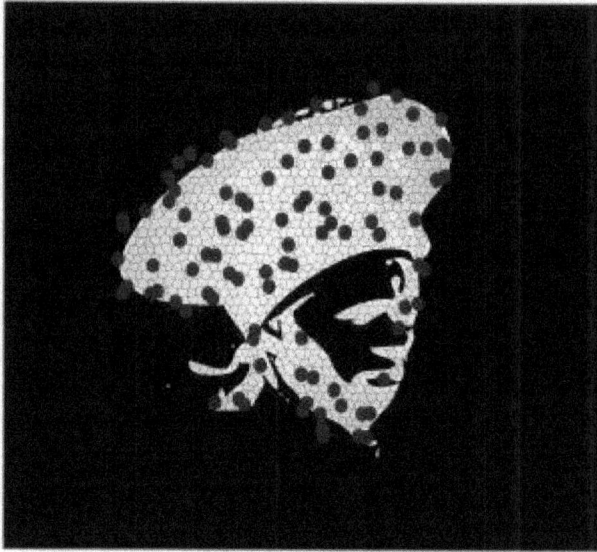

Earning a Yoga-Siddha Body

This afternoon I resumed the schedule for exercises before sunset. I got sunlight energy into the lower trunk of the body, as well as into the thighs. Usually those parts of the subtle body are filled with heavy subtle energy. To change the system into being a yoga siddha form, a yogi should displace such energy which will take the astral body to the lower astral planes when the physical system dies.

This heavy energy can be replaced with sunlight subtle energy such that when one looks down within the psyche into the subtle thigh, there is nothing but light or there is nothing there besides clear transparent energy.

A yoga siddha body must be earned by doing the right practices which affect the vibration and energy content of the subtle form. Methods of doing this are not the issue. If a method works it is valid. If it does not change the subtle body, it proves to be useless.

During the meditation session which followed the breath infusion, I worked on an instruction which was given by Swami Muktananda. This was an instruction to make the inside of the psyche attractive to the cosmic levels of consciousness. There is more than one cosmic level but the yogi begins by reaching the lower levels of cosmic consciousness. From there gradually he elevates the practice to go higher.

The main adjuncts in the psyche are the intellect, kundalini, and sense of identity. Kundalini is part of the cosmic kundalini. The other adjuncts are disconnected parts of a colossal cosmic force which is vast and infinite in comparison.

Kundalini is easy to deal with, because on this level it operates the body in terms of physical creature existence.

There is also cosmic memory and individual memory. There is cosmic sensual energy and individual sensory energy.

For this specific practice, I contacted the cosmic intellect. From inside the psyche, taking the position of the intellect itself, the coreSelf may express an influence which would cause the energy in the psyche to be attractive to the cosmic intellect. This would cause the vast cosmic light of the aggregate unused intellects to reach the yogi's individual intellect.

A blast of light from the cosmic intellect would completely transform the intellect of the yogi, converting it into a supernatural means of perception.

Infusing the Subtle Head

One aspect of breath infusion is to notice how the energy in the atmosphere changes daily. It is never the same. It fluctuates. This is the subtle atmosphere. In the subtle world, circumstances may change at a more rapid pace than in the physical environment. Sometimes it seems that nothing changes there or that time stands still as if waiting for a jolt.

The infusion session this morning was great. For about the last fifteen minutes I infused the subtle head. I used two procedures which are shown below. The first had to do with an attack on the intellect. In this situation the intellect was spinning up to the front.

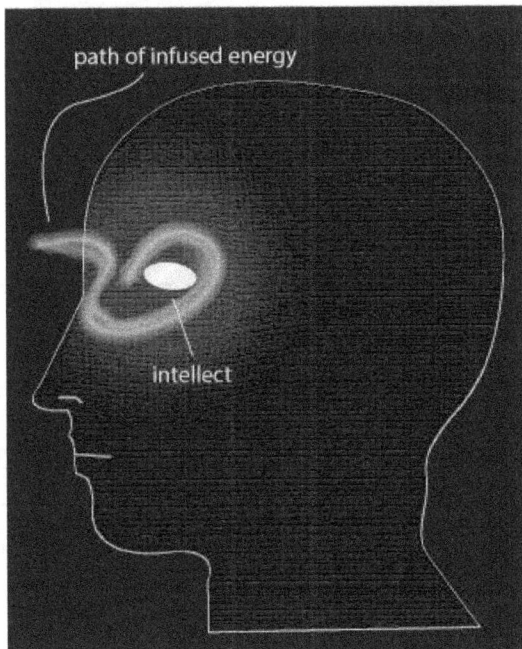

path of infused energy

intellect

Then I used a procedure for passing infused energy through the third eye into the head using a third eye flush-way or energy passing oblong tunnel.

Why do this?

This is part of developing a yoga siddha body with emphasis on the intellect, moving it away from its favorite interest which is to manipulate physical existence. When the intellect is sufficiently energized the yogi knows it since when he sits to meditate, there are no thoughts to watch, no thoughts to avoid, no thoughts to hash over and no thoughts to be entertained by. But that is not all. That is the accomplishment in the fifth stage of yoga, pratyahar. Beyond that there is linkage with higher persons, places and things.

At the end of the meditation session, suddenly after about fifteen seconds there appeared a gold energy at the third eye. This was gold in a brown-black darkness.

Most of the meditation was involved in trying to reach the cosmic intellect, to invite that energy to penetrate and saturate the psyche. In that sense it was an unsuccessful effort but it was successful from the angle of just doing as instructed by a yoga guru.

Sex Pleasure / Yogi Bhajan

Breath infusion practice this morning was successful. Somehow, I experience an energy flare where a kundalini force saturated the entire trunk, even the arms. A pearl-like energy vibrated through the trunk. It went into the arms with a bliss aspect and with distribution of small pearly molecules.

After this, I shifted and focused on infusing the head of the subtle body, beginning with the area where thoughts are generated and then moving to the back top.

For a short time near the end of the session, Yogi Bhajan's head appeared. He said this:

You cannot assume that you know what an advanced yogi experiences during practice, because you may not be on his level. In the West most of my students were stymied by sex desire. Thus, they underestimated what the Indians who do kundalini yoga experienced. It is not that all Indians are advanced. Some are just as restricted in the practice as those who took bodies in the West.

But it is a fact that when you take a body from the Western culture, you are automatically restricted because of the nature of the environment and because of the stress on sexual freedom. The focus of the culture in the West is for personal sexual gratification. The society is designed to facilitate that. But sex pleasure has little use in yoga.

Kundalini keeps the individual spiritual beings restricted in one way or the other but its hold on them through sexual facility is near complete. Imagine that you are in solitary confinement in a maximum-security prison. When one is attracted to sex and when one is sex-centered, and when one feels that sex pleasure is the ultimate enjoyment nature offers, one is under the maximum confinement. This may continue even when one does kundalini practice.

When I was alive and I stressed responsibility as a replacement for sex, hardly a person understood that. They looked as if I was uninformed. In the case of sex, the enjoyment is real and immediate. In the case of responsibility, the enjoyment is postponed for the future. I know about sex pleasure but in the long run, responsibility will give a greater profit in the cultural world if pleasure is what one desires.

After high school, youths usually try to rent apartments. This concerns the privacy needed for sex. As soon as puberty sets in one is confronted with this need for privacy which becomes an obsession. However, along with the need for sex the aspect of responsibility faces the individual. Sex offers enjoyment upfront while responsibility attenuates the pleasure, and demands service in return.

Yogi Bhajan spoke of those who confronted him as disciples when he came to the United States. Many youths from the counter-culture were attracted to him. They wanted enlightenment along the lines they discovered while using hallucinogenic drugs like LSD. However, behind the scenes there was an aggressive need for sex. This over-shadowed the need for enlightenment.

The sense of responsibility had no voice in the matter, because the sex pleasure need held the priority and did not allow any other function to predominate. As far as the experience they derived from hallucinogenic drugs, that too involved sex pleasure. That shrouded the sense of responsibility.

Responsibility for progeny is inclusive in the range of aspects for which we are accountable to providence. Ultimately in terms of reincarnation the responsibility for progeny is the biggest bill which one will be held accountable for. This is because to get the next body, someone must be induced to take responsibility for the infant.

Suppose my parent(s) beget my baby form and leave it to fend for itself while they procure more sexual pleasure. That pleasure will be the cause of my neglect. For them it would be pleasure and fulfillment of personal needs. For me it is parental neglect.

Responsibility includes responsibility for the progeny produced while using the sex force. If I could get a body but my would-be father or mother uses a contraceptive, they skirt responsibility for my upbringing. They get what they desire the most which is sexual pleasure. I would get what I do not desire which is the frustration of not getting an infant form.

Thought Location

Meditation this morning was the practice of taking advantage of the stoppage of thought generation. Students should find an infallible, all-time method which works for shutting down thought, image and idea production in the mind. There is no point in arguing about methods, whether it be chanting mantras, observing breathing, observing thoughts, ignoring thoughts, being detached from thoughts, breath infusion, walking meditation or whatever. That is not the point.

Use the method that works. Be sure that it shuts down the thought operations. Once you achieve that by a method which works time and time again, use it to achieve the thought-less, image-less, idea-less state of mind. Sit in the mind in the same location within it where the thoughts were generated.

This location is specific, it is not here, there and everywhere. Thoughts are created in a specific place in the mind. Once the generation process ceases, go to the generation location. Sit in the mind in that silence.

Imagine for a moment that you used to go to a theatre to see movies. You went there repeatedly. You know the screen's location. You know your seat. You know how you sat to enjoy the actions on the screen. You were not specific for looking at the projection booth which was behind you. You had some idea where that booth was, because there were times when you arrived late to see the movie and as you walked in the theatre to take your seat, you noticed a stream of light coming from an opening behind the seats.

I instruct that you should sit in the projection room. At first you misunderstood because you thought that the projection room is the screen. In that case, sit where the screen is. That is the beginning of this practice.

The idea is that you should not sit in your seat. Every time you enter the theatre go to the screen. Sit there. Do so in silence, because now the movie projector projects no images. It shows nothing.

Astral Changes

Each soul has an astral body but each soul does not have a physical form. When one has a physical body, it means that in addition one has an astral one. However, once the physical body is dead, and until one reincarnates as a baby one is left with only an astral form. This means that those who are embodied can be astral or physical. Those who are deceased and who are not again embodied are astral only.

If someone passed on and assumed a new body, that soul can communicate astrally and physically. In addition, the astral form can change shape. For instance, if my grandfather passed some years ago and is now a human being as a child somewhere, his astral body can meet mine in the astral world. It may assume the grandfather form temporarily just to relate to me as it did before. The astral body is capable of rapid adaptations.

Subjective Experience

Proof requires objective evidence which cannot be acquired from subjective experiences. For subjective experiences one should hold discussions with others who have similar experiences.

Two madmen may understand each other quite well but other people think that they are crazy. This is because their condition of mind cannot be externalized in an objective way. Because one madman had an experience, another fellow who had the same subjective expression can agree that it exist.

Question is:

Why should one prove a subjective experience to another person?

If one has an experience and is confidence of it, why bother with others. Unless someone is insecure about it and feels the necessity to convince others of it, a man does not have to convince everyone about his reality.

The way our minds are constructed, they are naturally extrovert. Most of the introvert actions are in support of extrovert pursuits. We have little or no confidence in genuine introvert tendencies of the mind. This is why we crave physical reality. That offsets the lack of confidence in psychic reality.

Most people feel that the mind is an expression of the brain and that when the brain is dead, there will be no mind.

If a person experiences astral projection, he/she can develop confidence that there is a mind which is separate from the brain and which will exist when the brain is done. But that is subjective. Only two subjectively mad people can agree on this.

Yogi as Ruler of Psychic Components

During breath infusion Muktananda appeared for a second. He said nothing. He went away. Then Yogesh appeared, looked, smiled and disappeared. These were astral encounters.

The air outdoors was cold but I did the practice. Better to practice than to leave this body and not have the subtle body changed into a yoga siddha form or at least into the habit of the practice which would yield a yoga siddha form hereafter. Who knows when nature will decide that it wants to get the materials which are used for maintaining this body? Once nature decides to reclaim these materials, no one will stop the death of this body. Nature is nobody's friend. Nature does whatever is convenient for nature, regardless of how inconvenient it is for anybody.

During the last fifteen minutes of breath infusion I focused on infusing subtle energy in the head of the subtle body. This is a new procedure but I was shown it some years ago by Yogi Bhajan with the brain breath infusion. With the help from other yoga teachers, I resumed that practice in a more thorough way.

Sometimes when one takes hallucinogenic drugs one may realize that the subtle head breathes subtle air into itself. It does not depend on the nose.

Doing the infusion the intake of breath was different in that it seems that the air appeared in the center of the head. It did not enter from the outside and then go inside. The air appearing magically in the center of the head and then moved in an upward curl on the inside around the intellect.

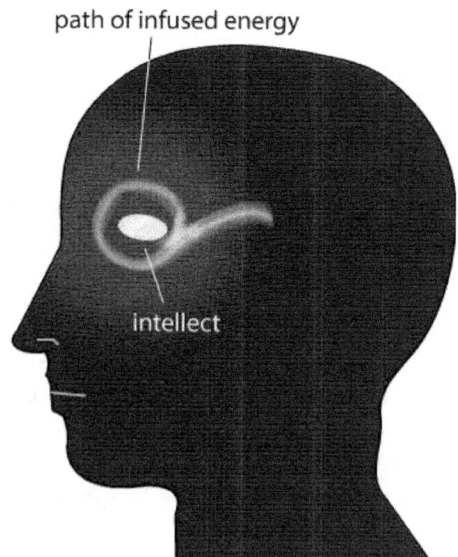

path of infused energy

intellect

When I sat to meditate, I went to the location of the intellect. In this case "I" means the coreSelf. The intellect, if it is not seen, is the place where the thoughts, images and ideas would occur. I went to that location. I sat there doing meditation.

After a bit Yogesh appeared in a miniature form. He said this.

Rule the domain. Take more control. Dismiss the intellect. Put your foot down as the conqueror of the psyche.

I listened and heard naad and as indicated by Yogesh, I called naad forward and sat with it where the intellect is usually located. There were some third eye dimensional openings and perceptions now and again during this meditation.

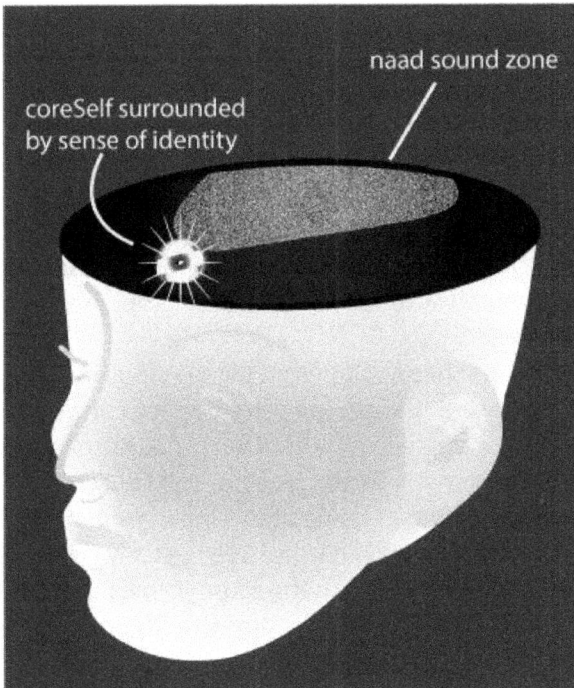

coreSelf surrounded by sense of identity

naad sound zone

Being God

Memories and tendencies are carried to the next life, but they are first carried to the afterlife. The carrier or conveyor is not the person but nature. Nature conveys it in its own way. For instance, many of the memories are compressed by nature and become instincts which are carried over to the next life. Personality traits are carried over mostly as predispositions.

Some memories cannot be retrieved because they are stored in the physical brain only and are not in stored in the subtle body. Leaving the physical body at will and dying as desired by killing the body and then leaving it, is possible if one spent the entire life-time mastering the lifeForce mechanism in the body. This mechanism, the kundalini, operates the breathing and other involuntary functions. That is the system that regulates sleeping and waking.

A more practical objective is to study how that system operates and learn how to make use of its functions and to take advantage of its methods.

Yogis study how the lifeForce releases the subtle body for astral projections and how it finally leaves the body at death. We can make use of this natural system. That may be all we can achieve. The way transmigration operates, only a few people get the best of the system.

Karma or consequential energy cannot be erased no more than one can rewrite history. Karma is what destiny produces as the new events which appears before us.

There is no way to erase a consequence? Whatever nature appears as is a production made from the raw materials of history.

Each plane has its own complete system of actions and reactions, but there is some energy exchange from one plane to another. One parallel world which jars into another may affect what happens in that other place. Still these are closed, isolated systems which have membranes which contain and restrict their contents.

The evolution is not happening from plane A to plane B but rather within Plane A and within Plane B. Usually we are stuck in a certain plane for millions of years. Jumping from one plane to another requires many permissions and radical changes in the psychic content of the individual. You may move from being a dog into being a human being but to move from being a human being into say an astral celestial being is hardly likely. Usually we move from a status within one plane to another status in the same plane. Rarely do we jump from one plane to the next, because usually during a lifetime, we do not upgrade the psychology sufficiently to make those changes.

Try not to confuse celestial beings who are astral beings permanently with earthly beings, like myself for instance, who make journeys into the celestial world but who are earth-bound spirits whose astral bodies cannot remain permanently on the astral plane but will always return to physical existence. Our psychological profiles at this time, will not permit us to stay in a celestial world because our tendencies will demand that we participate in the earth's history.

When you are on one plane, you get bogged down during that lifetime with the ideas, symbols and methods which relate to that plane.

Subsequently you do not develop the habits and qualities which are natural to another level. One is limited to a familiar plane.

Physical beings are usually repeatedly rebirthing as physical beings. They rarely evolve or become upgraded to being celestial people. Their psychology remains with physical habits and methods.

There is a verse in the *Bhagavad Gita*, where it is said that according to the psychological profile one has at the time of death, one attains the next living state. That means that if my mind is tracked for physical existence, I will again get only life in the physical world. After death my remnant self will be turned in that way and will desire that in actuality. Even if I imagine something else, it will have little or no effect because my basic profile is that of a physical being.

How did the physical universe come to be?

This is one question which cannot be answered in a scientific way because I cannot go back in time to the event. Even if I could do so the problem remains that I cannot take someone and show how it was done.

Each religious discourse has its proposition about this. Science also presents ideas. Which opinion is valid?

It is reasonable to accept the scientific proposal that the universe existed for thirteen billion years. If we can accept that, it is reasonable to accept that after thirteen billion years, a few tiny miniscule existences discuss how it started. They claim to know how it occurred. That is good comedy.

The evidence supports spontaneous occurrence. Development happens mostly by outgrowing potencies and their urges. Like for instance how a human infant develops a body which exhibits sexual urge at puberty. That happens spontaneously. It is not that the kid plans the sexual urge. It happens naturally.

We also have personality and non-personality, animate and inanimate aspects to the creation. We have planetary and dimensional environments. We have persons in these environments. We can assume that these aspects are perpetual. Anytime we have personalities, we will have social interactions. One will be inferior in some aspect and another will be superior. These features may be accepted as being causeless and spontaneous.

By astral projection, I experienced many dimensions and subworlds. I experienced deities or god-controllers of dimensions and worlds. In some phases of the astral body, one experiences a universal consciousness of a creative zone. From this one can get the idea that there are controllers or gods of cosmic systems. But it all depends on where one goes and what experiences one is afforded.

Everything outside of that is belief based on conjecture or faith in a person or book.

Will one eventually reach the point where one can create a universe?

Why would anyone wish to do that? Currently we are in a confused and conflicting situation. There is constant threat of political chaos. Why would anyone desire to create worlds, unless one thinks that one can do better than the person or force which created the one we are subjects of.

If we live in a deity's mind, as part of his fantasy, why would we want to take a position like that deity, and create another chaotic scene like the one we exist in?

There is this physical level. There is the subtle level which we experience in lucid dreaming and astral projection. Beyond that is the higher astral or supernatural level and beyond that there is the causal plane. In the causal plane the potential for this creation is existent. If one goes into the causal plane, one cannot act there. It is as if one was in a deep dreamless sleep. Some yogis retain a slight objective awareness there but mostly it is subjectivity folded into itself, which means absolutely no objective manifestation.

One of my yoga gurus who is now departed, entered the causal plane. I cannot reach him for instructions. Every so often he comes out. Then I can speak with him but while he is there, his existence is suspended.

To understand what it is like to be a creation of somebody's mind, of a deity, observe the mind when you think. Regard yourself as an idea. There is a story in the Srimad Bhagavatam, where it states that once the deity who caused this creation, suspended the lives of some farm boys for one year. The boys never realized that they de-existed for that year. If you live in somebody's mind, that is the type of situation you would be in. If right now we are some deity's idea then at any moment our existence may be cancelled like a blown light bulb. Thus, when one thinks of being such a creator, it means that others will be dependent on one's mental power for existence.

There is a story in the Puranas about two brothers name Madhu and Kaitabha. These two were great mystics but they had ulterior motives. They knew that they were creations of a deity. They wanted to out-exist the deity and take his powers.

They learned that he slept after many millions of years. They perfected psychic skills. When the deity slept, they remained awake. Their plan was to steal his creative skills because they could not by themselves develop those abilities. As he fell asleep, they took his subconscious memories so that they could access his magical skills and create their own worlds when he was unconscious.

Unfortunately for them, there was another person who was the deity in whose mind their deity was created. That other person, knew their plan. He objected to it and de-existed them.

This means that even if one produces a creation, there may be hassles in it. After all, if this world is imperfect, if we are imperfect by virtue of being produced in an imperfect world, it stands to reason, that whatever we produce would be flawed to some degree.

As far as guidelines for higher planes, the body one surfaces in on those planes is itself aware of the guidelines just as the body one uses now is aware of the force of gravity. One may see in real life or in a video, how a fawn runs some minutes after it is born. How is that possible? It is not that the fawn does that. Nature arranged that. The fawn is like a consumer in a store. The consumer cannot make the products but he/she can certainly use them.

The subtle body according to the level it is manifested in, exhibits certain abilities or mystic skills. Once in my astral body, a tube protruded from the third eye. It could see anything on the atomic scale. It is not that I produced the tube or wished for it. It happened. This means that I was on a subtle plane in which the astral body has the microscopic ability.

Yogi Assumes Thought Location

This morning during meditation, I continued the practice of relocating the coreSelf where the thoughts usually occur in the front center of the mental space. For those who have no idea that there is an intellect which functions to create ideas, this is a location. When I was first located there, I noticed naad sound in the back near the right ear. It blared in the subtle head, almost touching me but originating near the right ear.

After a time, I looked forward. I saw copper colored shapes at the third eye opening. At the opening it was dark except for the glow of these random copper shapes.

The main objective of this meditation was to control the place where the thoughts were produced and to be sure that no other thoughts arose.

The coreSelf does this with unfettered unsupported willpower. This is technical. Usually the willpower is a supported force. The first reinforcement comes from the sense of identity. When that reinforcement occurs, we experience it as attention, or the bare willpower becomes channeled as attention. The second reinforcement comes from the intellect. That attention changes into mental action. The third reinforcement comes from the emotions; this is interpreted as urge or desire. The word emotions pertain to the sensual energy of the kundalini.

Usually when the unsupported willpower is expressed, nothing happens. This is like when a king signs a decree and his prime minister refused to look at it. At that time, the king feels powerless. Suppose it is a decree for war on another king. Then even if the prime minister signs it, if the commander of the army rejects it, the king will be powerless because unless the warriors are given the order by the commander war will not be declared. Like that, the self for all it is, is merely a shadow ruler. It must take assistance from the adjuncts. Its big mouth and glorious acclaim about itself in philosophy and scriptures, have no practical value.

In this meditation however, by dismissing the intellect and doing its task, this whim of a king attempts to be the ruler.

The coreSelf in this case moved itself by itself. It broke away from its default position as an observer of the operations of the intellect. It moved itself to the place of the intellect. The energy to do this comes directly from the core. Formerly the core could not to do this. It was crippled. It took years of practice in meditation, a great struggle, before the core developed the strength to do this. A wimp does not become strong overnight. It takes years of effort to build muscles and shed the supports upon which it once relied.

That is what it is like to suspend kundalini and take over its operations in the body. Obviously, this is risky because the kundalini has some power and may do something treasonous to sabotage the core. Unless a yogi can manhandle kundalini, he cannot do this. The kundalini is allied to the intellect. Unless the core can break that friendship, it cannot command the psyche.

To be honest the coreSelf cannot function without the attention energy. In fact, on this side of existence the core is always accompanied by the attention energy. It can separate itself from everything except the sense of identity.

Getting rid of the sense of identity is not within the range of a limited self's ability. However, when the sense of identity is bared association with the intellect and the kundalini, the identity changes its attitude. It no longer expresses a strong attentive force which is focused for serving the intellect and kundalini.

The sense of identity produces the attention energy. It forms part of itself as the attention energy, which projects like a ray going out of the sun. A ray is from the sun and is made of the same energy as the sun but it is still not the entire solar orb.

Imagine if you are enclosed in a balloon in such a way that you cannot get out of it. If you want to relate to what is outside of the balloon you must do so through the membrane. If you want to hold an exterior object you must push the membrane.

The self is surrounded on all sides by the sense of identity. Any time the coreSelf tries to act, it must push its willpower which is the attention energy. The willpower is inside the attention energy, the way a hand would be inside the membrane of a glove which it pushes to grab an object.

Even though it appears to change as it transmigrates in the physical creation and passes through phases of subtle existence, the coreSelf does not go through the alterations.

The sense of identity is colorless and translucent. It absorbs colors and attitudes in association with the intellect and the kundalini lifeForce. This influence is then related to the core which is victimized by it.

Erasing Fated Consequences

The best way to erase consequences is to patch whatever it is on the subconscious level where the energy lays in dormancy in one's nature. This does nothing to help the other person(s) involved. The victim will still remain with energies for settling whatever happened but one may escape from having to be there to settle with the victim personally.

An example may be given in a court case, where I unfairly injured a man and then left the scene of the crime and went to another country. The police opened a case and serve a warrant for my arrest. Since I relocated out of the jurisdiction and they do not know my location, they had only the injured man and his problems.

I considered the matter and realize that I was wrong but I was unwilling to return to the area in which the incidence took place. I made a decision to do everything possible to compensate the man. I hired an attorney to go to the location of the incidence and to find how I could compensate in absentia.

He is informed that I could pay medical expenses and give money for punitive damages. I must give the man a pension for the rest of his life. I agree to this. I release the money to an attorney. This does not remove the man's resentment. He will carry that in his nature until it is resolved.

However, there is still one payment I must make and that is to nature. If nature took offense when I injured the man, I still have to settle with nature. It will not accept my ideas of how to resolve this.

CoreSelf as a Wimp

During the first part of the session, breath infusion was focused on the center of the trunk of the subtle body. Then I shifted focus to the head. Thoughts during practice can serve to alert the yogi about the impulsive activities of the intellect.

If I gave you a meditation procedure and advocate that it will do this and it will do that and then you apply it and it does not work, it means that for you it is an invalid process. Still, do not be frustrated. Keep at it by trying to discover for yourself an effective method. Go to another teacher. Get a process that works. It does not matter to me if my method failed for anyone. The important thing is that the student persists and persevere for success, either by discovering a method or by getting an effective one from someone else.

In any case, the student's success is my success. Sticking to my method which does not work does not assist me either. We both win and can enjoy the success if you discover a method that is effective or if you get a valid process from another teacher.

While meditating the student should observe the effects of the particular practice but he/she should give each process a chance to take effect. If for instance I do breath infusion and it does not work to shut down the impulsive thought-creation mechanism of the mind, I need to see the teacher who recommended that. I should hold a discussion to discover if I applied the method properly.

When I sat to meditate, I sunk into the central trunk of the subtle body to see if the energy there was in a clarified condition, to see if dense energy remained. There was no dense energy but there was a white misty energy. It was like going through a large vertical shaft, dropping deep into the earth. Observing this condition which was satisfactory, I rose into the head and went to the place where the thoughts usually arise. There were none. I took a seat in the center of the thought-production location. I listened to naad sound. It blared from the usual place in the back-right side of the head near the ear.

After this the third eye had light-filled clouds of white energy which passed through it now and again. These never cleared so the space of the third eye was never cleared to be a wide bay window into another world. So long as the third eye space remains unclear, the yogi is barred from clearly perceiving anything in those other dimensions. If you are in a house by a bay window and if there is a dense white smoke passing through the window, you cannot see what is beyond the window. Even if the white smoke is filled with light, it will hamper visibility.

During this meditation every so often, I drifted into nothingness. Then I would realize what happened and resituate myself at the intellect location and continue the meditation. This happened about three times.

This occured because of demands placed on the psyche by the kundalini lifeForce. Kundalini is the chairman of the department of energy in the subtle body. It controls energy distribution. It is up to the coreSelf to manage kundalini. It takes deliberate actions on the part of the core to do so. If it fails to manage the powers of kundalini, the core will continue depending on kundalini to make decisions about the sleep-wake-relax schedule for the psyche.

Breath infusion is the first serious step in taking power control over from kundalini because in breath infusion, the coreSelf can supply energy to run the psyche and does not have to be under the thumb of kundalini to get fresh air.

The coreSelf, imagines itself as a controller because it is rendered so many services by the various adjuncts but the truth is that the core is a wimp with a big mouth. It can however strive for real power by gradually outfitting itself with the necessary skills.

Army Marches through a Yogi's Body

Last night I was asked to give a short lecture and supervise a class about the *Ramayana* of Valmiki which is a standard religious book from India. After the function, I was offered a meal, which due to the tradition of these events, I could not refuse. It was 8 pm when I finished the meal. I knew it was punitive. Still, due to social requirements I indulged.

The result was that during the night there was a small army moving through my intestines, at a time when there is usually total silence and rest of most of the cells. The meal was about one-third the size of a full meal. A full meal would have been like ten battalions with heavy tanks bombarding a large city, pulverizing it to dust. Instead this was like a small squadron with a few snipers and two or three regiments with light artillery.

During the night I awoke twice when there was some firing of the artillery. I thought to myself, "I wish this infantry would fall and die or go to sleep for the night."

The question is:

How do people eat heavy meals night after night and then sleep and snore away? That is like when you are in the city which is shelled by an enemy and you get so accustomed to the loud explosions that you fall asleep anyway even though when you awaken the next morning the building you slept in vaporized due to the explosions?

I was late to do the breath infusion, doing it near 6 am rather than near 4 am. This is one of the disadvantages of night eating. One becomes inclined to rising later. I struggled to push some heavy energy through the chest, down into the navel area and then out through the bottom of the trunk. I worked on this for about twenty minutes.

After that I worked on infusing the head. I worked on blasting the thought, image, idea area of the subtle head. I had some success. During the exercises which I did outdoors, I heard the front door open.

After about fifteen minutes I looked and saw someone there. One of the visitors watched my exercises and breath infusion routine. This is a person who learnt this some years ago and who also was trained in meditation but who is so overpowered by a reluctance to practice, that he is unable to bring himself into even five minutes of breath infusion daily.

That is like when one is late to catch a train. One hurries and gets to the station but when one gets there a station attendant says that the train will be 10 minutes late. In the meantime, as one waits, one feels hungry but instead of going back home to prepare a meal, one stays at the station in fear of missing the train. Then after ten minutes, the train still does not arrive in the station. There is an announcement that there is another delay. The train will be twenty minutes late.

But then again one waits for an additional ten minutes. There is yet another announcement about the late train being delayed further. In the meantime, one remains with the hunger and the fear that if one goes for a meal, one will miss the train.

In this way many students fail to complete the practice because of social pressures which stall them at the station of social affairs and deprive them of the spiritually-nutrient practice of yoga.

In the Astral with Relatives

During the night in the astral world, I met some relatives who still use physical bodies but who are the last of their family lines. With their parents, grandparents and siblings deceased, they can no longer hide under the cover of having other elderly people in the family, feeling that someone else is older and will die shortly.

In this case, they are the pending subjects of death, waiting for the bell of time to toll with their name and number. They examined my subtle body, wondering why it has so much light and life as compared to their own.

The big secret is not meditation, it is breath infusion. Anybody can sit and meditate or can at least think that he/she meditates even if the person has no idea what that actually entails. But breath infusion is different; it takes effort and consistent daily practice.

These relatives asked me about diet. As far as they were concerned it had to do with vegetarian meals. They kept asking, "What do you eat? Give the secret!"

One lady, a cousin, came to me. She said, "Really, tell us the diet. We can adopt it. That may relieve the aches and pains of old age."

I told her that the first thing to do is to make sure one has something green in the daily meal, a green leafy vegetable. I suggested that she consume more than carbohydrate or starchy foods and meat.

After this one relative, another elderly lady, send a mental message, that I need not bother with the others and that I should come to see her later, since she wanted to learn yoga.

CoreSelf Occupies Intellect's Space

During meditation practice, I had some luck staying at the location of the intellect. The way to do this is to repeatedly make efforts to differentiate the coreSelf, the observing iSelf, from the antics and machinations of the thoughts, images and ideas which flash in the mind.

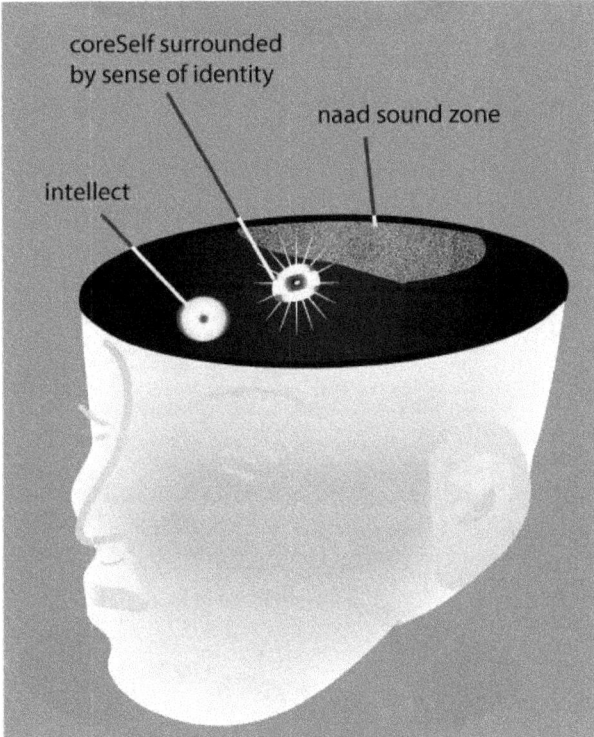

default locations of intellect, sense of identity,
coreSelf and naad

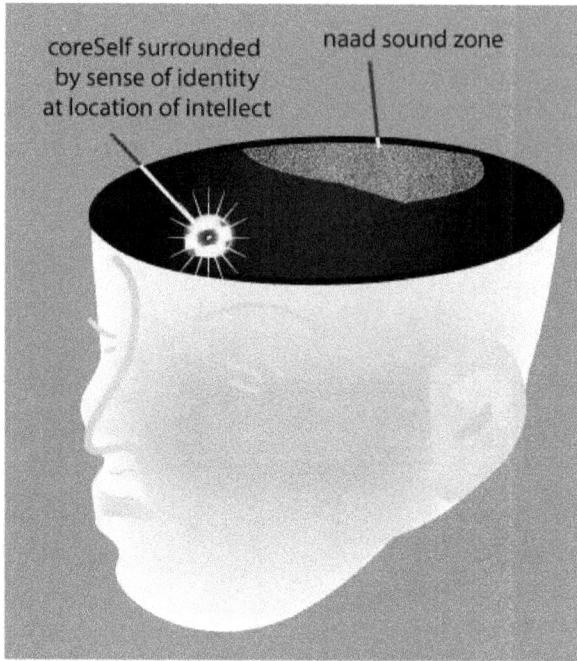

coreSelf surrounded by sense of identity at location of intellect

naad sound zone

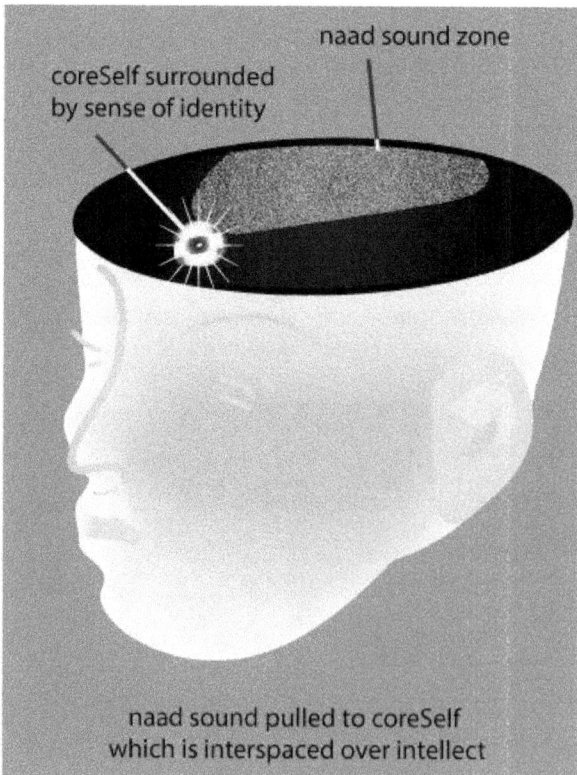

coreSelf surrounded by sense of identity

naad sound zone

naad sound pulled to coreSelf which is interspaced over intellect

The first part of this is to locate where images occur in the mind. Are the images all-pervasive, happening at random everywhere in the mind space? Are they occurring in one, or say two places only? For instance, a computer screen is usually on a table or mounted on a wall. It is not all-pervasive but sunlight is all pervasive on a cloudless day. Is the imaging in the mind like sunlight or is it like a computer screen?

If it is all-pervasive, one is in trouble. This procedure is useless. But if one finds that it is in at a specific location or is usually in one or two places, this procedure is valid. Note the location. Do so repeatedly to be sure that you are correct.

Once you note that place of the images, move the observing self there, so that there is no mental distance between the iSelf and that place.

What happens next is that the images will cease. If you are in a theatre viewing a movie or if you are at home viewing a video on your television, if you sit inside the TV, then obviously the viewing will cease.

However, I left out one small detail which is that to do this one must change the relationship with the viewing place, with the intellect. Naturally the relationship with that is one of being a passive observer, a consumer who is compelled to view whatever is shown on the screen. That would be changed.

There will be a resistance where the viewing place will not allow you to replace it. It will try to keep you at bay, so that you stay in your assigned seat and look helplessly at the images. You must act to change that.

The ashtanga yoga system recommends pranayama breath infusion as the way to destroy that resistance. Some persons have a less aggressive way of doing that. If you kill the enemy by gunshot that is okay, but if you can do it in a nice way say like by kissing him or by feeding him a cake, that is to your credit.

As I sat where the images usually occur, I heard naad sound which was way in the distance in the back. I called it to come forward which it did. I linked to it. After sometime when I looked forward, I noticed that at the third eye there was light. I also checked the condition of the mind space. In it there was no fear of the intellect. Usually in the mind there is this fear energy of the intellect where the coreSelf has this fear that it should not object to the intellect or it will face dire consequences. This fear was not present in the mind.

The fear in the coreSelf where it is afraid to object to the plans of the intellect, causes many persons who set out to meditate, to be afraid of challenging the mind. By the word mind, they really mean the thought-construction, image-producing, idea-formatting part of the mind which is the intellect.

For instance, most meditation procedures for dealing with the mind, for controlling it, are methods for attempting to silence the intellect but since the coreSelf is afraid of the intellect and because the coreSelf is not sure of its position in the psyche, these methods do everything but confront the intellect and take control of its operations.

Conquest of the intellect shows up as two developments.

- thoughts stop being generated
- thoughts are generated in slow motion only or they are generated directly by the coreSelf without the automatic expansion of such thoughts by the intellect or by the intellect in alliance with the memory.

A student must realize that as the coreSelf, he/she is deadly afraid of the intellect. It has the upper hand. We got this body with an intellect and kundalini being in charge of the body. That is the natural way from the time this body was pushed through the mother's channel. Nature did not design it with the coreSelf in control. It positioned the core to serve as a battery for providing power.

In that format, the coreSelf is important as a power-supply not as a power consumer. The adjuncts are the consumers. The core is required to stay put and give power and permissions at its expense.

This arrangement is fearful because it means that the coreSelf is a wimp. A scrawny little dogie will be afraid in the presence of a well-fed canine. But if the little dogie is nourished, it may challenge other canines.

This practice begins with observing where in the mind thoughts, images and ideas appear. It is a subjective space (the mind environment). The observation of what occurs in it, is the only information which will help the yogi. These are two locations, one observer and a thought.

Consider it in another way of there being a witness to an incidence, the incidence itself, the location of the witness and the location of the incidence.

In meditation first determine the incidence. Then try to determine its mental or emotional location. Then try to determine the distance between the incidence and the observing self. Then try to determine the observing self.

If you find that you cannot do this or that there is no differentiation between the incidence and the observing self, report that like this:

I saw something in my mind, something like a teapot but to me there was no distance between me and teapot. I felt that I was the teapot. In such a report it seems that the observing self was itself configured to be the incidence and the witness simultaneously.

Swami Rama / Reserving the Sexual Energies

The afternoon session of breath infusion went well. During the practice I felt the presence of Swami Rama on my right. He spoke as I practiced. His discussion was about these Patanjali verses.

अविद्यास्मितारागद्वेषाभिनिवेशाः क्लेशाः ॥३॥

avidyā asmitā rāga dveṣa abhiniveśaḥ kleśāḥ

avidyā – spiritual ignorance; asmitā – misplaced identity; rāga – a tendency of emotional attachment; dveṣa – impulsive emotional disaffection; abhiniveśaḥ – strong focus on mundane existence which is due to an instinctive fear of death; kleśāḥ – the mento-emotional afflictions.

The mental and emotional afflictions are spiritual ignorance, misplaced identity, emotional attachment, impulsive emotional disaffection and a strong focus on mundane existence, which is due to an instinctive fear of death. (Yoga sutras 2.3)

स्वरसवाही विदुषोऽपि तथारूढोऽभिनिवेशः ॥९॥

svarasavāhī viduṣaḥ 'pi tatha rūḍho 'bhiniveśaḥ

svarasavāhī = sva – own + rasa – essence + vāhī – flow, current, instinct for self-preservation (svarasavāhī – its own flow of energy of self-preservation); viduṣaḥ – the wise man; 'pi = api – also; tatha – just as, so it is; rūḍho = rūḍhah – developed produced; 'bhiniveśaḥ = abhiniveśaḥ – strong focus on mundane existence due to instinctive fear of death.

As it is, the strong focus on mundane existence, which is due to the instinctive fear of death, which is sustained by its own potencies, and which operates for self-preservation, is developed even in the wise man. (Yoga sutras 2.9)

ते प्रतिप्रसवहेयाः सूक्ष्माः ॥१०॥

te pratiprasavaheyāḥ sūkṣmāḥ

te – these, they; prati – opposing, reverting back; prasava – expressing, going outwards; heyāḥ – what is fit to be left or abandoned; sūkṣmāḥ – subtle energies.

These subtle motivations are to be abandoned by reverting their expression backwards. (Yoga sutras 2.10)

Swami Rama said this:

Each person who assumes a physical body must at some point in the initial formation of that form, submit to the curling action of kundalini. In this curling action, kundalini concentrates certain energies which are required as an initiation of the new body.

Even a great yogin who takes an embryo, is subjected to this. Few persons however can break the choke-hold of kundalini and its temperament which is to create a concentration of energy for sexual enjoyment.

Before puberty there is no carnal knowledge in the body. In fact, if one takes a juvenile who has not reached puberty and expose that person to sexual intercourse, there would be no experience of a climax. At that stage the body does not develop sexual pleasure.

However, for an adult, if there is exposure, that converts into an impulsion. Because of this forcefulness a student yogi may practice in a half-hearted way, whereby he/she cannot concentrate fully on the internal plane.

Kundalini is on the alert to procure pleasure. After puberty that becomes it main focus. When the student begins, he/she is stymied by the need for pleasure. Kundalini for its own part, stores hormones with the intention of using that energy during sexual expression.

Why should the student yogi go all out, when he or she can practice partially and make-by? Why infuse the sexual energy and then by a thorough infusion scatter it evenly through the body? You may not get intense pleasure if the energy is scattered. Hence, why do yoga to that proficiency if it will deprive one of the pleasure intensity yielded by reserving the sexual energy for the genitals?

Swamis and Sex Desire

A swami who passed on about a week ago, came this morning just when I awoke to do exercises. Now that he is departed, he wanted to learn yoga. This is a swami who was an officiating spiritual master in the Hare Krishna Movement. Due to prohibitions in their society concerning yoga; he could not do it while he used a physical body.

Due to having homosexual tendencies, he indulged in pedophile activities with boys who were in the boarding school in the religious society. He said to me,

Yoga was not allowed by our teacher but I feel that perhaps it would have helped many of us to curb sex desire. We could have done it for half-an-hour or even one hour, early in the morning. Then we could have cleaned up and attended to the chanting schedule and worship procedures. There was time for it.

Many of us had to deal with sex desire. We had no way to counteract it. Yoga especially the asanas and the pranayama practice could have been effective.

When I began the postures and breath infusion, he followed what I did. After ten minutes another Swami who was his main assistant and co-disciple came there. This person used to be the main teacher at a boarding school where I taught when I was in the society. He also had homosexual tendencies and was accused of sexual abusing boys in the religious boarding school. Seeing the Swami doing the exercises, he did the exercises as well. Even though he was hostile to me when I lived in the ashram and worked in the school under his supervision, he showed some congeniality towards me.

Once when I lived in their ashram, this other Swami approached to inform me that I could take time off, nights off, to visit my wife. He was concerned that I was not getting sexual intercourse. Since they discovered that I was not as needy for sex as they thought I should be, they began to wonder about the cause of it. Eventually they felt that yoga practice was the cause, even though in their ashram yoga it was banned and I never did any of it while I was there because it was prohibited.

It is interesting how human beings get a religious belief and then become crazy and fanatical, to the extent that they cannot properly evaluate it for what it really is. Because they become afraid of losing status in the religious society, they cannot adjust themselves until they leave the physical body,.

Mind Environment (November 2011)

Breath infusion practice was efficient with a mild rise of bliss bubbles which came up the trunk of the subtle body like tiny pearl energies which rose up into the shoulders. After flushing the trunk, I shifted to the head and worked on clearing images, thoughts and their potential for expansions from the intellect. The intellect did not resist because it was like a badly battered wrestler who was beaten to a pulp by an abled opponent.

During meditation there was a flash of energy. I saw Siddhanath Hamsa Yogi. On his face there was a smile. I sat where the intellect has its default position. I looked forward to the third eye. I was at this time in touch with naad sound which came from the back right near the subtle ear. The mind environment felt like the space in a distant galaxy with a sheer quietness and potent energy.

Past Life Relationships

We carry the past relationships which we had with each other, as predispositions. Memory of the past life is there as an instinct which surfaces in the emotions and in the mind in the present life, as a predisposition or an attitude or mood towards the other person.

However always take into account that if you took a new body in a different time, place and society, the relationship cannot continue without difficulty. This is because all relations were formed under particular cultural situations. When those cultural mediums are removed, the new situations may not respond suitably. No person is so powerful and resourceful that he/she can be successful without the agency of providence. Hence, if one has a conjugal relationship with someone in a past life, if one again meets that person and again enters into such a relationship, there will be a certain percentage of difficulty because of the altered time and place.

Each person had multiples relationships in various other lives. If I am married, I am not protected from meeting someone with whom I had a conjugal relationship in a past life. We are confronted with multiple possibilities for relationships because of the intertwining relationships from the past.

Many such relational energies exist in the creation. Hence any partner can be assailed with attractions to other persons on the basis of having similar relationships with such persons in one or the other past life.

In relationships, affection is currency. It is convertible. The same affection which is between mother and son can be converted into some other relationship. A wife in one life can be a daughter or mother in another life.

Morality means that we regulate these relationships in such a way as to keep them restricted according to how they are formed in socially acceptable ways in each particular life. In this situation, the question is:

Do you want to be a sexual partner with this person? If you do you should be honest about it. If this person cannot agree because of a stronger attraction to another person, one should drop the matter and propose to someone else.

Wherever one goes, one may find someone to love. One may find someone who loves one. What should one do?

Significance of the Astral Planes

In most cases the astral precedes the physical, and is a predictor of what will happen physically. Sometimes there are departures from this which means that something will occur on the astral level and it will not be mimicked on the physical side.

The physical side has more limitations. There one has to deal with inhibitions and moral restrictions. Thus, something that happens astrally may be prohibited physically.

Seeing Things in the Mind

Abstract perception comes about or develops by sticking to the routine of meditation in silence. Initially there is no result from this and one may get the idea that anything spiritual is void. If one is not patience one will be stuck with this idea and will not develop the abstract perceptions.

During breath infusion, a person reached me with some thoughts about social matters. To this person who is a relative, these affairs are of the utmost importance but social affairs from this life are mostly superficial instances which we need not focus on. In terms of many lives, in terms of going through many species of life, lowly and advanced ones, a single life and its social concerns may have very little value. It may be incidental.

One should repeatedly go back to the psychic plane in meditation. One should stay there for as long as possible because that is the method for developing psychic perception.

The meditation I did after the breath infusion practice was great. The mind created no images, thoughts or ideas. Everything of that nature was absent. The mental space was empty except from naad sound rising from the back part of the head.

Once during this session, I became aware of a man and his two children. One was an eight-year-old girl. The father was a European. They live in an older castle house in Europe. The father wanted the two children to go outside with him. The children were resistant. They ignored him but when he walked out of the room, they followed.

This perception occurred in the space between where the intellect and the third eye are located. It was neither at the third eye nor in the intellect itself.

Sometimes scenes which are similar appear in meditation. The yogi sees things which are far away. In this experience it was like I was in the room and also it was like the room was in my mind. Both perceptions occured simultaneously.

Someone may ask as people usually do: What does this perception signify?

The answer is that it signifies only that I developed that perception. Suppose someone is blind. Somehow by a miracle or by medical treatment he developes vision, would you ask for the significance of his sight?

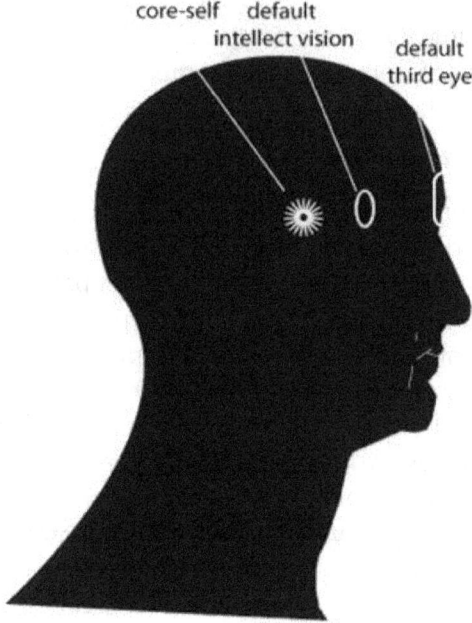

core-self   default
       intellect vision   default
                          third eye

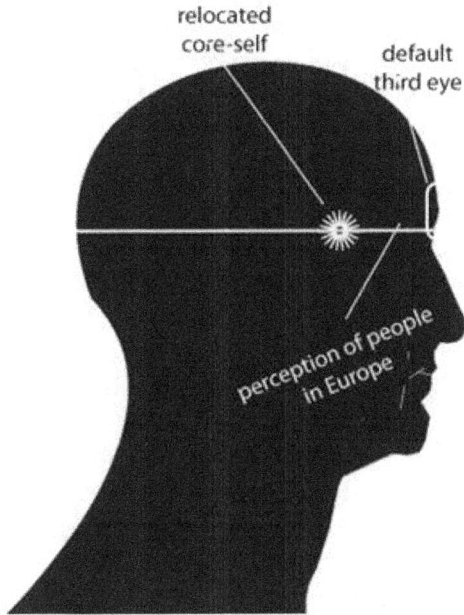

relocated
core-self

default
third eye

perception of people
in Europe

Part 4

Crown Chakra Hanging Bulb

This session of breath infusion resulted in an out-of-the-spine kundalini. This is when kundalini runs the length of the spine outside the spine, outside the body. This type of kundalini has a white-hot look. It produced a coolish heat energy when it rises or spreads in the subtle body.

As I did this, Yogesh appeared. He was in a happy mood. For one reason or the other, he came from the causal level. He handed me something which when I took it, it vanished into the head of my subtle body.

In the last ten minutes of the breath infusion, I got a teleported visit from Yogesh, where he showed how to move from working with the intellect to the brahmrandra location.

When I sat to meditate, I got another teleported communication with him, where he listed a *1-2-3* progression from the trunk of the subtle body, to the buddhi intellect organ and then to the brahmrandra hung bulb.

This bulb appears at a location in the head of the subtle body, just below the crown chakra.

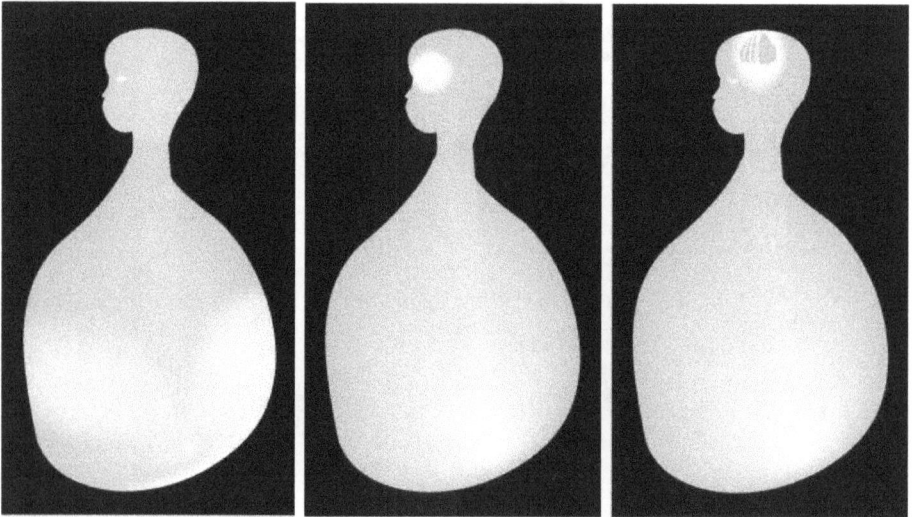

The *1-2-3* progression may be followed if the yogi curbed kundalini, and pulled it to the base of the brain. Once this is done the yogi has to spend weeks, months or years curbing the trunk of the subtle body, by using breath infusion to blast and burn the dark dense zones in the trunk.

After clearing the trunk, he should attack the intellect. When that is subdued, he should work on manifesting the hung bulb below the brahmrandra.

If the yogi can, he/she should, during meditation float in the hung bulb. From that location he can reach deities and advanced entities. He can get information about the supernatural world.

Brahmrandra Pull-up

Yogesh left instruction energy in my psyche yesterday. When doing breath infusion, I cleared the trunk and then worked on the head of the body, but there was a pulling force left by Yogesh from the brahmrandra pull-up area

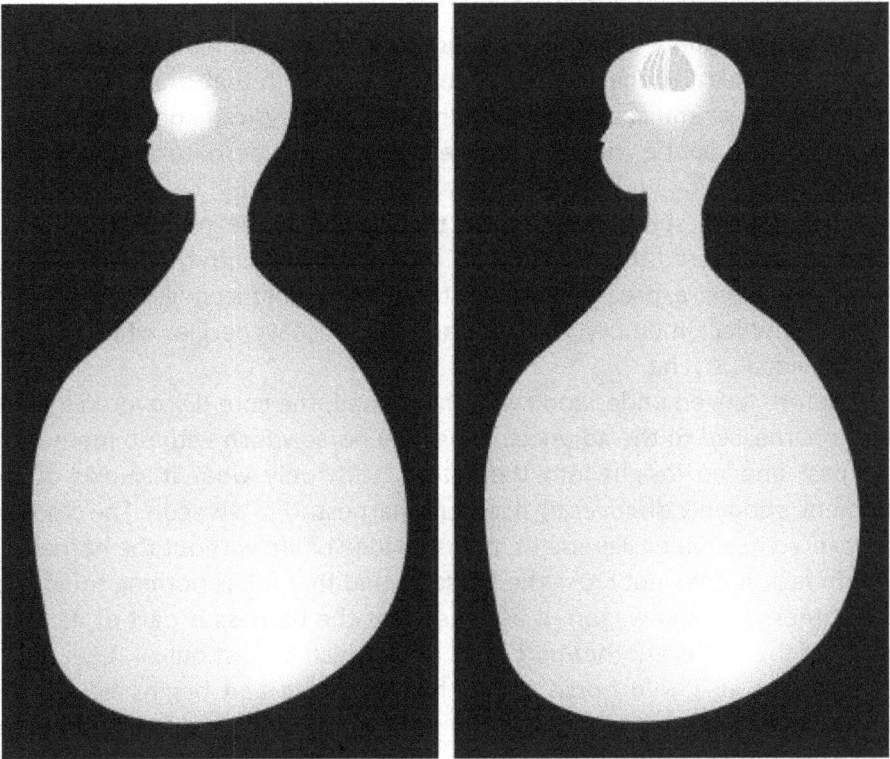

When I sat to meditate, I situated the coreSelf where the thoughts and images usually appear. I did not pay much attention to naad sound. This was because of a focus energy which Yogesh left in my psyche.

This energy had a notation which read that the third eye could serve as a distraction and therefore to conserve time, one should force the intellect to abandon its reliance on the third eye. But this is like asking a human being to give up physical eyes for no eyes, for a blank mind and some imaginative power.

There are subtle eyes but a human being has no faith in these. There is a natural faith in two types of vision, one being physical perception which was developed recently in the womb of the mother and blank psychic perception which adds up to no vision besides thought visualization and blind sensing energy in the mind.

During the meditation, I jumped to the brahmrandra. There was a pulling force which pulled the intellect into the bulb under the brahmrandra. With a guru who has the stature of Yogesh, the student's best bet is to do as instructed.

Yogi Escapes from Psychic Enslavement

It appears that Yogesh has a procedure for relocating the intellect into the crown chakra. If the student yogi is successful in that practice, it would mean that he or she ceased the peering into the physical world and into the regions of the subtle material nature which is a supernatural power unto itself.

The limited spirits who found themselves to be manifested in this creation, discovered themselves with awareness and with the application of awareness being expressed through the psychic adjuncts, like the sense of identity, intellect, memory, kundalini and the sensual energies which pervade the individual psyche.

Before it even understood what happened, the core discovered itself as it was harnessed to the adjuncts. Imagine a horse which with no memory of the past and no insight into the future, with only what it knows at the moment, suddenly discovering itself fully harnessed to a wagon. The creature discovered itself in enslavement. It has no idea of life without the harness.

In fact, it does not cross the horse's mind that it has nothing to do with the harness and the wagon. It assumes that the harness is part of its body, and that the cart is another part of its body which it must pull.

Imagine if a wild horse comes to that horse and begins neighing in anxiety over the enslavement of one of its kind. How would the harnessed horse understand what the wild one relates? Mentally, the wild horse will say,

"Release yourself. Slip away from the harness. You do not have to pull the cart. Come with me. Be free of the adjuncts."

Yogesh's technique:

Make sure that kundalini is pulled from the spinal column into the brain.
- Do breath infusion while focusing on the intellect.
- Until the intellect disappears attack it with breath infusion.
- Relocate the coreSelf at the location which is the default position of the intellect.
- If there are thoughts, images or ideas when this happens, stop the practice since you are not at the stage to complete this. In that case resume normal meditation practice.
- If there are no thoughts, images or ideas when this happens, connect the attention to the brahmrandra bulb. If you do not perceive the bulb, you may still direct your attention to the top of the head.
- After this connection becomes stabilized which may take days, weeks, months or years of practice, there will be a pulling force from the brahmrandra top-of-the-head chakra. The coreSelf will be pulled into the bulb under brahmrandra.

Yogi's Enemies Down-Under

Rishi Singh Gherwal appeared during breath infusion this morning. He explained an intellect pratyahar practice. Pratyahar is the fifth stage of yoga. Yet after one advanced into the practice further, one finds it necessary to review the fifth stage.

This is like when one conquers an enemy territory. One gets news that some pockets of the enemy are in a mountainous region. They resist. To consolidate the conquest, one must then venture and take those strongholds.

Some student yogis are scared of challenging the internal enemies. Some think that the internal environment is one cohesive whole, a oneness. They distrust any instruction which seems to suggest that the psyche is a composition of more than one psychic object.

In the _Meditation Pictorial_ book there is a basic course for the pratyahar practice. This concerns retracting the sensual energies which course out of the psyche into the world. However, beyond that practice, there is the way of pulling in sensual energies that are rebellious towards the coreSelf but which are within the psyche.

Many students of meditation feel that the problem with this existence is the external environment. They are satisfied to retreat from the world into the mind. They consider that psychic withdrawal to be meditation.

However, this practice is different in that this *retreating into the self* idea is changed when one sees that the word *self* in that case means the *psyche*. This psyche is not the self but is an existential compartment in which is housed a coreSelf and psychic adjuncts.

The battle begins when one understands this and accepts that the unity of the self is a temporary cohesion, because the core is one part of the psyche. It is not the entire composite.

During breath infusion, this retrieval-of-energy practice, takes place when the yogi develops the ability to move the intellect and coreSelf from their respective default positions. So long as the yogi is unable to relocate the coreSelf, this practice cannot be completed.

During the practice of asana postures in combination with breath infusion, a yogi finds that the pains of the postures helps considerable in relocating both the core and the intellect. This is because the pains felt in the postures helps to relocate the mind to specific places in the psyche. Some like the knees for instance, or the thigh bones or the toes, are easily reached by the postures and breath infusion. When this is done the yogi can relocate the intellect into these areas.

Once the kundalini is curbed and especially when it is pulled into the base of the brain and changed into being just a stub of white energy, the yogi is free to roam through the kingdom of the psyche (territory of the self).

By taking the intellect into the trunk of the subtle body, the energy which was allied to the intellect, will cling to the intellect and will be drawn into the intellect.

To understand how this works, one may consider the situation of sex desire. There are basically two parts to sex desire, the internal and the external influences. The internal is the creation of sexual facilities in the subtle body. The external one is the procurement of sex facilities outside of the body. In this practice the concern is the facilities in the body. The intellect invested both internally and externally in sex desire. The yogi must locate all of its internal investments and withdraw those from within the psyche.

This same withdrawal process must be done in reference to other needs like for instance the need for mobility which is in the thighs of the body, the need for digestion which is in the gut areas, the need for conversation which is in the vocal cord. In this way, over time when the intellect is taken into the trunk of the body, its allied energies will be recalled into it.

When one takes the intellect down, one will realize that there are bunches of grayish energies here and there which become manifest. These should be pulled into the intellect.

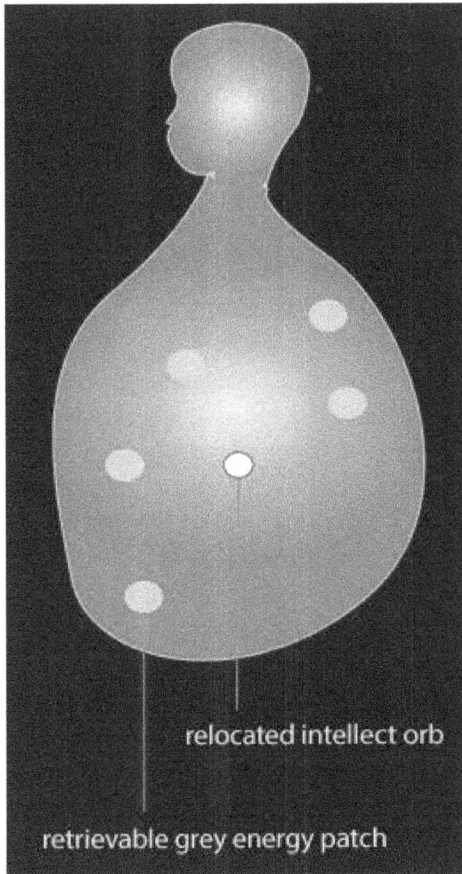

relocated intellect orb

retrievable grey energy patch

Later in the practice, this intellect with these energies within it, should be subjected to breath infusion, until the intellect becomes white hot.

So long as the kundalini is not curbed, the yogi will be unable to achieve this because the kundalini will protect these energies in various parts of the psyche by hiding them from the coreSelf, which will be of the view that these energies do not exist since it cannot perceive them. Kundalini conquest is important in yoga. Many of the higher practices are off-limits to the students who do not achieve that conquest.

Self as a Composite

Initially the God of the world produced a massive pool of individual willpowers. This is the cosmic sense of identity. This energy is supernatural. It is so abstract that the individual entities who got a tiny portion of this energy, cannot differentiate the self from it.

Take the example of ice in water. The ice has a very difficult time finding where it ends and where the water begins. In fact, as far as the ice is concerned it is the water and the water surrounding it is the ice.

Another example is if water is chilled to just one or two degrees above freezing. The water will never freeze in that way but all the same the water will hardly be able to discern itself from the chill. In that case we know for sure that the coldness is not the water and yet, as far as the water is concerned, it is the coldness. But the water realizes that it is not the coldness as soon we remove it from the refrigerator.

When the individual selves are on the causal plane of existence, a portion of the cosmic sense of identity latches on to each self but these senses of identity are so subtle, so close in vibrational energy to the self, that the selves have no idea that a parasite surrounded each of them.

As soon as the sense of identity senses anything, it alerts the self but the self assumes that such an alert is its own doing. It then pushes out of itself a research energy which in turn causes the sense of identity to form into a willpower force.

A man who uses a jackhammer may get the shakes, which means that the vibration of the tool enters and passes through his body. It is so effective, that even at the end of the day after he stops using the tool, he feels as if his body continues to vibrate.

Because of being linked intimately to the tool, the worker vibrates when the tool stutters in and out of concrete. As far as the worker is concerned his body vibrates and the influence of that continues even after he stops using the tool.

The sense of identity is not the observing self but it is fused to the self. Its actions are mistaken to be that of the self.

Still a yogi has it as a task to sort this for clarity.

Patanjali's first instruction about *kaivalyam* is for the observing self to segregate itself from its subtle perception adjunct but he refers mostly to the intellect and not the sense of identity.

तदभावात्संयोगाभावो हानं तद्दृशेः कैवल्यम्॥ २५ ॥

tad abhāvāt saṁyogā abhāvaḥ
hānaṁ taddṛśeḥ kaivalyam

tad = tat – that spiritual ignorance; abhāvāt – resulting from the elimination; saṁyogā – conjunction; abhāvaḥ – disappearance, elimination; hānaṁ – withdrawal, escape; tad = tat – that; dṛśeḥ – of the perceiver; kaivalyam – total separation from the mundane psychology.

The elimination of the conjunction which results from the elimination of that spiritual ignorance is the withdrawal that is the total separation of the perceiver from the mundane psychology. (Yoga Sutras 2.25)

The reason is that the observing self does not have the power to completely segregate itself from the sense of identity but it can separate itself from the intellect. Still, even though it cannot do this, it can perceive psychically that the sense of identity is an adjunct.

A horse in service pulling a cart cannot remove the harness. It is simply not possible because the body of the horse restricts what it can do. To say that the horse should have the power to free itself is really a lofty but impractical idea. The horse cannot have that power. In the same way the individual selves cannot remove the sense of identity, but they should do everything possible to realize its existence, how they are connected to it, and how they are influenced by it.

Uncertainty of Reincarnation

Due to pressing social concerns of others which penetrated the psyche and disrupted the focus, exercises this morning was a longer session than usual.

Last night in the astral world, someone asked of social affairs, about how a yogi should have the advantage where the social affairs are taken care of and the spiritual progress is also attained. Such a conversation is a total waste of time because it has to do with reducing spiritual disciplines and increasing social affairs.

Some people are willing to pursue social matters with earnest. They spend most of the time completing real or imagined duties. For spiritual life, they hatchet the whole thing, chopping it here and there to reduce its requirements.

The aspect which needs to be butchered is the social concerns but somehow students do not understand that. The reason is obvious. Human nature is slanted into the way of social affairs for deriving pleasures and superficial security in the physical world.

This morning it was a good meditation session in the effort to infuse the trunk of the subtle body below the neck but it was a disaster when it was time to deal with the head of the subtle body. This was due to pressing social concerns which burst into the head like fireworks in the sky. As with fireworks, the eyes want to see it. The ears want to hear it. One is distracted.

There should be no thoughts bursting in the mind during meditation. It is not a matter of observing passing thoughts, or ignoring them. Thoughts should not arise period.

The thoughts were persistent. They carried such a forceful charge that even the breath infusion did not banish them. All in all, eventually after infusing fresh air for about twenty minutes, the energies of these thoughts fizzed and vanished.

Why did the thoughts have such power? The reason is twofold.

- karmic obligation
- attachments to others

The world is so constructed that there are pressing obligations, even for a yogi. If one has a physical body one has consequential obligations automatically. That is a given fact. One gets the body with obligations. When anyone to whom one is obligated from this life or from a previous life, wants to be compensated, one is expected to serve the occasion.

Besides the basic services which one received from others in the past life, one has attachment to certain persons. Inevitably one forms these biases like a madman who does not assess his reckless acts.

All attachments lead to heavy obligations just like when one takes a substantial loan from a bank. It is nice to get that money but it is a stab in the back because later it will be a burden which will, like a lead weight, drag one into an inconvenient circumstance.

Yogis also form attachments not because they want to, but due to the fact that this is the nature of the world. It so happens that attachment is inevitable. A yogi sees the attachments and knows that they are dangerous. Still, he cannot stop their formations.

It is like a surgery. The surgeon knows that there is the probability that he will cut the wrong vein or nerve which may well incapacitate the patient. Still, the surgeon must take the risk.

Because of the uncertainty principle of reincarnation, a yogi takes the risk of forming attachments with certain entities. No one can remove the uncertainty principle. The risk of these attachments is ongoing. We must accept this.

During the session when I made efforts to remove those thought-energies, one person psychically asked for assistance to help with her children. What do I care about them?

In this life material nature is hostile to them. So what? On occasion, the parents of my body were not nice to it either.

There was another relative who sent a thought package stating that I should relocate so that I can act as a social senior to family members.

Many relatives passed on after acting as seniors. Now as infants they do not see their mothers or fathers, because their mother is busy completing her career and the father is busy maintaining the status quo and avoiding being insulted for not having sufficient income. Why should I be concerned? What will be my situation if I take another body?

Will the economy of the world, favor me? Will my next mother not have a career so that she can be there for me when I am an infant? Will she love her job and see it as being a better deal for her life by putting me in a daycare?

Khechari Mudra (November 2012)

A student yogi inquired about *khechari mudra*, which is the lengthening of the tongue or the cutting of the frenum under the tongue so that the tongue can close the throat passage during meditation practice.

This procedure is prohibited for students who follow the kriya path from Babaji Mahashaya. Lahiri Mahashaya particularly prohibited this. In fact, there is an instance in which he rejected a disciple who did this.

Before anyone takes surgical action to cut the frenum, one should be sure that the person who recommends this action, guarantees that one will get the result intended. Do not do this whimsically in the hope that one will become an enlightened being by the action. Be sure that you get a guarantee from the yogi who recommends this. I cannot guarantee anything in this regard. Subsequently I do not recommend it.

There are many kriyas with many objectives. *Khechari* became famous because of the promises mentioned in books in India about what would happen if one did it.

The main thing is to understand which guru recommends it and what he says you would achieve by it. It is not a general practice that can be used by anyone anywhere without a guru who used it. The reason for this is the fact that it has a mystic side to the practice. The mere physical act will not give results.

For instance, kundalini yoga is supposed to cause the student to control the sex urge but some students find that it does the opposite which is to increase sex desire.

Once I spoke to someone who lives in Upstate New York. He told me that he liked to attend yoga classes in the expensive parts of Manhattan in New York City. At the end of the explanation, he said this, "I love the women who come there with tights. There is sex expression everywhere. I love it."

Yoga as it is defined by Patanjali does not include interest in women in skimpy clothing doing postures. These women are doing the postures physically but on the psychological plane they are doing everything but yoga. A physical action of yoga which is without the corresponding psychic motive, actually pushes the student away from yoga.

Cutting the frenum, will not give the student the results of years of practice. The thing to do is to get insight into why yogis stretched the tongue back into the throat.

Formerly the Nath yogis, who follow the lineage from Gorakshnath stretched the tongue by sticking it out as far as it will go out of the mouth. Then they used the right hand to squeeze it forward so that eventually it stretches. There is also another practice which is to curl the tongue up and push it back as far as possible. These practices gave benefits when the yogi mastered pranayama practice for *kumblaka* breath suspension.

Kumblaka is mastered after many years of practicing to infuse fresh air into the body, and then mastering at last holding air out of the body. If one reads for instance the *Mahabharata*, one will be informed of the villain, Duryodhana. Even though he was a warrior he mastered *kumblaka*. He went into a lake and submerged his body. He did not need to breath fresh air.

In that practice, there is a need for *khechari mudra* because with it the yogi makes sure that water or air does not enter his esophagus, because if water enters the lung, the body will die. If air enters the yogi will be pulled back into the physical body. The dimensional transfer will come to an end.

The view that a yogi will taste nectar or subtle fluids when doing this practice, will only happen to someone who permanently energized and mastered kundalini before doing the practice. Those results are not experienced unless the yogi conquered the chakras and the kundalini system which is below the throat.

But if one plans on having the body enter *samadhi* and if one is proficient at that but wishes to be in *samadhi* for days or weeks at a time, a *khechari* practice can be used. Please note that when a yogi did this, he assigned to a trusted disciple the task of waking his body from the trance condition. Yogi Matsyendranath did this.

The other more important value of this practice is to kill the body. Sometimes a yogi is instructed by his departed guru, to kill the body, to forget about the mission of teaching physical people. Then the yogi who is already proficient in transcendence will sit in lotus posture and do pranayama until he reaches the stage where he can stop breathing. This kills the body. This is a classic method of yogi suicide.

On the battlefield of Kurukshetra, before both armies, Drona, a warrior who was a master pranayama yogi, sat down to kill his body after he heard a false rumor which indicated that his son was dead. He did not achieve that because a competing warrior severed his head while he made the effort.

This is fascinating but such suicide cannot be done by someone who did not mastered trance consciousness prior. It cannot be done by someone whose psyche is resistant and disobedient to the willpower.

Khechari mudra cannot work if one did not curbed kundalini and does not consistently do transcendence absorption in real time. There is another related more basic practice which must be mastered. That is the one with cleaning food matter from the lower and upper intestines.

Before long absorptions, a yogi is required to clear food matter from the intestines and colon. If this is not done, then during *samadhi* the digestive process will keep working at a slow rate, the matter will harden to become almost like a brick. It will give the yogi trouble when he comes out of the transcendence state or it may even cause the *samadhi* to stop as the life force may obstruct the absorption as it feels that it should act to keep the body alive.

It is important to understand that the *khecari mudra* procedure is an action of forcing the kundalini to switch over to not having fresh air during meditation. Why would a yogi do this?

First of all, if one cuts off kundalini's access to fresh air it means that one intends to kill the physical body. One can do that easily by locking the body in a car which is sealed once the windows are wound up, or even in a tightly sealed garage which has air tight windows and doors.

One can do this easier and quicker by buying a plastic bag and putting it over the head and using a very tight rubber band around the bag around the neck. In a short time, one would be deprived of air. Doing this would cause the same blockage of the air passage to the lungs.

Some students think that if the tongue is cut and forced back into the palate the person will go into a transcendence state. Perhaps, but what kind of trance state?

Will it be a transfer in the mode of ignorance which is stupor *(jada) samadhi*? Will it be a white-out, black-out or gold-out?

If one tied a plastic bag around the head, one will quickly go into stupor *samadhi*. One will not have to cut the frenum. But here is the catch. There were two types of objective with this. One was the system of increasing the carbon dioxide dulling energy (apana) and letting the kundalini live on that. The other is increasing the enthusing energy (prana) and letting the kundalini live on that.

Which is preferred?

Trees also have kundalini. They live on carbon dioxide. That proves that it is possible to exist without oxygen intake.

Which state of consciousness will it be? The carbon dioxide supported state or the fresh air supported one?

Duryodhana, the villain of the *Mahabharata*, escaped from the battlefield and went to the bottom of a lake where his body survived on carbon dioxide. That means he did yoga to such an extent that he could apply *khecari mudra* and block air from entering that passage to the lungs while his kundalini lived on carbon dioxide which was generated in his body from cell activity.

Usually if one deprives kundalini from fresh air for a long period, it leaves the body and people declare that one is dead, but Duryodhana coaxed the kundalini and got it to stay in the body living on carbon dioxide energy. He was an accomplished negative yogi.

Other yogis used the other system of compressing fresh air into the subtle body in reserve and then going into transcendence states while kundalini lived on that reserve oxygen energy. That is a fresh air-based state, which is different to what Duryodhana did but the *khechari mudra* can be used in either case.

In both examples the mudra was used to block air from going into the lungs but in one the kundalini was supported by carbon dioxide while in the other it was supported by compressed fresh air.

The Late Yogi

This morning the air was cold. It did not have much solar energy. This type of air is not so good for breath infusion. Still, a yogi should persevere and complete a practice session.

There were few thought attacks here and there during the session but I used the method of infusing the location in the mind where the thoughts occurred. If you are in a war zone and then a grenade is thrown by the enemy, you can either take the grenade and thrown it back or do something to neutralize it.

Thoughts which come from others may sometimes wait outside the psyche and then enter at a particular time according to how the thoughts were processed by the sender and by the power of the relationship the sender has with the yogi. Some thoughts have a time fuse where they remain dormant and then attach themselves to the yogi and burst in the mind commanding the yogi's attention at a particular time.

A student should know how this operates and learn how to handle these energies. Each type of ammunition, like a bullet, grenade or small missile, requires a particular type of dismantling if they are to do no damage. Those thoughts which the yogi fails to dismantle before they explode must be handled in a specific way to reduce the damage they do to the psyche.

The incidence of material existence is a fabulous joke. It is like a Broadway play with lights, costumes and actors who take the roles seriously.

Sometimes on a movie set, something goes amiss when a star develops a grudge for another actor. Then the star asks the set-up men to put some live ammunition in a gun. Subsequently that other actor whom the star is supposed to shoot with a blank bullet is killed. It is declared to be an accident even though the star intended by all means to kill the other actor.

I took this body in a particular family. Sometimes a family member gets the idea that my position in the family is forever and that I should do this and do that. That person plans for my life and considers my literary work and yoga practice to lack priority.

During the meditation session, I practiced a procedure which was left in my psyche by Yogesh. Last week I saw him but he did not give instructions. He simply smiled and disappeared into the causal plane. Later I realized that he deposited instructions in my psyche.

He insisted that I move the intellect into the bell housing which hangs below the brahmrandra. There was a small note which when processed and converted into language read like this:

Pay no attention to it at this time. You are late. Time is short. Flush the intellect with white heat. Then shift to the bell housing. Draw it up. Use the capsule in the end and escape. I may see you again; otherwise it is doubtful what will happen.

This terse coded message may be translated as follows:

Pay no attention to the third eye brow chakra. Your time to be in this body is short. You will not have sufficient time to skip out if you keep working with that chakra. Social overload reduced your time. You should cease some practices and do the essential ones.

Attack the intellect with breath infusion. Always infuse it until it seems to be white-hot with infused energy which causes it to skip from the lower planes to higher levels.

The liabilities and demands of social relationships utilize much time. That time cannot be retrieved. In an emergency one should do the essential only. To reach me later you should use the bell housing for transport, otherwise you will remain on lower levels, where I am not available.

To complete this instruction, I must complete these disciplines.
- Infuse the trunk of the subtle body
- Be sure that kundalini no longer runs its sex energy show in the trunk of the subtle body
- Shift and infuse the head of the subtle body with focus on the intellect
- Make sure that the intellect ceased its independent conspiracies which contravene yoga progress.
- Move the intellect to the bell housing under the brahmrandra

Dead Swami Reviews his Life

Kirtanananda Swami who recently departed his body in India, and who was imprisoned, disgraced and also disenfranchised from the spiritual society which he invested his life into, visited me during the daylight hours around 5 pm on the date of November 24, 2011.

On the subtle side, his subtle body recovered from its deenergized condition. It still walks with the limp and shows a pot belly just as his physical body did, but it is not in a wheel chair. He moves on two subtle feet. He said this,

I do not know if anyone will believe you but write this:

Those negative things which I did or which I influenced others to do, were done because of the mixture of my energy and Srila Prabhupada's. Those who feel that it is I alone who am responsible are mistaken. Srila Prabhupada's energy is mixed in with this.

Take for example that if I did not meet Srila Prabhupada, I would not do such things. My life would be simpler. I would not develop in the same way. Those circumstances would not manifest.

Prabhupada's process did not work to completion for any of my prominent co-disciples. Not one single one went to Krishna's place. I checked to see if those who are deceased are on the astral planes. Not one of them is missing. Nor does anyone who still uses a physical body, have energies in them which are different to what was in our subtle forms, which implies that they will fail to get to Krishna's place.

We were not objective with Srila Prabhupada. That is the cause of this failure. We were inundated by his supreme confidence in what he believed. I do not want to be pardoned or forgiven for what I did. After all, since the potential is there, this history of deviations can be repeated unless we develop some means of discrimination in our personal selves and can travel life after life with that protection as an instinct.

How did it happen? That is the million-dollar question. How to stop this from recurring again if again I meet a Srila Prabhupada or a spiritual master with such confidence?

There is nothing wrong in believing in Krishna but there is definitely the flaw of not testing every step of the way. The flaw is the desire to convert others, even though one is not fully purified of the animal instincts.

I am not sorry for the persons who got hurt. I realize that I was an agent of nature. The question, and it is an eternal one, is, how can one

effectively resist nature and not be its puppet? The deviant behavior will be repeated by me or by anyone who does not carry an instinct to resist the influences which originate and support such behavios. The real guru is the one who can show one how to develop that resistance, because otherwise, no matter if one apologizes sincerely, one will still return into the world and again express those behaviors.

coreSelf Controls Tendencies

Due to rising two hours late, the exercise session was not the very best. During the night there were numerous counterproductive associations. In the astral world, the worse thing is to meet people who are not yogis but who are aware of the power of yoga in one's life. This is similar to the case of a man who was in a criminal gang. His family heard of it. Instead of asking him to desist, they were silent and tolerant because they realized that he was useful for an income from the criminal acts. They had no intentions of being criminal but they did not mind if he was deviant, provided he acquired money.

People who think that yoga is good for nothing and that it obstructs materialistic living, may find a yogi to be useful if they can use his accrued psychological energies, either to relieve stress or to get some type of enjoyment.

People who are old or sick, sometimes realize that they are relieved when they stand near to a yogi. Once this is discovered they pursue yogis to get the rejuvenating energies.

Sometimes people meet me in that astral world and request that I deliver certain energies. I usually comply with the request even though it results in a loss of energy in the subtle body. It also misaligns kundalini resulting in a two- or three-day stagnation in practice.

When I sat to meditate, I did a coreSelf relocation practice. This is a location switching exercise. It begins with the coreSelf at its default location listening to naad sound.

Then the coreSelf moves into naad and grabs naad. Then the coreSelf moves back to its default location with naad by its side. Then the coreSelf moves to the location of the intellect.

Then the coreSelf checks to be sure that the naad sound is still by its side and is not in the back of the subtle head. If the naad sound retreated to the back of the head, the core should begin this process again.

When it reaches the position of the intellect, it should take its seat there just like a proud king who seized the throne of a rival ruler and who uses the rival's head as his footstool with full intention to dominate the territory of that defeated monarch.

In this situation naad does not act as a shield but it acts as a reference. If it is not there, the self will assume its default location or it will remain in the thought-image location and struggle with the thought-image process which it endeavors to control. To get naad to act as a shield, the yogi must go into naad in the back of the head wherever it is located there.

In this practice the idea is to test to see if the self can wrestle successfully with the intellect thought-creating mechanism. One runs a test by going forward to the frontal part of the subtle head and seeing if the intellect simply ignores one and continues in its usual way or if it is respectful of the core and remains silent.

By bringing naad forward one creates an anchor point but it may not protect one from an attack from the thought-image production organ.

Yogi and the Television

Some inquired about the value of using naad as an anchor and reference during meditation.

Naad causes the self to be objective to the thought-image-idea making feature of the mind. Mostly people feel that this feature is created in the blank space of the mind. I state that there is a psychic organ which creates the images, idea and thoughts.

In either case thought production should cease during meditation. If one is successful doing this using one method or the other, or even if this happens spontaneously of its own choosing, even then the experience does not happen for very long, before one finds oneself again viewing images, ideas and thoughts.

Listening to naad, or even bringing naad close to the coreSelf helps in the effort to create a resistance to the thought lures which are formed in the mind.

Make a test. Sit to meditate. If you reach the stage of having no images, thoughts or ideas, make a mental note of that and then wait in the blankness. See how long it takes before you find yourself again viewing thoughts. When this happens, it is usually realized after one already began viewing the images rather than just when the viewing begins.

Why does this happen that one does not realize the self when the viewing first begins but only after it developed further?

A detailed study of this will give one some idea about the operations of the consciousness. But when one sits to meditate, one should join the naad sound. One should make contact with it, listen to it, and keep it nearby.

Communicating with Dead Relatives

Most people leave this world reluctantly. At the time of dying, most people do not indulge in the fantasy about a great afterlife. Rather they focus on the diseased crippled failing condition of the physical body.

Usually they do not experience a subtle body at that time. They do not think that people are left behind. Most people think that they are being deprived of the physical world, which was for the most part the center of attention for the previous years of that lifetime.

However, once the person is separated permanently from a body, and cannot return into it as they usually did after sleeping and dreaming, that person is no longer in a position to worry about whether that dead body is cremated, buried or left in the open for scavengers.

It is the relatives who are left behind in this world, who become concerned about the method of disposal. Usually those persons want that to happen along the lines of their religious beliefs. As for example say a Christian relative who feels that the body needs to be in a coffin to be resurrected by Christ, or a Hindu relative, who feels that the body should go to Gaya in India or to Hardwar, to have the body cremated in a religious ceremony with prayers which are supposed to convey the deceased to the promised place hereafter.

As far as communicating with the deceased person, that happens just as it was before when the person was on this side with the exemption of the physical body not being used as an amplifier. Without that person's living physical form, the persons on this side are left with their intuition and psychic feelings. Everything psychological which was that person continues after the physical body dies. Thus, there can be communication, though it is psychic only.

The condition of disposal of the physical body of that person does not affect this. It is affected by the way persons on this side focus. If the relatives on this side are mostly physically focused, there will be little communication but if anyone has psychic ability, there can be coherent communication.

Dimensional Quarantine

The focus we maintain during the physical life remains with us in the afterlife. There will be no rash or sudden change in that focus merely because of the death of the physical body.

If one hopes to go to a spiritual place or some nice hereafter fantasy location after death, that may happen for an instant but soon after the usual focus on the physical existence will resume.

Night after night, I see deceased persons who reside for the time being in the astral existence on a level which is adjacent to this earthly place. Some of these people were religious officials. Some were ordinary people without firm beliefs. They do exactly what they did before. They maintain an interest in the physical side of life which is now inaccessible to them. Even though they are gone over to the other side, their interest in this world remains. They are eager to know what happens on this side. They want to discuss life on this side.

As soon as one loses a body, one becomes determined to come back into the world as part of its history. One envies those who are physical because they have some part to play in the fold out of physical events.

There is a range of existence in the astral world, both upper astral heavens and lower astral hellish places, as well as lower astral enjoyment places, and still a person who departs from the physical body will usually not perceive those places but will instead detect information coming from the minds of the physical beings.

Unless one secures a footing in the higher astral dimensions before leaving the body, it is hardly likely that one will be going to such places or will synchronize with such places after being deprived of the body. In a sense the astral world has dimensional quarantine.

Persons who meditate should consider that even though one may reach a desirable state in the mind, still one must again be aware of this physical environment and function here, and if one does not behave in a way which is amenable to society, one will be arrested and will have to meditate in a prison. The same type of situation will be there in the astral world hereafter, where one will have to be in an environment. One will be limited in that place unless one relocates to a higher astral realm. How will one do that hereafter if one cannot do so now?

At this time one can meditate and then one must refocus into the physical world. One must participate in society. The same will apply in the hereafter. This means that simple meditating in the mind does not solve the situation of the environment where one functions in a society as a mandatory feature. To believe that astrally one will not have to function in an environment is totally unscientific but it may serve the purpose of having a pleasant self-delusion.

Astral Body is Indulgent

The subtle body will do whatever it can. That is its nature. It will push the limits to express itself under freewill. In this world, if I go into a shop, I will hesitate to shoplift but in the astral world there is no hesitation usually. One does whatever one is urged to do.

However, if one implanted a morality in the subtle body during the earthly life, those reforms may surface to keep the subtle body from behaving in a totally careless way.

People do not develop moral behaviors in the astral world. They either have the proper instincts or they do not. There is no opportunity to develop that there as there is here. This place is the world of social action in which one can develop behaviors that ultimately benefit one and all.

Because that body is careless and is not concerned with anything but immediate fulfillments, we cannot rely on the subtle body to do what is conducive to our wellbeing. Suppose I meet an attractive woman and luckily, she falls in love with me, then naturally the course will be that I will sexually indulge her. But while that happens, I may not think of the pregnancy which may result.

Similarly, actions in the subtle world are spontaneous and careless without regard for the long-ranged implication of the behavior. That is the danger on the subtle side.

A yogi can train the subtle body to have the long-ranged perspective but he/she must do that while using a physical form. If you have a kite in the air and if you tie a ribbon to it and hang a weight, you will find that the kite remains stable in the wind. But if you raise a kite and do not attach a ribbon with a weight, the kite will sway even to the extent that it will make a big scoop and crash into the ground. The subtle body needs a physical system to balance and stabilize it.

A physical body is a sure pain-in-the-neck. Of that one can be certain, but it has a great value in that it can help us to bring the permissive sensually-craved subtle form under control.

Yogi's Loss of Focus

Imagine that I repair an appliance in my house but someone puts sleeping gas in the vent system through an outside duct. This gas is colorless and odorless. Hence there is no way for me to realize what happened.

I breathe it. I become unconscious.

After this the person who inserted the gas into the duct, enters my house, and removes my unconscious body to his theater hall and puts my body to sit in such a way, that when I awaken, I will be before a screen.

After half hour I awaken but due to the sleeping gas residual effects, I gain consciousness over a period of ten minutes, where I see the video on the screen and can make no coherence of it. However, after those ten minutes when the drowsiness ceases, I become objectively conscious of what I view on the screen.

I continue looking at the screen for about five minutes, trying to make sense of the story line of the images seen. Then a memory surfaces that I was repairing the appliance in the house. I get up from the seat in the theatre and go to the house.

When I get to my house, I return to the task of fixing the appliance.

Naad has a valuable use for removing those blank spaces which occur when meditating, when one blanks out and then finds oneself aware looking at images in the mind or looking at imagined scenes which the mind produced and which commands the attention.

Up to this date, I found no other sure way to remove these blanks slots except for naad sound. To be more explicit, it happens that when one meditates with a particular focus or even with a lack of focus, one discovers the observing self looking at images in the mind. These images were displayed for some time before one realized that one viewed them. After one realizes this, one may resume the focus or lack of focus as the case may be.

Yogi as Victorious Proud Conqueror (December 2011)

During meditation this afternoon, I had a visit by Swami Rama. He was in his usual jovial mood. Even though he is disciplined with students, he is an easy-going teacher. He said this:

Conquest of the inner self is necessary. Of course, what people think is the inner self is not that. They feel that there is one inner self as the entire mind. They do not perceive components of consciousness in the mind space This is due to the lack of keen psychic perception.

Behind closed eyes, the neophyte thinks that everything in the mind space is the self but that is not true. It will however do in the beginning but as the student penetrates more and more, and as the subtle becomes more and more visible, the student will understand that this is the beginning of a long journey of discovery regarding what is the self.

It is due to the strong focus on material existence, that the spirits have no spiritual perception and have settled for a physical reference and a single idea about the self being everything which is psychologically within the reach of the individual consciousness.

How many words are there in the Upanishads, the Yoga Sutras and related literature from India, about the self? Why is there more than one word? Why do we have atma, brahma, chitta, vritti, jiva, paramatma, purusha, bhagavan, manas, kundalini, dhi, buddhi, indriya and smrtih?

In the West we have the reverse where there are many words for each category of matter. Just take for example a mineral. There are so many

*words for that based on the kind of mineral, where it is found in the earth,
how it is used and so on.*

During the meditation session this Swami gave a procedure for using naad as an assistant or ally in the effort to conquer the frontal part of the mind space, the forehead region of the subtle body.

Procedure

Immediately after breath infusion sit in the center of the energies of the head of the subtle body. Grab the naad sound. Keep it close to the observing self.

Once you are assured that you have naad, move forward and sit where the thoughts, images and ideas usually occur.

Sit there as a victorious proud conqueror who will not allow an old enemy who was defeated to regain power.

Sit there for some time. Hold naad there.

If you can, move upwards and stay under brahmrandra.

If you cannot begin the procedure, make the effort again.

If you still cannot, it means that you have not completed the pratyahar sensual withdrawal meditation. You should complete that.

How Kundalini Leaves the Body at Death

During breath infusion this morning Swami Rama came. He discussed how a yogi should handle the psyche when the physical body is on the verse of dying. He said this:

Many meditators have no idea of what to do when death comes. Their belief is that it will be all good since they will merge into the Absolute or go to an astral paradise. That is not the way of the yogis. For yogis we desire to know what kundalini will do just before the time of death. We can either comply with kundalini's method, try to resist it or force it to do something else.

Some persons think that God will make it good for the devotee at the time of death. They feel that he will compensate the deficiencies but this idea is only as good as what God did in terms of preventing the material body from disease.

If we accept that there is a God, if that God will help one in the subtle body at the time of death, what is the explanation as to why that God did nothing to adjust the diseased condition of the physical body as it approached its death? Has that God said that he will fix the subtle body's

condition at death even though he rendered no care for the physical one?
Let us be real with these issues.

Kundalini is the single element which controls what will happen at death, regarding where the individual will transit. The condition of kundalini and its condition alone determines that.

When the body gets to an elderly stage and when the functions of it begin to deteriorate, kundalini uses one standard method which is to close down one part of the body after another, beginning with the extremities. Even parts of the brain are closed down. It is like when a person is to sleep at night. He turns off the lights one by one and leaves a small lamp in the bedroom. Kundalini does this by shutting down various functions and various organs one by one.

A yogi should take note of this and should not, like modern people, take medication which affords one the luxury of not knowing what kundalini does.

The student yogis like other human beings are forced to consent to the actions of kundalini which it commits when death is near. This means focusing on the one or two major health defects in the system at that time. This health defect serves as gateways to the afterlife for kundalini. But an advanced yogi should not use such easy gateways because they lead to lower astral planes and to haphazard rebirths in which the person has no idea what will happen and how things will be in the next life.

At first kundalini closes itself off at the base chakra. It shuts the exit points or sensual orifices. This is experienced as lack of sense of smell, lack of taste, blindness, numbness and deafness.

This is similar a king who governs a large territory and is attacked by rulers from other places. At that time the king builds a central fort in his territory. The idea is that he can be barricaded from rivals and live in peace behind the walls of a stockade.

Unfortunately, his rivals, who went away when he first did that. They returned with siege engines and battering-rams. They pound his city walls.

Hearing the constant threat of the rivals and being aware that his end may be near; this king planned to escape from the city, which was designed to protect him but which became a trap for him.

At last when the enemy breached the city wall, the king disguised and tried to escape through the same breach which his enemies made in the city wall

Kundalini is like this in that at death it tries to leave through the main disease which kills the body. Say for instance, that it is tuberculosis, then kundalini will leave through the lungs. If it is a venereal disease, it will leave through the genitals, if it is constipation or diarrhea, it will leave through the anus. If it is dimentia, it will leave through the malfunctioned brain cells which caused that. If it is heart failure it will leave through the faulty heart valve or muscle.

A yogi must however try to get kundalini to take a difference course at the time of death so that it does not travel along the lines of the terminal disease which the body will have.

Naad Diffuses Through the coreSelf (December 2011)

During breath infusion I generated a kundalini force which travelled up the left and right edges of the trunk into the neck of the subtle body. Once it reached into the neck, the force vanished as if it disappeared into nowhere but then it came out on the left and right side of the subtle head. I was unable to investigate the subtle material into which it vanished because there was a blank space where the energy which was like a shriek of lightning disappeared into subtle grey area of the neck.

At one time I felt Swami Rama touch my subtle head, but that was all. He said nothing. He left.

During the breath infusion, for the last fifteen minutes, I infused the intellect in the front part of the subtle head. That was effective in totally silencing the intellect which produced a few thoughts and one flash of a scene from a movie I saw some months ago.

Movies and videos are a death knell to the yogi because the images remain embedded in the mind and then forcibly work their way out of the mind before they are flushed out of the psyche. There is no point in feeling that there will be no negative influence from viewing videos.

Those yogis and meditators who think they can clear the mind of such images, indulge a fantasy but that is all. The way of the mind is not changed by mantras or by intentions. The mind has a way of doing things. One should study its methods and create solutions.

When I got to meditate, the first thing I did was to assume the default position of the coreSelf. Unless one has a special process, this is really the standard method for beginning a meditation session. One should assume the normal position of the coreSelf wherever that may be. For those persons who feel that the self is the whole psyche or who feel that the self has no set place and that it is all-pervasive, this instruction is useless, obviously, since something that is everywhere is in a sense nowhere and cannot be positioned.

The method which I describe is for those who experience a set limited location for the core. One assumes the default position. Then one should locate naad.

The normal way of the mind is for the self to assume its default position without realizing that it did so. Then the mind, quickly, in a flash, faster than the eye could see, usually links the self to the intellect but the self does not realize these actions because they are rapid. The self, mistakenly, realizes this as itself viewing images, thoughts and ideas in the mind.

After connecting with naad sound, I got an instruction which was left in my psyche by Swami Rama. This was an instruction to pull naad into the coreSelf, into the center of it. I did this. When I complied some shrieks of naad energy traversed the coreSelf. I saw these visually.

There was another instruction for naad to be pulled all the way through the core to its other side, passing through the center meridian of the core.

When I did that, naad switched and penetrated the self from all sides. After a while it retracted to where it is usually found in its default position near the right ear.

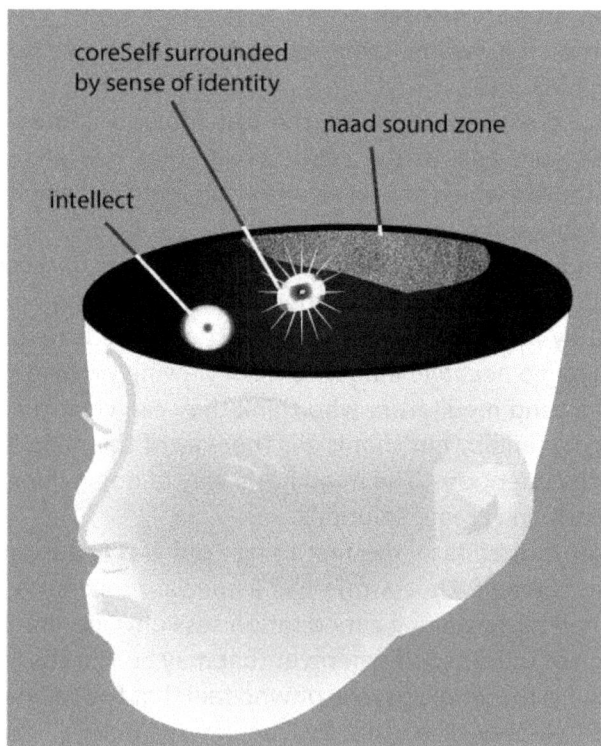

default locations of intellect, sense of identity,
coreSelf and naad

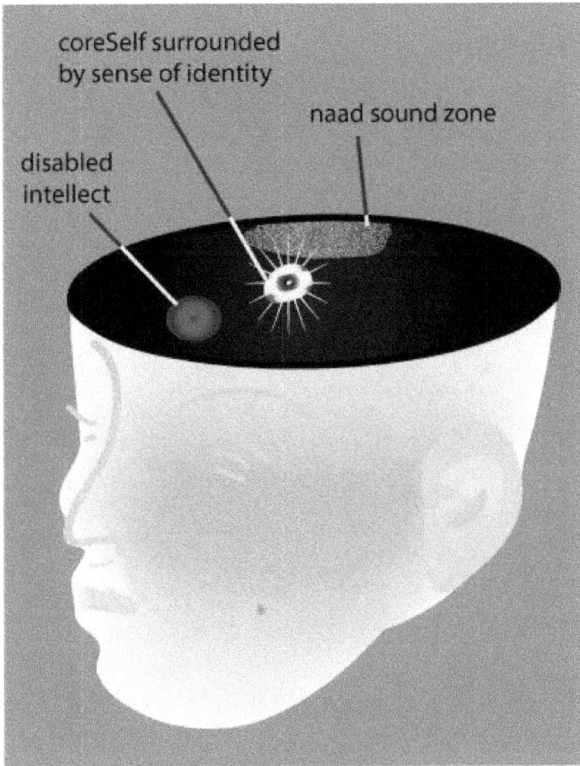

coreSelf surrounded by sense of identity

naad sound zone

disabled intellect

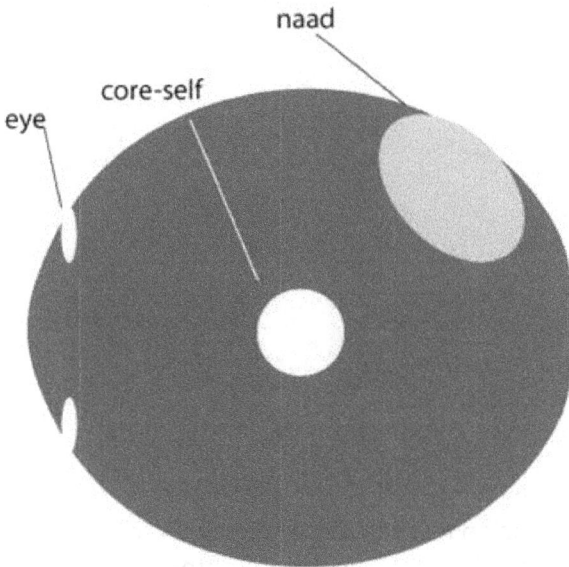

naad

core-self

eye

naad pull through core-self

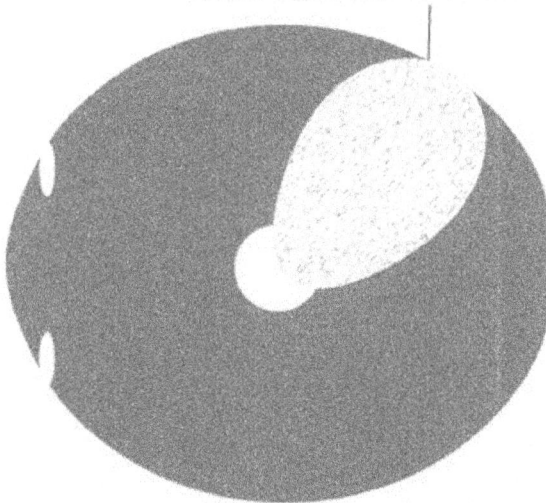

Then there was an instruction to repeat the procedure beginning with pulling naad through the right side to the center.

There was a notation of Swami Rama which was left in my psyche. It is a procedure of attracting or pulling naad through the core. Here it is:

Self needs sensations. There is no escaping this need. No amount of philosophy or belief can eliminate this need. Even if like Gautama Buddha one decides to forego sensation completely and even if the meditation is as good as his, which is doubtful, even then one will have to continue dealing with sensation. The need for it in certain aspects of the psyche will remain.

For a yogi who wants to go into the Absolute, into the supernatural no-man's land, he should beforehand feed the self with some sensation, so that while he is in transcendence, it does not call for that.

This is similar to breath infusion, which fills up the system with subtle energy in such a way, that the kundalini no longer seeks that energy. The yogi can practice without being called repeatedly to supply energy.

This practice is such that the yogi regards naad as a sensation energy which will be eaten or ingested into the core. When you are linked into naad you will sometimes see it as you would something visual even though usually it is audible. Sometimes you will feel it as something with feelings.

Mostly naad is heard but sometimes there will be a flash. You will see it or there will be an inset embedded vision of it as it passes through the psyche or the coreSelf even.

This practice of ingesting naad is required to be performed for at least six months in the case of an advanced student. Others may have to do it for years.

In the primitive stage, human beings got as close to electricity as they did to lightning and thunder. Those who lived in the north got some of it manifested in the winter when they used animal skins, which by rubbing, generated static electricity.

Electricity was known but it was not generated, controlled and exploited. Humans were mostly controlled by nature and did not know how to generate electric power. Now it is mostly the same because most human beings cannot explain how electricity is generated. We use it but there are only a few humans who understand how it is done. Among that few they are fewer who could manufacture a generator.

The same type of ignorance prevails in regards to kundalini. All the creatures, the humans and the lesser species use it but few know what it is. Fewer yet can energize and arouse it except through nature's methods like sex pleasure and other types of sensual stimulation or chemical alteration through eating plants and minerals which have a hallucinogenic effect.

In my case kundalini is permanently detached and retracted into the subtle head. This gives the yogi the opportunity to take control of the trunk of the body because otherwise, at the time of the death of the body, the yogi no matter what he/she says, must transit with kundalini. There will be no independence. But while, before, the kundalini did everything and the coreSelf functioned as a tourist under the control of a travel guide, now the core must do many things itself. It must be more attentive to what happens in the psyche.

There is an advantage in being a tourist in that you can awaken late, sit on the tour bus and everything is done for you. Taking control from kundalini adds to the tasks the coreSelf must perform. Instead of having a jolly good time going along for the ride while kundalini is put to the task of figuring everything, the coreSelf should better manage what happens in the psyche

The generations of the little kundalinis occur by the infusion of breath and the buildup of that force in particular parts of the body. Just by the accumulation those mini kundalinis are produced.

It is like the idea of flash-points in flammable substances. Let say that I release petroleum gas in a closed building. So long as there is no heat, it will not explode but if there is heat in any part of that building or if there is a spark there will be an instant flash.

But it is not easy to determine where the flash point will occur. When doing the practice, one knows that there will be a flash point or that a little or extended kundalini will occur, but one does not know where it will occur until it happens. This is because of variables in the atmosphere and in the psyche.

The yogi keeps doing the infusion until the flash occurs. Then he/she may apply locks and check to see how the energy flashed, where it went and what are its effects.

The involuntary activities in the body will continue even if the kundalini is withdrawn. This is due to the fact that those functions are impulsive and transpire by the grace of nature.

A gruesome example of that is like when in previous times, when warriors used swords on the battlefield, sometimes when a warrior's head was cut off by another warrior, the headless body continued its fighting action for one minute or so. Even though the head which has the motor and nerve controls was removed, the cells in the trunk of the body kept performing even though they had no support from the sophisticated biological functions in the head, which lay on the ground.

Another example of this is like when a chicken is beheaded by a human farmer. If the body is not held down, it may run heedlessly for two feet for about five or fifteen seconds even to relieve itself of the amputation. Then it will drop and go through several spasms until the body actually dies. The cells have a coding or process which they follow if the main directional force is removed.

We can understand this better if we study the reverse by observing what happens when we increase the work of kundalini in certain areas. In my practice the effort is to reduce the power of kundalini and to take charge of its duties directly, but let us look at the circumstance when we increase its powers and force it to work beyond its normal capacity.

In some countries there is usually a restriction on long-haul truck drivers where they are prohibited from driving continuously without resting for a certain number of hours. These rules came about because the government became aware of the fact that many drivers used caffeine, methamphetamine and other drugs which alter the sleep-wake cycle of the body. These truck drivers remained driving for many hours trying to increase their income but the hazard of it was that sometimes they crashed on highways when their bodies lost consciousness while driving. These are cases of forcing kundalini to act beyond its natural capacity, so that one caused it to remain in the waking state way beyond its capacity.

Here we can agree that we can adjust the operation of the kundalini in the body to maximize certain of its function, to curtail some or extend some.

Another example is the increase frequency of sexual indulgence in modern human beings over ancient human beings. On the average the frequency of sexual indulgence increased. We discovered ways of stimulating the body to increase sexual participation. These are ways of affecting kundalini. In the same way we can decrease the influence of kundalini, just as we can increase it for sex or for staying awake.

A simple test can be made to see if you can override the authority and function of kundalini. Sit quietly. Observe the natural breathing of the body, especially the rhythm of the in-breaths and out-breaths. When you made a mental idea of the duration of these breaths, take control by willfully breathing so that it is no longer an automatic function being performed by kundalini but it is being done by willful efforts.

That is a simply way to see that you can take charge of some kundalini functions. In yoga one may take a large share of the work which kundalini does, if one can divert oneself from the usual outside interests and refocus in introversion to inside concerns.

By inside I mean within the psyche. Here it is not that you are going inside yourself or inside the self but rather inside the psyche where the self and its adjuncts operate. Kundalini is one adjunct. Kundalini teaches the self about digestion, sex expression and many other functions.

In kundalini yoga, the self can learn how to direct kundalini to rise through the spine and enter the head. As this practice progresses, the self can learn how to elevate kundalini. Then the self will see what happens when that is done. It is in the realm of subjective experience, but if a yogi is persistent it can be done. The yogi can make sense of what happens in the psychic realm of existence.

In this body, the routes for energy transmission and distribution were designed and established by kundalini when this body was formed in the father's and then the mothers' body. That is already there, so even if kundalini is relieve of some duties; those routes will still be used. To build a city one must take assistance from engineers but once it is built; one may not require their services.

The body can function even if kundalini is relocated from the lower trunk and is retracted and controlled in the head. If the yogi fails to control kundalini in that way, his religion, beliefs and philosophy will not help him when the body dies and for better or worse, he will be forced to take the course that kundalini favors at that time.

Part 5

Memory and CoreSelf Battle it out (December 2011)

In the kriya yoga memory must be investigated.

Is there one memory chamber?

Is there two or three?

Where are these located?

Even if you cannot sort and find psychic components because in your experience, your head consciousness is one diffused or concentrated energy, still the questions remain about the operation of reasoning and memory.

In meditation one may find that besides the screen of images, thoughts and ideas in the mind, there is another factor which frequently and involuntarily mixes in. That is memory.

Here is an experience during meditation which may throw some light on this topic:

While meditating, I first captured the naad sound. The coreSelf was in its default position in the head. After capturing naad and keeping it close, I moved to the frontal part of the subtle head to the place where the thoughts, images and ideas occur.

At that place due to an earlier breath infusion, there were no thoughts, images or ideas. I then moved upward because there was a pushing force pushing energy upward.

This force was so powerful that it pushed the chin and eyes upwards. It was a subtle force but it affected the physical system. I carefully switched back to physical consciousness and moved the chin downwards to its normal position. I left the eyes upwards. When I did this the pressure to push the eyes upwards and to cause them to roll upwards in the head, increased. I then move to the crown chakra and began an upward pulling force to pull the intellect upward under that chakra.

Initially this was successful but then about ten minutes after when I lost touch with naad sound, I felt a pulling force which pulled the intellect back to its default position. When I looked down to see that pulling force and to identify it, I found it to be a memory which travelled up through the neck and which demanded that it be involved with the intellect. I immediately yanked on the intellect to pull it up. I did not want it to link with the memory energy.

However, at that time the memory energy sensed my intentions. It immediately released pictures of past scenes in order to weaken my resolve and gain control of the intellect. I then released a dismissal energy which causes that memory energy to sink into the neck but it did so while releasing disappointment energy.

Where did the memory originate?

How did it expressed enough power to pull the intellect away from the coreSelf?

Yogi is Visited by Deity (December 2011)

अभ्यन्तरं शरीरस्य प्रविष्टोऽसि यदा मम

दृष्ट्वा लोकं समस्तं च विस्मितो नावबुध्यसे (2.43)

abhyantaraṁ śarīrasya praviṣṭo'si yadā mama
dṛṣṭvā lokaṁ samastaṁ ca vismito nāvabudhyase

abhyantaraṁ - inside; śarīrasya – of the body; praviṣṭo = praviṣṭaḥ = entered; 'si = asi = you are; yadā – when; mama – my; dṛṣṭvā – having seen; lokaṁ - world; samastaṁ - everything; ca – and; vismito = vismitaḥ = astonished; nāvabudhyase = na (not) + avabudhyase (you will thoroughly understand)

Entering the inside of my body, you were astonished. Having seen everything in the world there; you became astonished and did not thoroughly understand. (Markandeya Samasya 2.43)

After translating this verse, I had an appearance of the divine boy Krishna whom Markandeya saw. This happened on the morning of December 3, 2011, on a Saturday morning while I sat to meditate on a couch in Mobile, Alabama.

I concluded the meditation session. Then I had a feeling to meditate more. In fact, on that morning I was late for meditation, some two hours late, but still I felt compelled to meditate just a little more.

As soon as I decided to do that, there was a pressure from the back of the head and then naad sound moved forward. I became aware of it. A hand held a finger of mine and drew tilak markings on a forehead. This was a Vaishnava tilak marking but it was a bit different to the one introduced by Bhaktivedanta Swami. This tilak was like this.

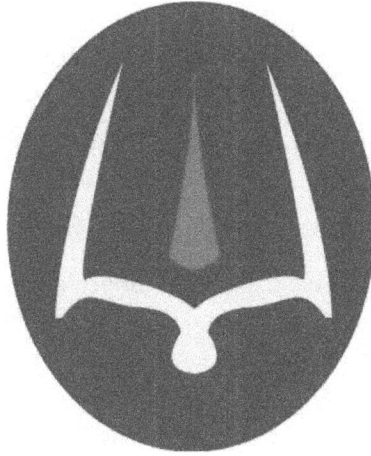

The hand that held my finger to draw this was the hand of the deity. He said, "Be sure to draw the tilak like this on both my and the Maharshi's illustrations."

I felt the existence of the deity but I could not see his body. It was transparent, emanating transparent light. He then said, "Is there anything I can do for you. Ask a favor, son."

I ran through my mind in a hurry because I felt pressed for time, before the deity would disappear. I had no desire. I meditated on the request. I was inspired. I said, "Help with this meditation. I need to reach the chit akasha more frequently."

He said, "That is strange because you are in touch with chit akash. Anyway, do this and go here."

Then he left.

The instruction to do this and go here, was an instruction for me to jump into the high part of the subtle forehead and then to put my attention forward just a little without having the attention go outside the forehead. This causes the membrane of the subtle head to dissolve. It allows the yogi to make contact with the chit akash.

This is a simple procedure, but there is a preliminary thing which is that the yogi must be proficient in breath infusion and kundalini pull-up process.

There was a notation which the Deity left in my psyche about this particular tilak mark. He said:

They have no use for this. They are not yogis. They feel yoga is useless. In this tilak that space is where the yogi makes contact with the chit akash. This is more than a mark. This is a meditation process.

Mark it externally or do not mark it externally. But that is not it. It has to do with contact with chit akash. It is the unseen mystic mark in the psyche of the accomplished yogi. What have they to do with this?

They believe in physical reality only. They lack confidence in this. Be blessed to continue this, my boy.

Yogi / Thoughts across the Border (December 2011)

There are different kinds of thought energies which disturb meditation and which cause a student to be stalled, sometimes for years, without making substantial progress.

Usually students feel that thought energy is thought energy and that is the end of it. Most meditation processes regard it in that way without segregating the different types of ideation. This general approach is great for beginners but it is insufficient for an advanced yogi. The reason is simple:

Thoughts are based on particular types of personal relationships. Even thinking to oneself is based on a relationship with someone else. The arrogance of a student is that he/she may feel that it is all about the self, that it concerns only the lack of self-control.

Actually, we are in a pool of influence at all times. We are never alone, never completely segregated. The faster we can realize this, the more successful we will be at the game of existing.

Can one stop this game of existence? Can one think a way out of existing? If it is all up to oneself, if one is God or even if one is potentially God, can one stop existing? Does one have the right?

We must understand the influences which bombard us and which prevail over us from time to time, for better or worse.

Many thoughts are created in the psyche on the basis of energy in the psyche but some penetrate and take control of the psyche. This happens even though one may be versed in advanced meditation.

Some thoughts are created in the psyche by the psyche. These are based on energy in the psyche. Other thoughts came about only after certain energies penetrated the psyche.

What does it matter? One may ask. After all a thought is a thought even if it is projected or smuggled into the psyche?

Default Location of the CoreSelf (December 2011)

For the coreSelf two aspects need be considered and adjusted. These are:

- Its location
- Its default activity

If I asked you where the coreSelf was located, what would you say? Do you know? Is that a definite location or are you all-pervasive, unified with all?

Are you not sure because to you it is vague and indistinct where you are not sure who or what you are?

What is the coreSelf's default activity? Is it thinking? Is it seeing images in the head? Is it creating ideas and visualizing scenes?

What does it do? Where does viewing occur in the mind? Where is sound heard? Where does the observer peer from? Is there anyone else in the psychic room of the mind?

This morning during meditation, I reviewed the practice to be sure that everything which was to be done in the preliminary stage was completed. It so happens that from time to time the student yogi should check to be sure that previous stages of practice which were completely half-heartedly or carelessly are reviewed and corrected.

Checking on the default activity of the coreSelf, I found that it was in a limbo where it was not sure if it should resume looking at images, ideas and thoughts or if it should go to naad sound.

Thus, I repeatedly reset it to be sure that it would do that. I would relax mentally and then see where the coreSelf would go and what it would do. If it hesitated, I moved to naad immediately. If it went to naad I reinforced that as the desired behavior. If it attempted to go for thoughts, images and ideas, I prevented that and took it to naad. It is amazing how repetitive the mind can be in an undesirable behavior.

If "I" is different than self, then who/what is the I which makes the adjustments and gyrations? Is the "I" which controls and adjusts the self facilitating desires to perceive, detect, recognize and will? Who perceives?

This inquiry is based on the assumption that the conventional self is mistaken for the coreSelf and that it would be impossible to sort identity. I agree that there may be confusion. One is forced to be and to use the conventional self as the total in social dealings. In fact, from day one, from the time one exited the womb of the mother, one was faced with this conventional self as the self and nothing but the self.

However, in meditation one is no longer forced to identify as the conventional self. One can relax it. The section of yoga which is the fifth stage, that of pratyahar, has to do with this relaxation from the convention. But if one is fearful of segregating and sorting the conventional self, the pratyahar sensual energy withdrawal will be uncomfortable.

The conventional self is a composite of various psychic adjuncts and the coreSelf or *bare nude self*. For meditation, one should split the composite self into parts. Then one should identify the core and its adjuncts.

Why?

Because in the conventional combination of adjuncts, the core and its adjuncts are termed as the self, these are experienced as one indivisible something, even though they are distinct when perceived from a higher level of consciousness. The core is fused with an observing faculty. When we say the observing self, we usually mean the coreSelf and that observing faculty. Patanjali advised us to do kevalam or kaivalyam which is to partition the coreSelf from that observing facility. Even when that is done the coreSelf is still an observer except that it is an observer without its analysis equipment.

When a student sits to meditate, he or she may rapidly or slowly, according to the degree of meditative skill developed, split up the components of the conventional self and be that observer by itself or be the observer with the observing faculty. For each student this must be determined according to the student's mastership of the practice of pratyahar sensual energy withdrawal.

There are many meditation processes. Some were adapted from methods of Indian yogis, where there is no sorting of the adjuncts and where students move from the conventional self to an absolute self or to a oneness self. But in the practice which I teach the student has to either rapidly or slowly sort the conventional self and be the segregated coreSelf with or without the observing faculty.

Initially when there is the effort or desire to meditate, the whole conventional self is involved. As soon as the meditation begins, the coreSelf finds itself in its default position at the center of the energies which are the psychological forces which comprise the conventional self.

The coreSelf has a tendency to unify itself with or to give attention to the observing mechanism which is usually used as an intellect and as an analyzing faculty. If the coreSelf is fused with that observing mechanism, it may be termed as an observing self with equipment. If it does not fuse with that but instead turns to the back of the subtle head, it will meet with the naad sound or it will meet with mental blankness.

Even by itself without the observing mechanism, the core can perceive and detect but not in the same way as is done by the mechanism. Its range of observing is greatly reduced when it is not fused into the mechanism.

When it is with naad or when it is in the mental blankness at the back of the head, it does not need to identify with varied realities. It still has a sense of identity but that sense is not applied to anything. That may be compared to having a vehicle in the neutral gear. The engine is not engaged even though the vehicle is operative. There is no torsion in the vehicle because the transmission is not engaged. Similarly, the sense of identity is present but it is not active.

Yogi and the Astral People (December 2011)

Last night I was in some humbug situations of one person after the next, like a central station at the end of the day with workers rushing to catch express trains to their homes.

In the *Bhagavad Gita*, in Chapter 8 there is mention of the influence of the sun and moon on the subtle bodies of those who are deceased, where if they are under the influence of the moon they take the path of return and if they are under the influence of the sun, they take the path of no-return and are projected to higher dimensions.

यत्र काले त्वनावृत्तिम्

आवृत्तिं चैव योगिनः ।

प्रयाता यान्ति तं कालं

वक्ष्यामि भरतर्षभ ॥८.२३॥

yatra kāle tvanāvṛttim
āvṛttiṁ caiva yoginaḥ
prayātā yānti taṁ kālaṁ
vakṣyāmi bharatarṣabha
(8.23)

yatra — where; kāle — in time; tv = tu — but; anāvṛttim — not return; āvṛttim — return; caiva = ca — and + eva — indeed; yoginaḥ — yogis; prayātā — departing; yānti — go; tam — this; kālam — time; vakṣyāmi — I will tell; bharatarṣabha — O bullish man of the Bharata family

O bullish man of the Bharata family, I will tell you of the departure for the yogis who do or do not return. (Bhagavad Gita 8.23)

अग्निर्ज्योतिरहः शुक्लः

षण्मासा उत्तरायणम् ।

तत्र प्रयाता गच्छन्ति

ब्रह्म ब्रह्मविदो जनाः ॥८.२४॥

agnirjyotirahaḥ śuklaḥ
ṣaṇmāsā uttarāyaṇam
tatra prayātā gacchanti
brahma brahmavido janāḥ
(8.24)

agnir = agniḥ — summer season; jyotir = jyotiḥ — bright atmosphere; ahaḥ — daytime; śuklaḥ — bright moonlight; ṣaṇmāsā — six months; uttarāyaṇam — the time when the sun appears to move north; tatra — at that time; prayātā — departing; gacchanti — they go; brahma — to the spiritual location; brahmavido = brahmavidaḥ — knowers of the spiritual dimension; janāḥ — people

The summer season, the bright atmosphere, the daytime, the bright moonlight, the six months when the sun appears to move north; if at that time, they depart the body, those people who know the spiritual dimension, go to the spiritual location. (Bhagavad Gita 8.24)

धूमो रात्रिस्तथा कृष्णः
षण्मासा दक्षिणायनम् ।
तत्र चान्द्रमसं ज्योतिर्
योगी प्राप्य निवर्तते ॥ ८.२५॥

dhūmo rātristathā kṛṣṇaḥ
ṣaṇmāsā dakṣiṇāyanam
tatra cāndramasaṁ jyotir
yogī prāpya nivartate (8.25)

dhūmo = dhūmaḥ — smoky, misty or hazy season; rātris — night time; tathā — as well as; kṛṣṇaḥ — the dark moon time; ṣaṇmāsā — six months; dakṣiṇāyanam — the time when the sun appears to move south; tatra — at that time; cāndramasam — moon; jyotir = jyotiḥ — light; yogī — yogi; prāpya — attaining; nivartate — is born again

The smoky, misty or hazy season, as well as in the night-time, the dark-moon time, the six months when the sun appears to move south; if the yogi departs at that time, he attains moonlight, after which he is born again. (Bhagavad Gita 8.25)

शुक्लकृष्णे गती ह्येते
जगतः शाश्वते मते ।
एकया यात्यनावृत्तिम्
अन्ययावर्तते पुनः ॥ ८.२६॥

śuklakṛṣṇe gatī hyete
jagataḥ śāśvate mate
ekayā yātyanāvṛttim
anyayāvartate punaḥ (8.26)

śuklakṛṣṇe — light and dark; gatī — two paths; hyete = hy (hi) — indeed + ete — these two; jagataḥ — of the universe; śāśvate — perpetual; mate — is considered; ekayā — by one; yāty = yāti — goes away; anāvṛttim — not return; anyayāvartate = anyayā — by other + āvartate — comes back; punaḥ = punar — again

The light and the dark times are two paths which are considered to be perpetually available for the universe. It is considered so by the authorities. By one, a person goes away not to return; by the other he comes back again. (Bhagavad Gita 8.26)

नैते सृती पार्थ जानन्

योगी मुह्यति कश्चन ।

तस्मात्सर्वेषु कालेषु

योगयुक्तो भवार्जुन ॥८.२७॥

naite sṛtī pārtha jānan
yogī muhyati kaścana
tasmātsarveṣu kāleṣu
yogayukto bhavārjuna (8.27)

naite = na — not + ete — these two; sṛtī — two paths; pārtha — O son of Pṛthā; jānan — knowing; yogī — yogi; muhyati — is confused; kaścana — at all; tasmāt — therefore; sarveṣu — in all; kāleṣu — in times; yogayukto = yogayuktaḥ — disciplined in yoga practice; bhavārjuna = bhava — be + arjuna — Arjuna

Knowing these two paths, O son of Pṛthā, the yogi is not confused at all. Therefore at all times, be disciplined in yoga practice, O Arjuna. (Bhagavad Gita 8.27)

Some say that this does not apply to them because they are devotees of Krishna who transcend such influences. But really? Are these people actually keeping track of the present performance of their subtle bodies? Are they happily living on assumptions which have no application to what they do in the astral world?

Last night the atmosphere where I was in Alabama was different. The air was imported from the Caribbean Sea. There were Caribbean and South American astral bodies in the astral atmosphere in this part of the USA.

It was like when you are on an island. There is a trade wind which comes from another place. It brings mosquitoes and makes it miserable for everyone. The bugs cannot fly such distances on their own. With a free ride in a trade wind, they traverse large distances.

First, I saw some persons from Trinidad whom I knew years ago. They were excited to be with each other and glad to see me. I dodged some and hid from some but those who had meaningful relationships with me years ago could not be avoided.

Some were the same as they were many years ago with the same ideas, mannerisms, and idiosyncrasies. Then I saw my father, who came from Guyana. He knew some Trinidadian persons but now he, like some of them, is deceased.

Looking at a few ladies who were there, and who were his age when he used his last physical body, he said, "I know you are required to be celibate to practice that. That is yoga. It requires celibacy. I know that much about that."

He pointed to me and said, "He helped us. There were some family difficulties, some liabilities but he covered the expenses. He helped us."

After this he asked me about one of his grandsons, as to whether that person had a family or not. I told him that he should speak to the person directly since I do not supervise such things. I did enough in helping the ancestors already.

Except for one person, these astral persons even though deceased have no spiritual interest. Their minds are honed to physical existence just as if the astral reality had no value and the physical world is the only reality.

Yogi in Room Full of Mirrors / The Battle Within

Bhagavad Gita took place on a battlefield with real warriors and real butchering of enemy combatants. It was about conquest. Funny thing is how *Bhagavad Gita* is carried and treasured by monks and pacifists.

Even Mahatma Gandhi, a person who became famous for his non-violent posturing, wrote a commentary on the *Gita* and tried to say in it, how the book was about non-violence. Gandhi is a credible figure of human history but a person would really have to be a fool to believe that about the *Gita*.

As they say even if God says that the sun rises in the West, it is not going to happen. Even with Gandhi talking about peace and nonviolence in his remarks about the *Gita*, that will still not cover over the truth about the slaughter of the warriors at Kurukshetra.

But there is another aspect to the *Gita* which is the war within the psyche, the fearsome gory details of which are left to be discovered in yoga practice. It is in the *Gita* but one must shift attention to the psychic level to see it.

Many of us want only peace and love, the better more desirable side of human nature.

A fantasy? Perhaps!

In meditation I propose that the head of the subtle body is a battlefield and for that matter whatever is lower than the head is another separate war-field.

The self must fight for its freedom. It will have to dominate if it wants to take control. Otherwise it will be under the thumb of the senses, intellect, memories, instincts and the needy sense of identity.

Some feel that these aspects are not to be segregated or that they cannot be sorted, that they are all one person, one noumenon called the self, the individual, or the higher self. The naming has to do with the preference, philosophy and concepts.

In the case where it is all one, there is no battle. Who is so crazy as to want to fight himself or herself? Who wants division where there is union?

But for those who are not particular about that and who prefer to sort. I give a diagram of locations to consider for conquest. Do battle in these zones. Bring them under control.

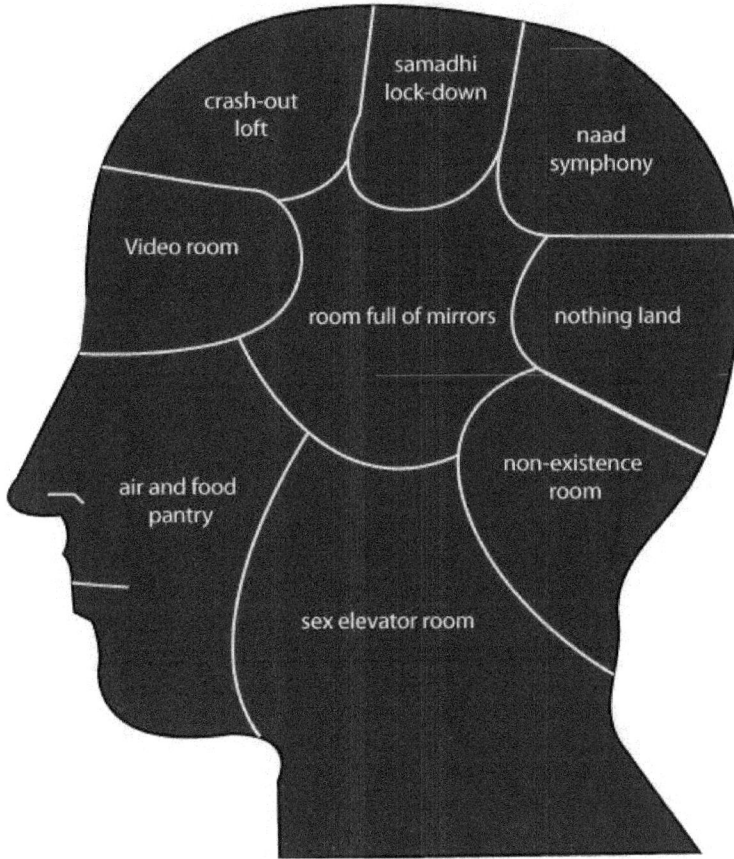

It would be a shame. Would it not be? If you as the master of the psyche, were captured and held as a prisoner by another aspect of the psyche. Maybe that is your situation already!

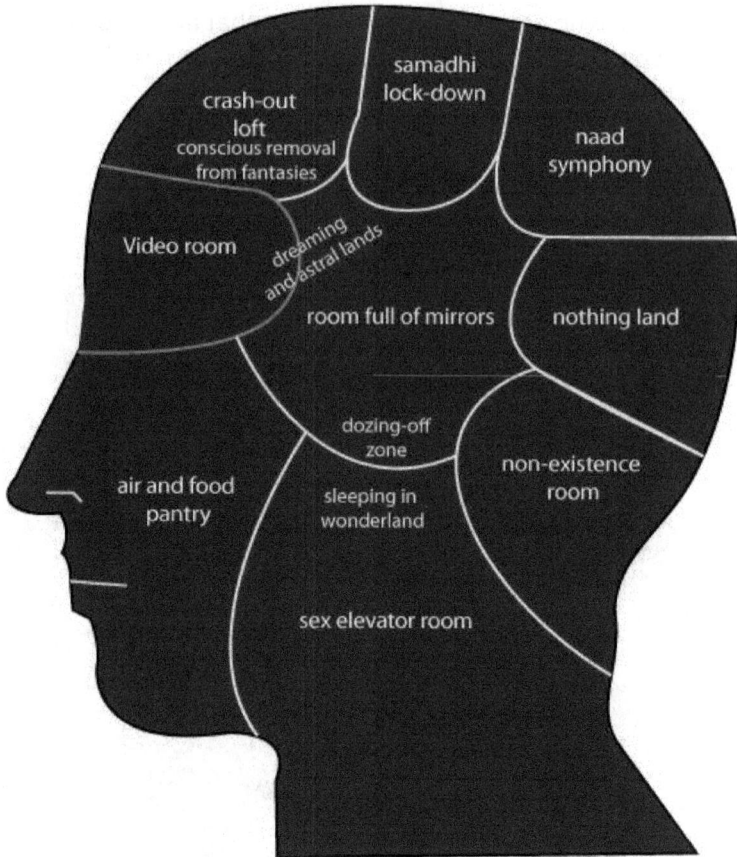

It is important that everyone draws diagrams of the mind as realized in meditation. A yogi should discover the locations used for different psychic operations.

Yogi and Eggs

I consume no eggs. I regard them as female reproductive fluid. Each egg to me is menstrual fluid in a shell. Of course, eggs are clear and yellow on the inside, but still it is in fact the reproductive fluid of the hen with or without the sperm of a rooster.

Everything hinges on the childhood upbringing. If that is counterproductive to yoga one must struggle to get free of it. In the *Bhagavad Gita,* in chapter six, Krishna discussed births a yogi may get. The one in the household of an advanced yogi is the rarest, most infrequent birth.

The sad part is that sometimes someone gets that birth and does not appreciate it. This is because a birth is attained because of service in a family, not because of past yoga practice. Many ascetics made the wrong assessment and think that one gets a body because of yoga practice but that is not a fact. One gets a body because of social contribution.

The sequence of birth then death is intertwined with social service, not with yoga and self-realization. This is why someone may be the son or daughter of a great yogi and that child may be totally against yoga and what it advocates. If a yogi takes a birth in a family, his social obligation for progeny is to that family. It is not to his yoga friends. His children may be disinclined to yoga because it is not their tendency from past lives. They have merits in the family based on social services committed prior to taking the new body.

Someone inquired of the yoga practice of my children. Why question that? Children means persons who contributed socially to the family. It has nothing to do with yoga. But yes, there are cases where the son or daughter of an ascetic becomes a great yogi. For instance, Vyasa the author of the *Mahabharata (Bhagavad Gita)* was the son of Parashar Yogi, who was the son of Shakti Yogi who was the son of Vasisht Yogi. Vyasa's son Shuka who told the story of Krishna to Parikshit was a mahayogin. Now and again there are yogis in succession in a family. But that is irregular. The usual situation is that a yogi is irregular in a family.

Even though Yogesh is not that famous he was the greatest yogi in these modern times. He ran away from the relatives when he was a teenager. He did that to become a yogi. That is the usual situation. Begetting children is a duty that one has as soon as one gets a body. It is an obligation as far as nature is concerned. If one is lucky to comply with it, one must save oneself from it as well because most of the entities under whose influence one will do that may be materialistic which means that they will influence one to abandon yoga. They will inspire and encourage the pursuit of status and wealth.

I advise students not to avoid responsibility. Compensate the family by raising progeny responsibly but practice yoga all the same. Yogesh ran away. He did that successfully because he is a son of Brahma. He can do that and be exempt from family obligations. If a lesser yogi does that, he will incur a fault which will abjectly affect the practice. It is better to efficiently reimburse the relatives for the body one got in their family line and be done with that, than to escape and have a demerit sink one later.

In terms of eating eggs, luckily, I was born in a meat-eating family which was in state of poverty. Eggs were expensive where I grew up. It was rarely cooked. I remember that sometimes the seniors in the family had a few hens. They took eggs from those chickens now and again. I was the last on the list in terms of diet and food because I was not an adult. I was the youngest in the household. I was a boy. When things were shared, I got the least. In retrospect that was in my interest because I was deprived of so many things.

I remember that the biggest use of eggs was for cakes which were baked for Christmas. My part in it had to do with cracking the shells, draining the liquid into a bowl and then spending about half hour or more beating these eggs. There were no electrical appliances. In fact, the only use of electricity was for a few light bulbs. Everything else was done manually.

In a child's body I used to marvel at boiled eggs, how they had to boil for many minutes and then the liquid would harden into a lily-white color with a gold orange color in the center.

But the thing that was of interest to me was a hen or two in the backyard. Early in the morning we would hear cocks crowing in the neighborhood, calling their rivals while announcing the arrival of daylight. The hens had a different attitude to the cocks. I noted that as a child.

I always wondered about the silent contract they signed to surrender their eggs in return for being in a pen under the protection of human beings. After laying an egg, a hen would pop out of her cubicle and make a clucking sound to announce that the egg was laid. She made her part of the bargain. She expected to be compensated with rice or corn.

Once there was a drawer in which some cockroaches hid. A senior in the family told me to take it quickly to where the chickens were. Those chickens were merciless on those roaches and gobbled them down. That was strange. Here were the roaches hiding safely in the drawer. Suddenly their lives were imperiled, just like in a war where innocent people get killed by soldiers.

From then on, I was afraid of the beak of birds. I developed a new respect for chickens because I realized that they were deadly killers. They spared no species which they considered to be food.

About this time, there was the introduction of small incubators which could heat about fourteen eggs at a time. There were imported eggs which produced white chickens. Everything changed because the white chickens were civilized and did not relate agreeably with the home owner, the way the brown chickens insisted on clucking after laying.

As a child I had a relationship with these animals. I did not regard them as a source of eggs. Later after I considered the habit of eating animals, I realized that it was an extension of animal life in the jungle in previous lives, and that as human beings; we still have those needs. Knowing that I was far away from primitive life, I left it aside easily. When I joined the US Air Force in 1968, the main breakfast meal was scrambled eggs. I was not used to it but it was served to the airmen. I ate that because of the circumstances. Over time I ceased that even though there was nothing else available besides bacon, milk and sugar loaded cereals.

The idea of keeping chickens stuck with me however. When I purchased a small property in Roosevelt, Minnesota some years later around 1976, I bought a few hens and a rooster. I did not eat their eggs or bodies. I kept them for company sake. I used to listen early in the morning to the daylight call of the rooster.

Sir Paul was there with us at this time. Once, his girlfriend came there. She was attacked by the rooster who flew to her thighs and tried to peck her. The rooster did not like that fact that she wore short pants which exposed her thighs.

I thought it was funny but the lady annoyed. These animals are living entities. They have opinions and views like everyone else. They want to live, have a family, express themselves and even enforce their opinions.

When you see it in that way, it is difficult to continue with the eat-the-animals habit. It depends on what species of life one is attracted to. If for instance I take a python body and that is possible even though it is not likely, I will have this understanding that everything which lives and moves is food. I will not have a sophisticated diet. I will have no need for fire in food preparation. I will not have to discard nails, hair and bones. I will digest even that.

It depends on what species I am most attracted to. We retain animal instincts from former lives even from millions of years prior. In Kriya yoga, one sees this and one makes a decision to strive for spiritual insight, so as to be with the divine beings.

There are two directions, up to the divine world or down to the animal kingdom. This is not religion. This is evolution and making a turn this way or that way, up or down.

I wish to be with the divine beings because I am tired of the riffraff existence with my brothers and sisters, the animals. I desperately learn about divine beings. I substitute their patterns for the animal instincts. I heard from siddhas. One said that after millions of births a living entity meets a divine being. Suddenly an insight surfaces in the mind. One feels that one can become divine. One could relocate to the divine world where viciousness is conspicuous by its absence.

A Yogi and a Subtle Body Swami

This morning during my exercises, I had a strange visitor on the subtle side. It was Kirtanananda Swami who is recently departed from a body in India. I am currently in USA. When I saw Kirtanananda, I realized that his subtle body came from a short distance, from about thirty miles in the physical sense.

He said, "I thought you could help him. These people are more inclined to Buddhism. Prabhupada did not like that but it is alright. I am at a farm nearby. I want to watch you do the pranayama exercises. As you know,

Prabhupada did not allow it. The whole thing about one system only, is invalid. People from different cultures must have something that is within their purview. But Prabhupada did not go for it."

I continued the practice as he observed. When I was finished, he followed me to a room where I did meditation. He sat to meditate and tried to do what I did mentally. Because he is on the astral side full time now, he has more subtle perception. He asked about why I was absorbed in naad sound resonance. I told him that it was the yogi mantra.

He said, "Prabhupada did not mention that. With him it was all Hare Krishna and nothing else. We did not know that Krishna discussed naad with Uddhava. Occasionally, I heard that sound but I did not heed it. Prabhupada never spoke of it."

Yogi / Thought Dissection (December 2011)

I skipped a few days on reporting the practice. This was due to time taken for teaching and discussing with others. Presently I practice on schedule but time is curtailed by teaching and holding discussions.

This morning I did breath infusion and sat to meditate. As soon as I sat naad sound was moved forward. I connected with it. After thirty seconds, there was an infusion subtle force which moved from the frontal part of the subtle head. It collected energy there. It pushed that energy into naad.

As the energy made contact with naad, it fell as if it was trash being pushed off a cliff by a bulldozer. This happened repeatedly. As soon as one mound of that energy was pushed into naad, it fell down into a chasm space and disappeared. Again, the same action was repeated over and over.

After a time for about eight minutes or so naad was everywhere. That energy which was being pushed and which dropped off was nowhere to be seen. Naad saturated the area.

After another ten minutes, a thought arose. It was from astral persons whom I was physically in discussion with the day before. From those persons thoughts penetrated my psyche as the breath infusion energy subsided. These persons are interested in spiritual life. For that reason, their thoughts penetrated. As soon as I noticed the thoughts, they were on the verge of bursting into a mental video display but I suppressed it. It shrunk in size and retreated.

I listened to naad again but again I found myself viewing thoughts. I shrunk them again and returned to naad. This happened eight times. I made a decision to study this deviation.

There is a switch which triggers when one is in naad. When this switch flips, the coreSelf is hurled into the theatre of the mind, and is compelled to view thoughts, images or ideas which are illustrated.

Does the self control this switch? If not, who or what controls it?

I did inResearch to find the answer to that question. In what I observed, this switch has no visible operator. Even in meditation, there appears to be no one triggering this switch but whenever it flips, the self is compelled to abandon naad and move to invest its attention in the frontal part of the subtle head.

I noticed that an energy leaves thoughts, images or ideas which enter the mind. This energy fires in a laser beam type of configuration and that hits the switch, then the switch flips and the coreSelf somehow is compelled to repeat this action or relocate into the theatre in the mind where it is inflicted with ideation.

Why is the core controlled by that switch? How is the core linked to it? Who or what designed this automatic switch? Is it serving the purpose intended? Is it malfunctioning?

I noticed something else. Certain thoughts which come from others, especially those which come from desperate or anxious persons, stop on the outside of the psyche, about two feet from the edge of the face. These thoughts then strengthen themselves by contracting. They release a laser beam which hits that same switch. The self is then drawn into the theater of the mind regardless of if it desires to go there or not. Once the self is there and peers into nowhere mentally, the thought package which entered the psyche is displayed. The self is subjected to those thoughts. It is usually not objective to the display.

Another important observation is that the subjective viewing of thoughts, images and ideas is related to the self's involuntary contribution of its power to the mental illustration feature of the mind.

If an idea in the mind is sustained by the voluntary and conscious contribution of energy by the self, that self will have the power to withdraw its energy but if the energy was taken involuntarily with the self just being victimized by the thought-creation apparatus of the mind, the self will experience itself as being powerless to disable the thinking operations.

Recreating the Past

Student's Inquiry

If I reincarnate from this life into the next, does the next life have to be in a time frame after death? Can it be well before, like sometime in the middle-ages or during the time of dinosaurs? If I die in year 2020, will it only be possible to reincarnate after that date? Can I reincarnate into the past, say in the year 1900?

Author's Response:

There is no reverse gear in the reincarnation machinery. There are several forward gears however.

If you are a first-class psychic you can surely go back in time as a neutral observer, with absolutely zero interference rights. You may switch to a realm where the current history is similar to your past or to the past of some other place but in that other place, you can neither adjust nor interfere.

Astral Friend and Me

Last night I was with a friend who lives near Tampa, Florida. This may be because my physical body was in Florida at this time. It can be reached easily by persons who physical bodies reside in Florida and who do not usually astral project far away from their physical forms.

Unless one makes an effort to free the subtle body from the physical one, that subtle form will be earth bound. Even on the astral side, it will usually act as if it is a physical form. For instance, the astral body can pass through a concrete wall, just as radio waves do, but if the person is focused on material existence, the astral body may mimic the physical one and be so dense that it is unable to pass through a concrete structure, even though in fact, it can.

Spiritual life includes more than the mind which is the subtle head. It is also concerned with the rest of the subtle form, its trunk and limbs. One should free both the mind and the lower part of the subtle body from the need for physical life. One should have experiences of being out of the physical body and into the subtle world where different laws of nature play out. There the subtle body can float or fly because it may not be subjected to the gravitational force which the physical body is controlled and restrained by.

Actually, there is a force which makes the subtle body earth-bound but it is the astral gravity not the physical one. However, a person can cause the subtle body to be physically bound by having and maintaining a materialistic demeanor. This has nothing to do with one's philosophy of life. I may have the most sublime philosophy in the world and still my astral form may be earth-bound. It may comprise of dense subtle matter which will make it remain on the near-physical end of the astral spectrum of energies.

In that encounter with my friend, his astral body was dense as was many of the other people who were out that night in the astral world in Florida. We saw some persons whom we knew years ago when we lived in an ashram in West Virginia. These persons were in astral bodies. Those forms were taller than their material bodies by about one foot, but each was earth bound. I spoke to my friend. I said, "Let us fly. We do not have to walk to go where we wish."

He was concerned that the others would see us flying and would object. I told him that I did not care for others. They could not prevent us even if they disapproved. These others he mentioned were his superiors in the Hare Krishna society which has its bosses and underdogs. He was an underdog. He was afraid to offend the superiors by flying which they may interpret to mean that he thought he was higher than they.

I told him not to worry about their echelon system of seniority. I said to him. "Unless you hold my subtle body, you cannot do it anyway. Your subtle body is dense like theirs."

He held on. We floated through the sky. Like a heavy piece of cargo in an air plane, I could feel his body weighing mine down. By concentrating a little both of our bodies raised into the sky to about 120 feet above the ground. We began moving in the direction he preferred. We quickly passed his superiors. Their faces turned sour seeing us flying in the distance further and further away.

As we flew, we lost vision. Then we regained astral vision but were in a dark-grey sky which was so dense that we could see nothing beyond one foot.

At that point I release him and told him that he would awaken on the physical side. His astral body trailed until it was not within range. I returned to my physical form. I awoke and wrote about the experience.

We lost vision because of the denseness of his astral form. It drained my astral form and caused it to vibrate at a lower frequency. Helping others in the astral world may deter and de-energize the helper.

Two human beings who are locked in this dimension using physical bodies, seeing the same sun and moon, may be at different levels of awareness internally. My friend was not aware that we were in the astral world. He may not recall the encounter on the physical side of existence. The astral body may play out many circumstances in the astral world and the person may not know of these on the physical side. The memory apparatus which logs astral events is not the same as the one which logs physical factors. Since the entity is mostly physically concerned, he/she may after returning from an astral projection not access what happened in the astral world.

Nature switched the person over to the physical memory system as soon as the astral body is recalled into the physical one. Then the person awakens and feels as his or her social identity on the physical side with no awareness or recall of what took place astrally.

On the physical side, my friend understands astral projection and the flight of the astral body. He has information which is based on what he heard from others but that does not guarantee that he could recall the astral projections of his subtle form.

Always remember that the master of astral projection is nature itself not the entities who are in nature as individuals. By observing how nature does it, we learn of it. In so far as we can penetrate into nature's private and hidden affairs which affect us, we can become aware of astral projection and other psychic events.

Thought-Reception Switch near CoreSelf

I found the location of the subtle switch which moves the coreSelf from a full focus on naad to a full focus on the images, ideas and thoughts. If the self is fully focused on naad, this switch operates automatically when it is triggered by incoming thoughts from others. Rarely does it operate merely because of internal thoughts unless those energies came from others, and then entered the psyche.

The diagrams below give the location of this switch and shows its way of operating. A thought comes from someone. It penetrates the psyche. It is accepted by the intellect (thinking-reasoning faculty). However, this happens only if the intellect operates and was not disabled.

If the intellect was silenced, the incoming thoughts are not attracted to it, simply because it does not have an energy charge which attracts the thought-energy. The intellect becomes attracted to the sense of identity which surrounds the coreSelf. As soon as the thought energy is pulled to the intellect, it is pulled to the switch which is located in the sense of identity. As soon as it contacts this switch, the coreSelf is drawn out of naad focus and finds itself staring into the intellect to see the contents of the thought energy in visual display. This happens in a split second. Usually, it is not perceived by the meditator.

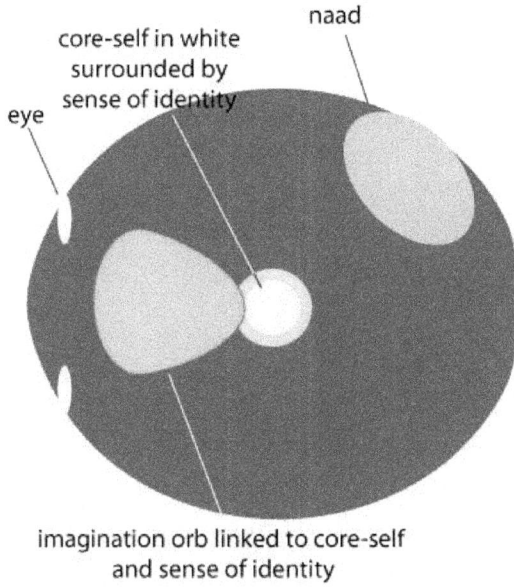

naad

core-self in white
surrounded by
sense of identity

eye

imagination orb linked to core-self
and sense of identity

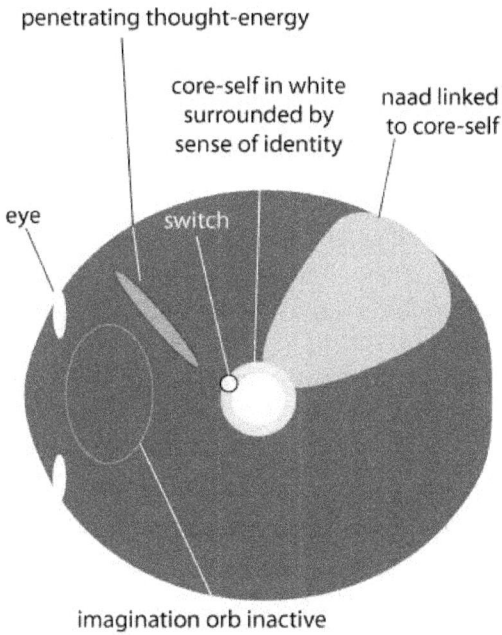

penetrating thought-energy

core-self in white   naad linked
surrounded by   to core-self
sense of identity

eye   switch

imagination orb inactive

penetrating thought-energy

core-self in white
surrounded by   naad
sense of identity

eye   switch
              inactive

imagination orb relinked to core-self
and saturated with thought-energy

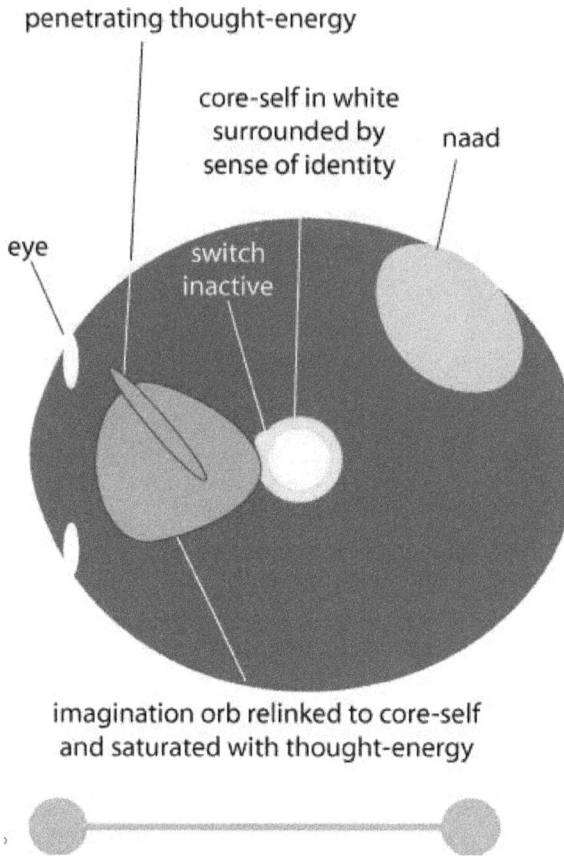

Muktananda's Guru Magic

In a conversation with Swami Muktananda's subtle body this afternoon, I discussed the issue of the Indian yogis who came to the West after performing yoga austerities in India and who downplay their austerities or do not describe the severity of the disciplines. They advocate an easy course, like sitting to meditate or like being touched by a Swami to be put into a sublime state.

I said to him,

"Why the silence? Patanjali clarified that yoga has eight parts. Why give people the idea that they can do meditation (samyama) without completing the preliminary stages?

"Do you really think, that with a touch to a disciple, you can erase the preliminary requirements and bestow meditation which consists of the three higher stages?"

He replied,

Before I got to the West, there were Indian yogis who established missions. They defined yoga in a certain way, especially as asana postures. Postures are one part but some people already had the idea, that asanas were yoga.

There were other persons who were influence by Indian swamis who felt that yoga is meditation only, which the Western people defined in their own way as sitting to concentrate or to focus on something selected.

These ideas were established. People wanted to hear nothing else unless the views were in support of that. I wanted to get at least a few people to come back to India to do the austerities because in the West the environment was not supportive. You know, people feel everything is easy and that they have a right to certain existential conditions of happiness.

They are told about their beauty, harmony and oneness with God or everything. They feel that they already achieved that. I could not change those attitudes.

I remarked,

"What about *pranayama* practice? You did much of it, months on end. But you pretended that Baba Nityananda blessed you with the insight? Why did you misrepresent that? Many others came to Nityananda. He touched them too. Still they did not get the insight. Why con people into thinking that it is merely a guru's touch that causes the insight."

He replied,

That is a good point. I did not remember every detail of the austerities I did. Pranayama, I did for years yes, and for a long time everyday sometimes. But what happens is that as one progresses one forgets or rather one does not focus the attention on what was done previously. When teaching one does not remember to mention every detail.

I replied:

"Tell it frankly: Can these persons develop the supernatural insight, the spiritual eye, without doing the *pranayama* practice to proficiency?"

He replied,

"I would not say that it is impossible to gain that without doing the pranayama practice to proficiency. But I will say this that most people cannot get it without that. The reason being that the subtle body will not be adjusted to the required level without it. Willpower is useless in this matter. Visualization is a waste of time. They cannot compel the subtle

*body to be elevated. The energy in it must be displaced by a higher
energy.*

Patanjali said it succinctly in that verse, you should quote it. You

know the verse.

I replied:

"Yes, I know the verse. I will note this. Thanks for the clarity. Thanks for
checking on my practice."

जात्यन्तरपरिणामः प्रकृत्यापूरात् ॥२॥

jātyantara pariṇāmaḥ prakṛtyāpūrāt

jātyantara = jāti – category + antara – other, another; pariṇāmaḥ –
transformation; prakṛiti – subtle material nature; āpūrāt – due to
filling up or saturation.

**The transformation from one category to another is by the saturation of the
subtle material nature. (Yoga Sutras 4.2)**

Samayama is the three higher stages of yoga as one sequential practice,
moving from linking of the attention to a higher reality, to effortless linking
of the attention, and then to continuous linking of the attention for extended
periods.

Yogi Attacked by Thoughts

I took time to check on the demand of thoughts, where in meditation
one feels compelled to look at an incoming or emerging thought. In some
experiences, one is forced to see the thought even though one intended not
to experience it.

Many persons who meditate indulge in the fantasy of themselves being
great people with infinite potential. They do not stop to observe how they
are man-handled by a tiny thought. The lack of thought control is so regular,
that only in deep meditation can one see how one helplessly indulges in the
thought-creating mechanism. In fact, one cannot understand that it is
necessary to gain control of this until one goes into deep meditation.

I did meditation this morning after a thorough breath infusion in both
the area below the neck and the area above the neck. Despite that, as soon
as I sat to meditate there were thoughts which attracted my attention. These
energies were in my psyche. Sometimes these energies are outside of the
psyche like aircraft near an airport waiting for permission to land. But these
thoughts landed, even without my permission. These were invaders. They
were armed for attack. They unfolded themselves and displayed themselves

but I closed the perception of them. This is a tactic which may be used for thoughts which are so powerful that even without permission they penetrate.

As soon as I closed the perception to them, they shrunk rapidly and disappeared. I refocused and reached for the naad sound. As soon as I did that another thought bunch appeared without permission. It slowly unfolded itself. I deprived it of my perception. It shrunk and disappeared.

Is this a victory?

Some thoughts have a power of their own, where they simply refuse to disappear. They have a compulsion energy. The real problem is not the thought itself but how it derived that compelling power. If one knows that one may deal with it. At least one may realize that the source of it is more powerful than the self.

Masturbation?

From the view point of reincarnation, masturbation is one of the methods we may use to deprive ancestors of bodies. In other words, if I have intercourse and I pass the semen outside the woman's body or if I use a condom, the would-be child would not develop because it would not be fostered in the woman's reproductive track. I would have, in effect, deprived that ancestor of a body.

On the other hand, if I masturbate, the same deprivation would occur. But here we are not concerned with fault or religion. We are concerned with providential reactions, in the sense that perhaps when I try to get the next body I may be subjected to the same treatment. Providence may flip it to me so that my next effort to get a body becomes one of frustration where my would-be father either masturbates or passes the semen which is to be my embryo into a condom or outside the body of my would-be mother.

Yogi Captured by Two Women

Last night was a night of horrors in the astral world. I was drawn into a parallel world where I met two persons who were church friends when this body was about thirteen years of age. Church was mandatory. The elder of the family attended religious services four times per week. In addition, we had duties at the church. On Saturday night we swept the church for the Sunday morning service. This was in the tropics, where bats lived in the bell tower. Dried bat down collected under the tower. It was swept and discarded.

We filled communion glasses with wine. These were miniature glasses which fitted into an ornate multi-level tray. At the top tray we put tiny round white wafers which represented the flesh of Jesus Christ. The wine was supposed to be his blood.

In retrospect, that Christian ritual, was similar to blood rites in a primitive culture. Anyway, on Sunday morning the elderly persons in the congregation took it seriously. They went to the altar, knelt and consumed the symbolic flesh and blood. They were confident that they and no one else would go to heaven hereafter. The rest of world would be fried in hell.

In the astral world I met two persons, two females who were girl members of this church years ago. Physically, I have not seen these persons for at least forty years, neither have I seen them astrally. Now suddenly, I was drawn into a parallel world where they prepare to live after leaving their physical bodies.

Each had this idea that I would be her companion in that astral place. How I would split myself into two they did not figure. Instead each thought to supersede the other.

What about all the other people whom I know? Each did not consider that. Each was sure that she would excel any other female. Suddenly while I was with them, one did an astral maneuver. I found myself on a large boat on an astral river in South America. We were the only two persons on the boat. There was no boat crew. This was a large boat which needed a crew to manage it. The lady operated it by her willpower. She smiled. From her mind came this idea:

"I take you to a place where we will be alone. It is what I always wanted. How do you feel about this? After you left the country, I always thought of you. I never forgot you. It is funny how in life you may never get what you desire but at death, all that may change for the better. Now we can be together forever."

Interestingly, there were no sexual overtones. It was a gender relationship without sexual flashes. I examined the astral body's energies and noted that it was ideal for this level of the astral existence. I thought I would have to leave since it was close to the time when my alarm would ring for practicing breath infusion practice. Just then I found myself with the other lady in another astral dimension.

I was on a dirt road, near to a car which was supposed to be mine. The lady came to me. She said that she would get a part for the car and I could install it. She was all smiles. Again, there was no sexual exchange. It was a sexless companion relationship.

I asked her, "You feel I should fix this car?"

She smiled broadly. She was happy to have me. I noted that there was no other desire in her mind. In those astral places, everything operates on the basis on one's imagination. Since she was absorbed in happiness, the dimension faded. I awoke on this side.

Think about it.

What would it be like if I am captured and held hostage after leaving this body? Whose world will I be in? What will be my role? How many years will I spend there?

Part 6

Yogi's Astral Address

When I am in New York, I stay in Brooklyn. In contrast, what is my astral address?

After some astral encounters last night with several people in Florida, I reflected that most human beings, even some seekers, have no idea of an astral address. They are aware of physical locations at properties or apartments. If you inquire of an astral address, they are at a loss for words.

I questioned some astral people. I asked, "What will be the address after death? Where can a deceased person be located then?"

Most persons at the astral meeting walked out. I thought to myself, "These folks do not realize that they are in the astral bodies. They think they are physical beings."

What is the astral address?

For me the physical address changes constantly. The astral address is more reliant because it is the physical body itself. Wherever that physical system may go, that is the location of the astral form which resumes residence in the physical body after sleep sessions. No matter where the physical body is located, it serves as the address for the astral form.

The second question about the astral address has importance to those who plan on finding a suitable situation in the astral world hereafter. Most of us do not care about the astral body. We feel secured in the physical world with the physical body as the address. For many years, we live in that reliable physical system. Somehow after dreaming, we find the physical body and awaken as it every morning. By the grace of nature that takes place. It happened reliably since as babies we realized ourselves as these bodies.

What will happen on that last sleep, that last dip in consciousness when we are no longer permitted to awaken as this form?

Where will one go?

What will be the new address?

Yogis take help from the Sun

During breath infusion, I had luck. I experienced small kundalinis. For the past week, because the atmosphere was not properly surcharged with sun energy, breath infusion was not as desired.

Still, I maintained the practice. Because of natural or man-made chemicals in the atmosphere and differing weather patterns, on some days sun-surcharged subtle air is hard to come by. A yogi should accept these variations. The main thing is to maintain the practice no matter what.

With sixty years and counting, with ultimate collapse of the body staring me in the face, it is in my interest to reinforce the practice. During the breath infusion, there were two small kundalinis which were in the face. These shot downwards into the cheeks on both sides. This felt like cool foam shooting through the cheeks. It was a bright white color

Five minutes after that occurred, there was a kundalini force in the frontal chest area. This shot through the neck on the right and left sides near the front. Neck clearance is important since the neck constricts and limits the exchange of energy between the trunk of the subtle body and the head of it.

If the neck is blasted in practice, the energy from the trunk will flow into the brain and visa versa. One of kundalini's bad habits is to keep the neck blocked. It allows food and breath energy to pass through the neck downwards. From this energy it manufactures hormones. It then hoards these hormones for sexual expression.

Kundalini is very stingy about passing any of that energy into the head, except that it sends some of that energy as sexual charges into the senses.

A yogi has a task to disrupt this process of kundalini. By punching open the neck, kundalini is no longer allowed to store this hormone energy just for sex. Instead, it can be used to increase clairvoyance and other psychic perceptions, which help the yogi to better manage social involvements and to discover methods of spiritual realization.

When I worked on the lower part of the body, there was a time when the thighs became surcharged with energy. This energy usually stays in the thighs and is used by kundalini to motivate the sexual urge and to drive the aggressive energy used during sexual intercourse. I pulled that energy from the thighs into the trunk of the body. Then I pulled it into the brain. This is part of what is called the *urdhva reta* practice, where a yogi pulls the sexual charge of energy into the brain

Sun-Charged Air:

Yogis are reliant on sun-charged air for progress. This is because the consciousness which we use on this plane is dependent on the sun. The sun planet though a physical furnace is also an astral reality. The astral bodies are dependent on it just as the physical ones are.

In India there is what is called the *gayatri* (Gai-tree or Gai-a-tree) mantra This has to do with brahmins praying to and making contact with the sungod three times per day, at sunrise, noon and sunset. It is for greeting the sun-god and taking assistance from him as well as remembering that we are dependent on him. Brahmins wrap a sacred thread around the right thumb thrice per day while saying this mantra and meditating to make astral contact with the sungod.

The words of *savitur, dhimahi, dhiyo (dhiyah)* mean the shining light of the sun god. Savitur is an altered word form of Savita who is the sun god Aditya or Surya, the son of Aditi, in the Vedic pantheon of deities.

As great a person as Krishna stated that the yogis use either sun or moon energy at the time of death to either go and not return to earthly rebirth or to return to the earth after staying in an adjacent parallel world. This is explained in *Bhagavad Gita.*

If the astral body is not properly surcharged with sun energy, a yogi is stuck. It will not matter what his philosophy is.

We are not independent. We will not be absolute anytime soon. This is why yogis are advised to take pranayama practice to infuse the subtle body with the energy which elevates and shifts it to higher planes.

Physically the sun is a nuclear furnace. But the sun is also personal. Of course, we cannot physical perceive any person on the sun but that does not mean there are no persons there.

Ancient yogis made formal contact and offered appreciation to the sun god *Savita (Surya, Narayana, Aditya).* Without sun energy both on the physical and subtle level, we would sink to a low existence, especially on the astral side.

Two Astral Swamis and a Yogi

Breath infusion went well this morning. I had an unusual visitor during the session, Swami Satchidananda. He is departed but is available on the astral planes. Usually I do not see this swami. I did not take instruction from him when he was physically present.

He wanted to discuss what I could do to help some of his students. I told him that if someone came to me, I would check the person's practice and advise as I see fit but beyond that I can do nothing.

Last evening, I was at a meditation session in a nearby town. During the session this same swami appeared but before he did, Swami Shivananda, His guru appeared.

I was surprised to see Swami Shivananda because he is no longer available in the astral world in India. It is understood that he went into the *brahma* as they say in India, which means that he went into the spiritual energy in fact.

In India it is the tradition that when a great spiritual master leaves his body people say that he went into final *samadhi* or *mahasamadhi,* indicating that he went to the spiritual world as defined by the particular sect. Those who believe in oneness say that the guru became one with everything. Those who believe in a deity, who has spiritual territories, say that the guru went to the spiritual world to be with God.

These are assumptions of loyal disciples which may or may not be the reality of the teacher who departed. For Swami Shivananda, I know that he did go into the *brahma* because I saw him in the subtle world. In the first place when Shivananda left his physical body he did not go into the *brahma* immediately. He remained at Rishikesha in India in an astral body which was similar to a yoga siddha body. But later, years later, he went into a transcendence environment.

Usually a spiritual master switches to his astral body after death of the physical one. Usually he does not go to any maha*samadhi* or to a spiritual place. Such things do happen but rarely. They certainly do not happen to a spiritual master who was involved in a large mission and who was aggressively making disciples, becoming famous, building large temples and shrines. Because their subtle bodies are saturated with concern energies for this place only, such gurus remain in the astral world which is adjacent to this place. Why should they go to a spiritual world to be nobodies when they can remain near the earth and have thousands of disciples treating them like gods?

During the meditation session, Swami Shivananda appeared in a savior body. Some gurus assume such bodies when they become qualified to be world teachers. It means that he left the transcendence level because of the desire to be a world teacher. After being qualified he was permitted by the cosmic deity to take a form of light to be a source of spirituality to others.

When he came to the hall where I was with others who were in a meditation session, he was in the distance about some twenty feet in the air in another dimension. Light-yellow light streamed from his world-savior subtle body. He was over one of the persons meditating indicating that he would grace the said person. He smiled brightly.

About one minute after this, Swami Satchidananda came there. He stood near to another person. Pointing to the two persons, he spoke astrally to me. He said, "He is a disciple. She is his student. Can you help?"

I replied, "There is not much I can do. They should practice and keep in touch with you. You are the teacher. If Dada blesses them, that is complete."

Satchidananda was not satisfied with the reply. He stayed for a while for the meditation session but Swami Shivananda whom we respect as Dada or Old Father, left. He faded in the sky at a great distance in space.

No one should tell anyone that when I leave this body, I went into maha*samadhi* or that I went into the *brahma* or that I went to the spiritual world. Why spread false rumors and try to give a yogi credit for something he may or may not achieve?

To find where I will go when I leave the body, simply check the meditation notes I wrote just before leaving the body. If in those notes, I regularly went into a maha*samadhi* or I met the Krishna deity in the spiritual world, or I transited to Shiva in his spiritual territory, or I met great yogis who use yoga-siddha bodies, then you can explain my achievement.

Otherwise if I had ordinary dreams just before departure, be honest. Say that I went to the astral world where the departed souls reside as they wait for an infant body.

If you credit me and if your motive is to encourage others to practice spiritual disciplines, you may say that I continue practice in the subtle body in some place which is near to this place but which is such that I can engage in practice and not be fully occupied with non-yogis who are deceased.

It may be explained that if I am successful my astral practice would cause me to go to a siddhaloka place where accomplished yogis may direct me in how to attain spiritual world access.

Yogi Links to Naad

During practice this morning I had a small kundalini rise in the front chest. This came up on either side and felt like tiny frost crystals changing from warm to cool alternately. I was up at about 4.30 am to do breath infusion. I supervised a student. His body was over 70. At that age the body is like an old cranky wagon.

When the body is young it may be disinclined to practice. When it is old and wisdom dawns and when one sees that something will happen which people label as death, one may be inspired to advance in psychic perception. Then, the body is like an old car and is resistant to change. But anyway, it is better to be late than never. Better to make an effort with an old body, than not to make the endeavor. Any attempt is good because it will be embedded in the subtle body which is the body one will have in the afterlife.

Yoga practice in old age is wonderful for keeping the subtle body from become filled with dense astral energies. The real benefit however is that one gets association with yogis hereafter.

When I sat to meditate, I focused on naad sound which blared in the psyche but last night during meditation naad blared outside the psyche.

When naad is outside the psyche one can use a *dharana* practice to reach it. *Dharana* is the sixth stage of yoga. Patanjali spoke about samyama which begins with this sixth stage. What is *dharana*? Mostly, people say it is concentration.

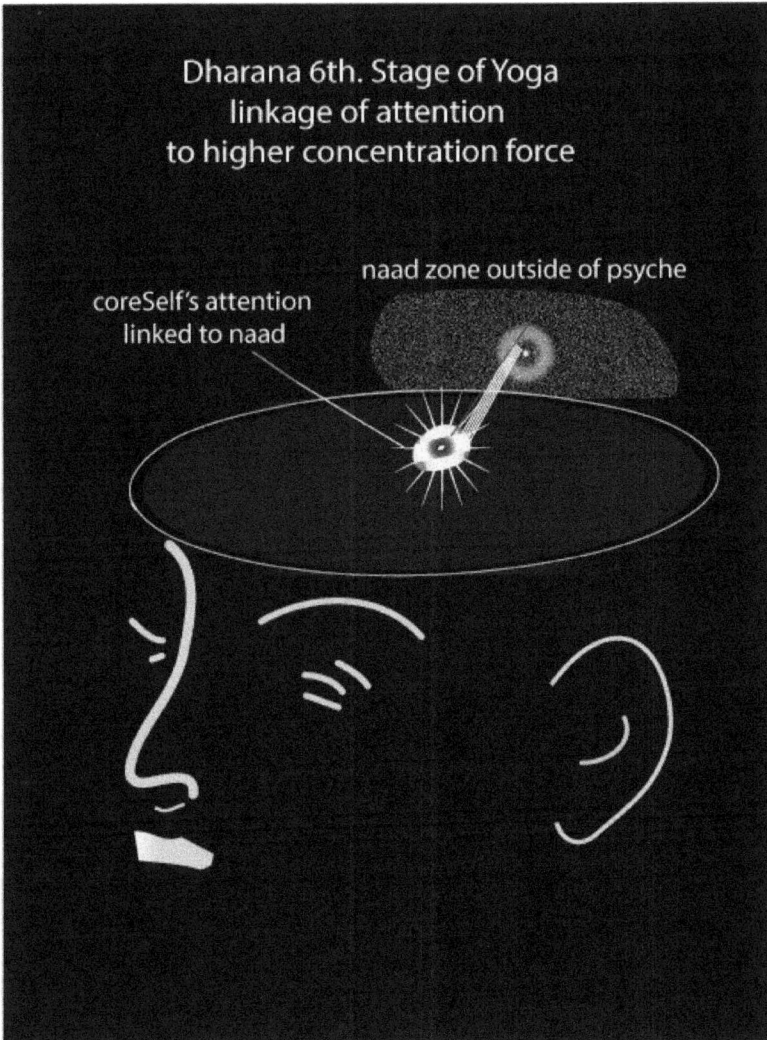

Dharana 6th. Stage of Yoga
linkage of attention
to higher concentration force

naad zone outside of psyche

coreSelf's attention
linked to naad

However, I am not concerned with that meaning of the word. Here I discuss linking with the naad sound at a source point outside the psyche. In this case I do not become naad. The coreSelf is itself what it is. It can link with other realities. If it is linked to a lower reality it feels as if it is lower. For instance, when it is fused into a material body it feels as if it is the identity of that body.

If it is linked into a higher reality, it feels elevated to that higher plane. In this practice of dharana, the coreSelf can link to naad in three distinct and clearly defined ways which are:

- Relocate from its default position and go to where the source point of naad is located outside of the psyche

- Relocate from its default position and go into naad but not go into naad's source point
- Remain at its default position and send a linking energy into the source point of naad or into the dispersed field of the naad sound

In neither of these cases does the coreSelf merge with naad. If the linkage or relocation linkage is done efficiently the core becomes aware of naad and loses its focus on anything else. This causes the thought-generating part of the mind to cease activity. The coreSelf gets freed from identifying itself as a material body.

Ultimately, this relocates the entire psyche to a higher plane such that it has perception of the chit akash spiritual planes of existence, some of which are inhabited by divine beings who use divine forms.

Samadhi with the Earth

During breath infusion this morning, I connected with the line of force which went through my physical body to the center of the earth. That means the gravitational center which may not be the geometric center. This line of force gripped all the atoms in the physical body.

One may want to know what *dharana* deliberate focus practice is. If one observes how the power at the gravitational center of the earth, pulls on the body with a steady force, one could understand what focus is.

A force that pushes or pulls is not static.

Dhyana spontaneous effortless focus on transcendence events, which is the seventh stage of yoga, can be understood by studying the gravitational force. *Dhyana* (dhee-an) is similar to *dharana* (dhuh-ruh-naa) but it is *dharana* which is effortless. When one becomes aware of the earth's gravitational force, when one realizes that it does so effortlessly, then one can understand how to do *dhyana*.

If, however when studying this, one notices that this force is ongoing, continuous and effortless that it seems to have no rhyme or reason, that it is inexplicable, that one cannot claim it as being caused by oneself, then one can understand what is continuous effortless focus *samadhi*.

In *samadhi*, the self is not the pulling force. It is not the pushing force. It is merely in the flow of the pulling or pushing force or it may be involved as part of this force. It is in this force which has a direction or a polarization, which may be the characteristic energy or socialization of a particular level or range of existence.

Samadhi is when the self remains in that time or place effortlessly and is penetrated, saturated, blended or infused with that level of existence or that nature of that divine person.

During practice when I became aware of the pulling force of the earth's gravity. It was like someone at the center peering through my form with laser vision, while exerting a mild pulling force, just enough to keep the body on the earth without causing the body to be crushed into the earth. This was a subtle force exerting a pulling energy on the subtle body.

Being in *samadhi* is one thing and having someone be in *samadhi* in reference to oneself is an entirely different matter. Is the fetus at any time in a *samadhi* force in reference to the mother's psyche? Are the energy forces of the mother penetrating the fetus, passing through it, influencing it?

The earth has my body in its *samadhi* range of energy. It claims my body as its own. The sun has this planet in its *samadhi* range, keeping it within limits. Deities are like the earth and the sun, in the sense that first we are in the control grip of the earth; then we along with the earth are in the control grip of the sun. Then the sun is within the control grip of the center of the galaxy.

Break away for a minute and try to understand how personalities may be configured in the same way. That gives insight into what is meant by deities.

Self / What is it?

I was asked a question yesterday about the small ego self and the true self. I was asked to discuss this in relation to the information of the *Bhagavad Gita* where Krishna declares three types of selves.

द्वाविमौ पुरुषौ लोके
क्षरश्चाक्षर एव च ।
क्षरः सर्वाणि भूतानि
कूटस्थोऽक्षर उच्यते ॥ १५.१६ ॥

dvāvimau puruṣau loke
kṣaraścākṣara eva ca
kṣaraḥ sarvāṇi bhūtāni
kūṭastho'kṣara ucyate (15.16)

dvau — two; *imau* — these two; *puruṣau* — two spirits; *loke* — in the world; *kṣaraścākṣara = kṣaraḥ* — affected + *ca* — and + *akṣara* — unaffected; *eva* — indeed; *ca* — and; *kṣaraḥ* — affected; *sarvāṇi* — all; *bhūtāni* — mundane creatures; *kūṭastho = kūṭasthaḥ* — stable soul ; *'kṣara = akṣara* — unaffected; *ucyate* — is said to be

These two types of spirits are in this world, namely the affected ones and the unaffected ones. All mundane creatures are affected. The stable soul is said to be unaffected. (Bhagavad Gita 15.16)

उत्तमः पुरुषस्त्वन्यः
परमात्मेत्युदाहृतः ।
यो लोकत्रयमाविश्य
बिभर्त्यव्यय ईश्वरः ॥ १५.१७॥

uttamaḥ puruṣastvanyaḥ
paramātmetyudāhṛtaḥ
yo lokatrayamāviśya
bibhartyavyaya īśvaraḥ (15.17)

uttamaḥ — higher: puruṣaḥ — spirit; tu — but; anyaḥ — another; paramātmeti = paramātmā — Supreme Spirit + iti — tims; udāhṛtaḥ — is called; yo = yaḥ — who; lokatrayam — three worlds; āviśya — entering; bibharti — supports; avyaya — eternal; īśvaraḥ — Lord

But the highest spirit is in another category. He is called the Supreme Spirit, Who having entered the three worlds as the eternal Lord, supports it. (Bhagavad Gita 15.17)

यस्मात्क्षरमतीतोऽहम्
अक्षरादपि चोत्तमः ।
अतोऽस्मि लोके वेदे च
प्रथितः पुरुषोत्तमः ॥१५.१८॥

yasmātkṣaramatīto'ham
akṣarādapi cottamaḥ
ato'smi loke vede ca
prathitaḥ puruṣottamaḥ (15.18)

yasmāt — since; kṣaram — effected; atīto = atītaḥ — beyond; 'ham = aham — I; akṣarāt — than the unaffected spirits; api — even; cottamaḥ = ca — and + uttamaḥ — higher; ato = ataḥ — hence; 'smi = asmi — I am; loke — in the world; vede — in the Veda; ca — and; prathitaḥ — known as; puruṣottamaḥ — Supreme Person

Since I am beyond the affected spirits and I am even higher than the unaffected ones, I am known in the world and in the Vedas as the Supreme Person. (Bhagavad Gita 15.18)

This gives a general categorization of three types of spirit, one being affected by the mundane energy, one being unaffected by it and a supreme spirit who is outside those two categories.

In this system, the higher self of the affected spirits can be realized by them by specific methods of introspection. But that higher self of the affected spirits is not the supreme spirit. They do have a higher self in their own right but that potential if realized in full does not make them into the supreme spirit.

The affected spirits are evolving through the mundane evolutionary cycle. They are individual spirits not a collective set of spirits or a universal spirit. To become liberated from nature's control of their energy, the affected spirits must take help from one of the unaffected spirits and from the Supreme Person as well. They must also take help from the very same nature which consumes their energy and subjects them to suffering and misplaced identity.

Bhagavad Gita does not ascribe to the idea that an individual spirit can become the Supreme Being. It gives processes for the individual limited spirit to be at its best and to reach its highest level of expression. It can attain a higher level of itself but that higher identity is not the Supreme Being and does not have the powers of the Supreme. *Bhagavad Gita* encourages the attainment of the higher potential of the affected spirits.

In relation to the unaffected spirits, these entities have a resistance to nature, whereby if they are in the physical world, they maintain themselves psychologically in the higher potential. But these beings are not as high as the Supreme Being.

Patanjali said that the Supreme Person is distinguished and that He taught the ancient superior beings long ago. The unaffected spirits help the affected ones to resist nature and to eventually shift to a dimension whereby they are not degraded.

As far as the limited self is concerned, it has an eternal coreSelf. When I use the words limited self to indicate the individual mind, in that case the word self should not be used. We should switch to a word like psyche or psychological environment. The eternal coreSelf lives in a psychological environment or container. It struggles to gain the upper hand in relation to what that psyche may do.

Because it is fused with other psychic principals, it has some difficulty discerning itself from its adjuncts. Sometimes it is of the opinion that it is the mind itself, that it is the psyche itself, while in fact, it is a component in the psyche which is liable for the activities of the entire psyche.

This may be compared to a father who has two sons. One, the eldest, cooperates with him frequently while the other, the youngest, is totally resistant. Since both boys are minors, the father is responsible for their activities. Once the younger son broke a neighbor's expensive window. The police came, arrested the father and took him to the precinct because he could not pay a fine. The younger son denied the act of breaking the window. The elder son being capable of reasoning observed when his brother broke the window but when questioned by the police, he denied. He said that his brother was not in the neighborhood when the window was shattered.

Later at the station, the police made a formal charge against the father for the crime of the youngest son. The elder son supported the father by stating that the police could not hold the father because they had no evidence that the younger brother broke the window.

In that story we see that the observing self, the elder son, may support the lower or the higher self. Instead of condemning the lower self outright, it tries to protect both the lower and higher selves. Therefore, it is also untrustworthy but the higher self is still dependent on it for reasoning and conclusions.

The lack of clarity has to do with the fact that one component in the psyche, namely the self, has to accept responsibility for the activities of the psyche even when that self objected to such activities and did not have the power to stop them.

Since it has to accept the responsibility for the psyche, the self is circumstantially conditioned to say that it is the entire psyche, even though this is not true.

The self is confused about its sense of identity. It is super-confused by the application of its sense of identity. It is uncertain as what it is and as to what other components exists in the psyche.

In this dilemma the self adopted the view that it has a higher self. It seeks to abandon its lower habits and to adopt its higher self as itself only. This is like if a prisoner admits to a crime but explains on the witness stand that it was his alter ego which committed the offence. He explains that he no longer identifies with the alter ego, and should be released as being innocent of the crime.

Of course, the authorities will have none of it. As far as they are concerned his partition of himself into an alter ego, observing self and higher self is a convenient ploy which they are not concerned with. They condemn him as the criminal.

In order to escape from the troubles of the psyche, the self splits itself into three parts namely the alter ego, which it considers to be insane, the observing self, which it considers to be a witness which is sometimes affected by the alter ego and sometimes unaffected by it, and the higher self which is supposed to be perfect.

However, what happens in fact is that this observing self is really the higher self with an objective view point. The alter ego is the same higher self when it is influenced by lower energies.

There is only one self. It is victimized by the subtlety of the other components in the psyche. It comes to think that it can partition itself into three and abandon at least one part of those partitions, which is the lower part or the alter ego.

The reason for this is the weakness of the higher self in that it is unable to control the observing self and the alter ego reflections of itself. It cannot figure a way to lift up its alter ego which is troublesome and untrustworthy. It cannot get the observing self to have supernatural vision, even though this observing part has intuitive and conclusive reasoning powers.

Because of this innate weakness of this higher self, it decides to abandon both the observing self and the alter ago and focus on its own nature as a diffused field of energy existing in a seemingly infinite energy field.

The story about the father and his two sons may clarify the relationship between the three selves of the psyche. This story does not solve any problems but it shows the relationship. From that one may reconstruct the relationship in a way which is helpful to the higher self getting the cooperation of the observing self and the alter ego.

Before we can get ahead with this situation, we must first abandon all attempts to eliminate the alter ego. In that relationship, the father should stop thinking of either killing the younger son or locking him in the cellar for good. The father must find a way to help the younger one to reform behavior so that he always serve usefully.

Once the father decides that he will keep the younger one, and patiently work to reform the boy, we can get somewhere; otherwise we are back to the dysfunctional relationship.

The key for the higher self is its relationship to the observing self. In other words, if the father could get the full cooperation of the elder son, then everything is settled. Here is why?

For all his trouble and stupidity, for his entire tendency to get carried away with whatever he does, for his habit of abandoning the authority of the higher self, the youngest son, the alter ego, cannot act unless it gets power from either the elder brother or the father.

But there is a catch which is that if the alter ego cannot get attention from the father, it can go to the brother for the attention. It can operate even if the father is not attentive to it. In other words, the troublesome boy can make problems for the father even when the father is not attentive to him.

But there is a catch to this, which is that the elder brother cannot give attention to anyone unless he takes attention from the father. If the father or the higher self could closely and fully regulate the distribution of its attention-energy to either son, especially to the observing self or elder son, all problems are solved, because the younger one, the alter ego, cannot act independently.

The process of doing this is the fifth stage of yoga which is *pratyahar*. The word *pratyahar* itself holds the key. It is a combination of a Sanskrit prefix and a noun word. The prefix is *prati* which means against or opposed to and *aahaar* which means to consume or eat. That process is the reverse of what we are usually interested in which is to enjoy and consume this existence. To control the boy, the father must abandon attempts to enjoy and consume the world.

However, there is a problem which is the relationship that the father has with the elder son. Even though the father speaks of living alone without children, even though he feels that he can get along fine without the elder son, the truth is that he cannot.

Why?

Because to live in the world requires calculation and analysis which is something that the father cannot do because he is not skilled for that process.

He needs the elder boy who is an intellect. This one weakness is the cause of his failure to control the younger boy. Because he must rely on the intellect or elder boy, the father cannot control the younger child, the alter ego, because that younger son takes energy from the elder one when the father gives the elder brother attention.

In this discussion, I did not give a solution. I explained why the father cannot deprive the younger child from attention.

Theoretically it is like this.

The secret to controlling and reforming the younger son, the alter ego, is to cut the attention which is given to the elder son, the observing self, but that cannot be done unless the father, the higher self, finds a way to absolutely control the elder boy. The father has one major hang-up which works against him and that is his idea that he must get rid of the mischievous little boy. He cannot get rid of the boy but he can imagine that he may do that. He is stuck with the boy. This is why I say that he should give up that idea and face the fact that he must elevate the boy.

The only way to get rid of the boy in real terms is the elevate the boy, not to deny the boy's existence or to pretend that the boy is a non-existent shadow. If it is troublesome then it exists. That is final. Imagining that it is not there or that it should not be there, will not eliminate it.

The father has one minor hang-up which is that even though he is the lofty higher self which is superior to the two sons he produced, still he is dependent on the elder son. By logic it makes no sense that you could produce a child who has attributes which you do not have but actually even though it is illogical, that happens. For example, some plants produce seeds. These seeds produce other infant plants but the parent plant does not have seeds within it. It cannot necessarily produce a plant from a cut of its branches.

This means that there are things in this existence which are contrary, which defy logical and even common sense. The higher self must come to terms with that aberration whereby it does not have an analyzing function in itself and has to depend on the observing self for that. If the father were to get rid of the elder son, the father would be deficient because the analytical function would be gone. In a way it is a good thing that the father does not, in fact, have that power. What he has is a sense of detachment along with hopes and wishes that perhaps he could live in the Absolute (whatever he conceives that to be) without the elder son.

The father must come to terms with this fact that he lacks certain things which manifested as his sons.

Yogi: Touching Students

I got an inquiry about touching students when showing yoga exercises. First of all, my training is that yoga should only be taught if one is commissioned by a teacher. The main reason for this is accountability. If one teaches but one is not commissioned by a more advanced person, who is one accountable to? What social standards should one observe in that case?

When there is a teacher, it is easy to determine what should be done and what is approved behavior. Patanjali listed a set of yamas and niyamas which define dos and don'ts. If there is no teacher from whom one gets a code of conduct, one has to create one and use it.

When teaching postures, it becomes necessary to hold someone's body but that carries with it the danger of sexual energy exchange. There is the question of what to do with the sexual energy which entered one's psyche from a student?

If possible, male teachers should have female assistants who demonstrate to and monitor female students. If a male teacher touches a female student there is a risk that sexual energy will pass in either direction. The result will be that either the teacher or student or both will be affected.

The teacher of the teacher may not approve of certain associations with some students. Once in 1973, I had an ashram. I taught kundalini yoga which I learnt from Yogi Bhajan and postures with third eye meditation which I learnt from Arthur Beverford. Once I called Beverford. I was in Springfield, Missouri. He was in California. When I explained to him how I managed the ashram, he did not like certain things. Like for instance he did not like that I woke students at 4 am for yoga class and meditation. He thought it was too early. He had other objections. If one teaches a certain method on behalf of a teacher, one must decide which of that teacher's method one will use.

Fated consequences is not an illusion. It is a real. It that affects people and frustrates their plans. Patanjali, near the end of his sutras, wrote of dharmamegha, which is the cloud *(megha)* of righteousness rules *(dharma)*. It means that as a spiritual teacher, one would be a fool not to know what the risks are when influencing people.

प्रसङ्ख्यानेऽप्यकुसीदस्य सर्वथा विवेकख्यातेर्धर्ममेघः समाधिः ॥ २९ ॥

prasaṁkhyāne api akusīdasya sarvathā
vivekakhyāteḥ dharmameghaḥ samādhiḥ

prasaṁkhyāna – in the abstract meditation; api – even so; akusīdasya – of one who has no interest or sees no gain in material nature; sarvathā – in all ways; vivekakhyāteḥ – with super discrimination;

dharmameghaḥ = dharma – nature's way of acting for beneficial results + meghaḥ – mento-emotional clouds of energy; samādhi – continuous effortless linkage of the attention to higher reality.

For one who sees no gains in material nature, even while perceiving it in abstract meditation, one has the super discrimination. One attains the continuous effortless linkage of the attention to higher reality which is described as knowing the mento-emotional clouds of energy which compel a person to perform according to nature's way of acting for beneficial results. (Yoga Sutras 4.29)

I am lucky because I teach one or two people. I am not required by any of my teachers to teach many. Teaching yoga in a sincere way is hard work. For me I must have coverage from yoga gurus and deities, especially from Shiva and Krishna.

If I hold a yoga class and begin teaching what Yogeshwaranand showed, I must remember that I teach on his behalf. If I explain the *Bhagavad Gita*, I explain that Krishna declared that he is God.

If I am teaching on behalf of Beverford then I explain that he believed in a Primal Creative Cause. He did not think that one person, an individual identity, was the Cause of all causes.

If someone wants to teach on my behalf, I give restrictions and explain where I am committed.

I hide so that only a few people know that I teach yoga. Just about an hour ago I heard a man telling a lady that there was a guy nearby who is an expert on yoga. When I heard that the hairs raised on my skin. I thought, "This person is the enemy."

Any association means exchange of energy which does not always go in one's favor. Personally, I do not believe that yoga should be taught to everyone. I feel that unless a person is supported by higher yogis, his/her yoga teaching will result in his/her undoing. For me it is easy to be a student yogi without ever being a teacher.

Yogi Enters Memory of Student

During breath infusion, suddenly there was a flash in the left thigh bone, on the top part of it. After this both thigh bones were infused and assumed the color of white-hot metal. I did some stretches which caused the thigh bone to be infused.

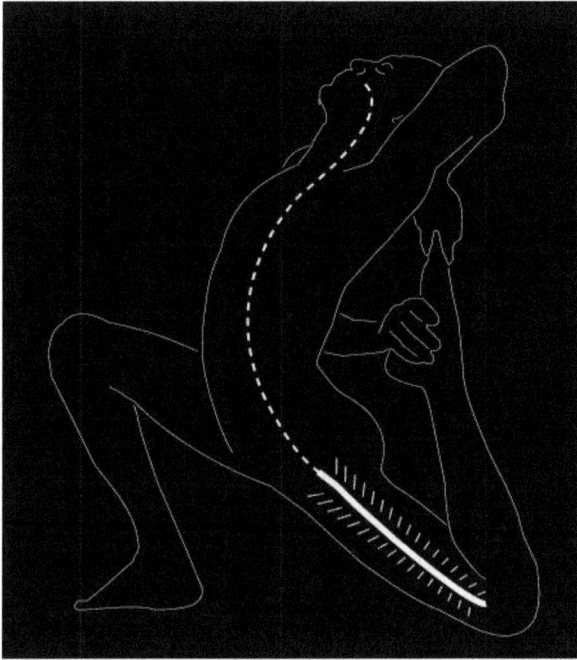

These lower parts of the body are important in the effort to uplift the kundalini and its outposts which are in remote parts of the body. For the development of a yoga siddha form after leaving this body, one must have the entire subtle body saturated with a high grade of subtle energy. If just the head, or if only certain chakras have that energy, while the rest of the system is with heavy astral force, one will fail to assume a yoga siddha form.

This is similar to the idea of being a mermaid. One is part human part aquatic such that one cannot be either and essentially the fish part predominates. This half state is that of a crocodile, where it lives on land part of the time and lives in water part of the time. It cannot stay on land all of the time and it must come out of the water some of the time.

Another example is that of peacock. Visually, it is a very beautiful creature to see but its habits are that of a vicious bird. Despite the beauty, mentally it thinks of killing and eating insects and worms.

Thus, if the subtle body is only partially filled with light, the person will go to a lower dimension which is suited to the heavy energy in that body. In the end the lowest level of the psyche will take the person to a lower category.

As I did the practice, Yogesh entered the subtle head. I really thought that I would never see him again since he transited into the causal ocean of energy from which yogis usually do not return to this side of existence.

This appearance of his in my head was such that I determined that he abandoned his endeavor to just stay in the causal energy. I did not question him about it.

However, he was in my psyche checking through a memory chamber which is down below the neck. It was funny because he pulled out something and threw it out of my subtle body, then he began pulling out more and more like a person pulling things out of a duffle bag and throwing them at a distance.

He said, "O what is this? What is this? Why did you do this?

Where did this happen? What sort of yogi are you?"

Since I did breath infusion while this took place, I did not dare to laugh since that would shatter my focus and ruin the session. Then he pulled up a scene from a movie which I saw years ago. He looked at it in disgust. This is because yogis are not supposed to do anything which creates more unwanted impressions in the mind. Patanjali prohibited yogis from doing anything which increases the chittavrittis or impressions in the mind which obstruct the practice of higher meditation.

Just after he pulled up that impression from the movie, he pulled out a few small impressions of insignificant things and then he pulled something and said, "This is it! How did this happen. This is what I search for."

That was an impression about my seeing the Krishna boy form in the divine world. This happened years ago. It was one of the memory impressions of it that Yogesh found. That was not the original impression but it was a copy of the original. He turned to me and said, "I have to work on this, the spiritual body. How did you achieve this? The deity picks and chooses. If you are not chosen, he does not appear to you in which case you will never know of that place."

This conversation happened while I did breath infusion. Yogesh said that I should increase the practice by at least one hour. He said that the first forty-five minutes was the warm up. There should be another hour with focus on the head. Then one should stop that and sit to meditate, doing *samyama*, absorption focus, as advised by Patanjali.

Basically, that means about 2 hours of *asanas* and *pranayama* and then meditating for an hour. Usually I do 40 minutes or more of *asana* and *pranayama* and then 40 minutes of more of meditation practice. But in his view that is not enough.

Yogesh showed some breath infusion practice which is done to the head of the subtle body, in different parts of the head here and there.

Spirit or Soul: What is it?

Emailed questions about the sex you! book:

I thought that spirits were the ones in the astral realm and souls not spirits incarnate?

Author's reply:

This idea is that there are spirits who are permanent residents in the astral world, persons who remain there all the time, in contrast to souls who are body-supported beings who must repeatedly incarnate in physical bodies.

In *sex you!* the terms soul and spirit are used interchangeable, even though soul really means a spirit who is earth-bound even when it is in the astral state between leaving one physical body and acquiring another.

It is a fact that there are spirits who remain permanently in the astral world. These spirits have neither need for, nor attraction to, physical existence. They are not drawn into birth situations in physical species.

However, most spirits who are in dimensions which are adjacent to this physical existence are earth-bound souls, meaning that even though they are spirits, they nevertheless have a need for physical existence.

To clarify:

A spirit is a spirit unit but if that unit has an affinity for physical existence, it is identified as a soul.

There is little difference between spirits and souls except for the cultural affinity of those spirits who are earth-bound and who are put into the soul category to differentiate them from the spirits who have no attraction to physical existence.

Question:

I thought the father's soul attracts a similar soul when the female is impregnated?

Author's reply:

In *sex you!* the cause of attraction to a set of parents is based mostly on social work which the deceased person did in a past life. Usually there is an attraction to the father or mother or to both simultaneously. But the crucial factor is the disembodied soul's beneficial social activities in that family in a past life.

Even if the father does not attract a soul, even if the father is hostile or indifferent to the disembodied soul who is to be the child, the effect-energy of the child will cause the father, even against his will, to beget a body for that disembodied person. This is explained in the *Anu Gita Explained* book.

The father and mother are under the influence of ancestors, but that is unknown to most parents because they assume that their thoughts, desires and urges are their very own.

When a person loses a body, we say, 'Mommy is dead' or 'Daddy is dead.' In reference to grandparents and great grandparents, we feel that they died long ago. However, usually a deceased relative lives in the body of a descendant. It lives in the body, unseen and unheard, until it becomes visible through a pregnancy.

Sex during Elderly Years

Last night in the astral world, a friend asked about the time when a person may stop sexual intercourse in an old body.

A great aunt of mine, told me that her husband could not perform sexually after he was about fifty-five years of age. She was distressed about it. She resented him. He had sexual dysfunction. When the elderly lady told me that I was surprised but I pretended that the statement did not jolt me.

In the skill of the kundalini yoga, sexual indulgence is an unwanted feature except when it is done to beget children which will cause a karmic obligation to be absolved. Besides using sex for generating progeny, classic yoga, Patanjali yoga, has no use for sexual indulgence.

But there are sects for tantric yoga and kundalini yoga which give process for increasing sexual pleasure, prolonging it and enjoying it. There are also subtle dimensions in the astral world where people engage in sexual intercourse for days, weeks or months even continuous. It all depends on what interest and culture one develops or is subjected to as one transmigrates

As far as doing it for the natural pleasure which it provides, in kundalini yoga we use the energy to get the pleasure in the head of the subtle body, by moving it up the spine. We consider the head pleasure to be higher. If the hormone and life force energies are mixed and then used for sex expression, they cannot be used for pleasure in the head. This is why yogis are concerned to conserve it from sexual expression.

Both sex pleasure and the pleasure of the aroused kundalini in the head are pleasure. Look at these terms and note that *ananda* is the end of each word:

prajananda = *prajaa* (begetting) + *ananda* (bliss pleasure)
brahmananda = *brahma* (spirit) + *ananda* (bliss pleasure)

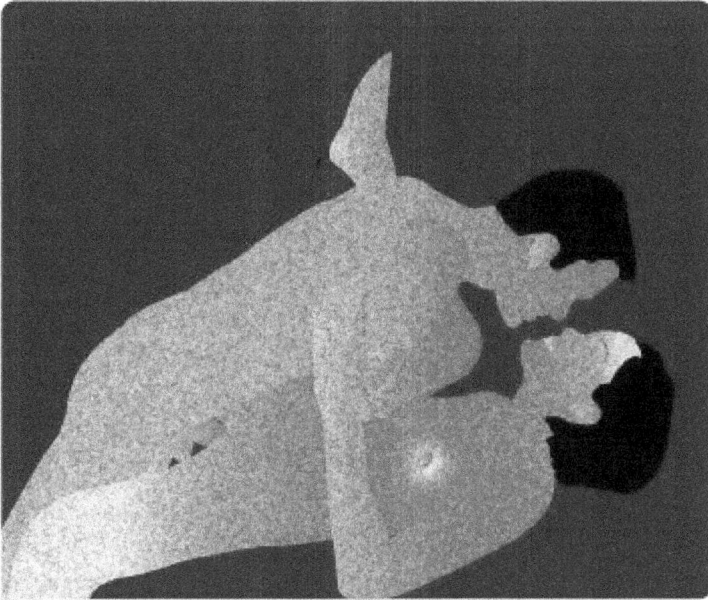

A yogi is interested in brahmananda or spiritual pleasure. To increase that the yogi avoids sex pleasure expression.

The question of when to stop at what age of the body, would hinge on a person's needs and desires.

I explained in my books that it is the same kundalini which expresses itself though sex pleasure which is use to trigger spiritual pleasure. It may be hard to understand that sex pleasure is conducted by the kundalini, but I insist on that.

A sure way to disable one's third eye if it is functional and open, is to get involved in sexual pleasure. It is a matter of defining one's objective. One should note the effects of one's activities and make decisions accordingly. Of course, sex pleasure is a basic instinct and even if one desires not to be involved with it, one's decision may prove to be ineffective because of the impulsive force of nature.

Attaching Spirit

Email Inquiry:

Any spirit who takes shelter in one's psyche for whatever reason and on whatever basis is an attaching spirit. The person does not have to be an ancestor of one's body. Someone from a previous life in a totally different family may become attached to someone else.

Even persons who are not related but who contributed socially to the well-being of the family have rights to take a body through a member of the family. The deceased one may become attached on the basis of former contributions.

People who need bodies are in desperation to locate or activate sexual intercourse which is their gateway to this side of existence.

Yogi: Preparations for Leaving the Body

Yogesh left a message in my psyche for me to do what is called the desire-intention-pull-back.

This concerns pulling back into the desire-need energies which were expressed from it when one was in the process of taking the present body. At the time, the energies of desire which were to be fulfilled in this life, were injected in the system of the father and the mother, so that the body created would be capable of endeavoring to fulfill the said desires.

Later in the life of the body, one finds twerks of time and twitches of providence which make it impossible for some desires to be fulfilled.

In some parts of one's life one feels that one found a perfect match in relationship, vocation, employment, leisure and other aspects. Many fulfilled desires are canceled but the unfilled ones are left in the psyche as needed endeavors.

A yogi should recall the unfulfilled desires-energies, returning them into the subtle body and then into the causal form if he can perceive that subtlety.

Whatever is not fulfilled in this life can be fulfilled sometime in the future either in a future life or in the next universe one is destined to appear in. But if one leaves the released energy in the atmosphere, it creates tensions for which one is liable.

The method for doing this is to cling to naad in the back of the head while allowing the subtle eyes to blink at about a rate of three blinks per minute. As the subtle eyes blink, that will retract one frame of desire with each blink. One should keep doing that until one feels that the energy is retracted, until one feels that the energy which was put into the environment before one got the body, is totally recalled.

This produces a clean departure at the time of death with no looking back to recover desire energies which were not fulfilled and which are embedded in the present layout of destiny.

Failure to do this could result in what is called, taking-another-body-to-do-something-trivial, or it may be taking another body to build a house, or taking another body to marry Mary, or taking another body to use a technology. Desires are so powerful that merely renouncing them or saying that one does not have them or that one reached a level where they do not exist, does absolutely nothing to stop their assertion.

Many desires which I had before taking this body and which I expressed for fulfillments when I took this form, are now totally irrelevant and cannot be fulfilled or can be fulfilled only by taking a contrary course in fate. Thus, all such desires should be recalled, reviewed and scrapped if necessary.

The best thing is to recall these energies into the psyche and push them into the causal body. However, if one cannot do that at least one should recall them and let them go into dormancy in the subtle form until another time when providence rolls out a situation in which one can manifest them and bring them to life in a suitable time and place.

Think of what you would do if you had to leave your native village or country. What would you carry? What would you leave behind as unnecessary? What would you regret that you could not take?

Low Quality Meditation (July 23, 2011)

In the past, students of meditation questioned about days of meditation when there is no progress, when even though efforts are made to elevate the self, the mind remains on the normal level with silly ideas.

Over the last two days, when there was a low energy during my meditation, I considered this. The answer to this is to consider that mental and emotional states are a kind of weather. As in atmospheric weather, one cannot control it and one knows that for sure, so in psychic energy one cannot have absolute control.

People resume their activities after a weather disaster for the very reason that they know that the weather is beyond control. They are at its mercy. But they are confident that it will change for the better and then will again go haywire.

This consideration should be used in meditation, where one knows that on a certain day the meditation was of low quality and then provided one keeps the habit, the meditation will be enriched on another day when the mental and emotional atmosphere accommodates higher energy.

A depressed or dull meditative state, one that is not inspiring, one that discourages, should not deter practice, no more than a hurricane or earthquake will stop human beings from proceeding with their lives, when the danger is past.

Continue the meditation even when it is of a low quality. Be confident that it will again resume a deep experience and then it will again digress. This will happen so long as one is in a world where the mental and emotional energies fluctuate.

Naad-Intellect Kriya by Buddha Deity (July 23, 2014)

Buddha deity showed procedure for making the intellect become absorbed in the naad sound. Usually the intellect stays away from naad. The coreSelf alone goes to naad with the sense of identity which is continuously fused to the core.

One may experience a mental space of about two inches or less between the coreSelf and the intellect but there is no space between the coreSelf and the sense of identity. That sense is fused to the core.

Usually, this Buddha Deity is strict. In this discourse, he was friendly and chatty. Being one of his sons, I am careful. In some communications, I am more like the son of an inferior concubine. But on this occasion, he was relaxed. He gave these details.

Many of the ascetics who are in my system and who regard themselves as Buddhists do not understand what it is to be an original buddha. They feel that all buddhas are the same. They think that they will become a buddha on my level.

That is ludicrous but I do not interfere with the idea because it hurts only the person who feels that way.

When I taught, I divulged only what a person needed at a particular stage. Some of what I did during austerities was told to no one.

Even though some of it is exactly what I did, the process which they divulge for a monk today is different to what I did. I do not need an assistant. I can give instruction to someone directly. If a person regards me as another buddha and not as a special unique one, it is hardly likely that he will have the disposition which is accommodating to personal instruction from me.

The kriya or procedure for causing the intellect to be absorbed in naad is based on clarifying the energy at and around the base chakra. Buddha said that once the base chakra is uprooted from its anchor position, the intellect changes so that it no longer adheres to the frontal part of the head.

Then it easily moves backward in the head and no longer exhibits the stubborn tendency which is to stay focused in the frontal part of the head creating images, sounds and ideas.

This would mean that the intellect has some subtle connection with the kundalini energy, such that if that kundalini is reformed and controlled, there is a corresponding increase in control over the intellect.

When this happens one can grab the intellect and move it back. Its resistance is neutralized. It seems to be a padded envelop of light frequency energy about the size of a 3 inch by 3 inch by ½ inch thick.

Naad Fusion Meditation with Mantra (July 22, 2011)

A Buddha deity *(Shakyamuni Gautama)* in South Korea, gave a mantra+naad sound mantra system which I was unable to test while in South Korea. There are many spiritual systems, but I test a process before I divulge it.

This system combines ajapa with naad sound. Ajapa as opposed to japa is mental recitation of a mantra where no sound is heard externally. The vocal cords are not involved. In japa the sound is made with the vocal cord. It is intoned externally with the mouth and heard physically with the ear.

For instance, in some of the Vaishnava societies *ajapa* or mentally-said mantras are outlawed while *japa* or physically-said mantras are said to be the only process. In the same societies there are confidential mantras which are *mula* mantras and *gayatri* mantras. Some of these are called *bija* mantras. Essentially these are call-prayers for reaching deities and divine beings in other worlds. The *bija* mantras are confidential. In some sects these are murmured. In others they are said mentally only.

For instance, if a priest conducts a ritual ceremony for a Krishna deity, the priest cannot barge into the deity's chamber. He must first stand outside, ring a bell and say certain prayers to the deity. This is for alerting the deity to his presence and to seek permission to enter the sacred area.

Most *bija* mantras concern a deity or a supernatural or spiritual being who is in another dimension, but there are a few which concerns *dhyana* meditation and *samadhi* trance states. *Bija* means seed or source.

For instance, there is a *bija* mantra for the base chakra. There is one for the causal body. There is one for the *sushumna* kundalini central spinal passage. These are sounds which are supposed to cause a particular chakra or location to resonate.

Just as in electronics, one can use a small device which projects a laser beam or a digital signal to open a lock or close a door, so one may use a *bija* mantra.

Om mani padme hum mantra is used primarily by Tibetan Buddhists. It is attributed to *Avalokiteshvara* Buddha. The first known description of the mantra appears in the *Karandavyuha Sutra*, which is part of certain *Mahayana* canons. In this sutra, the Buddha says:

"This is the most beneficial mantra. Even I made this aspiration to all the million Buddhas and subsequently received this teaching from Buddha *Amitabha*."

The *Shakyamuni* Deity said that when this mantra is chanted mentally, the yogi should loop the *hum* intonation mentally to the naad resonance.

He said that *hum* is harmonious with naad. Naad absorbes it with full efficiency. When one is told something by a deity or by someone who is in another dimension, one should check to make sure that the source of it was authoritative. To do this one should test the advice.

When a yogi sits to meditate, if he finds that the coreSelf has no interest in naad or cannot stay focused or be absorbed, or that it drifts in and out of naad, he should go to naad. While focusing on naad and being absorbed, he should observe the drifting self. As soon as it drifts, he should mentally begin reciting the mantra. When saying the first three words he should focus on the mantra but as soon as he says the last word mentally, the *hum* sound, he should loop attention to naad. This procedure should continue until the self remains fused on naad.

Special Note:

In terms of location the yogi would usually find naad on the right or left back of the head near an ear. The self usually drifts from that place to the frontal part of the brain where it indulges in images, thought constructions, ideas and memories. As soon as the self drifts, the yogi should begin the mantra. When the last word, the *hum* sound, is mentally intoned, the yogi should loop his attention to naad.

In my experience I found that the *hum* sound fuses with naad perfectly. One finds oneself again listening to naad.

Since this was given directly by the deity *Shakyamuni* Buddha (*Gautama*), it has tremendous potency if practiced with sincerity. Do not say the mantra hastily. It should be said slowly. It should be mental only.

Psychic Criminal Acts

Either in this life or in the next, the resultant effects of a person's psychic criminal acts will find him. If one becomes liberated the effects will stay in this dimension. Its energy will adhere to some other person.

Physical nature and subtle material nature are reactive to whatever one may do. Hence there will always be a return-effect or consequence which will loop through future time and strike the offender.

I may forget what I did in the past life, and I may focus on what is current, but Time never forgets my previous acts. It victimizes even those who have no memory of the past.

The subtle body has a subconscious compartment. In advanced yoga, this is regarded as a memory storage. While it is subconscious to the average human being, it is conscious and compressed to the yogi.

Subconscious means what is below the threshold of objective observational awareness. A yogi can use special tools of insight to read the information in the subconscious.

Every unfavorable act of the past, even incidental criminal ones, can be dealt with effectively in the subconscious, rather than to wait until such acts burst by the sprouting action of inscrutable time.

To deal with such acts, one should learn how to enter into the subconscious stockpile of energies and apply neutralizing energies to the residual potencies which are in the process of converting into history.

A criminal, if he or she can reach the law enforcement officials before they write a warrant for arrest, may be absolved of crimes committed. Once a warrant is released, he or she must attend a court. Thus, if he or she could compensate society before charges are filed, imprisonment may be avoided.

Samadhi Practice

The idea of doing yoga which includes meditation, is to develop familiarity with higher bodies and to learn how to use these, so that after leaving the physical form when it dies, one can go to a divine world.

A living entity requires an environment. Right now, by the grace of nature, we are familiar with this physical place. If we fail to develop an interest in another higher location, we will return to this world as infants in a species. This will happen because we did not become familiar with anything but the physical body.

Many people meditate but how many become aware even of the astral body, what to speak of the super-energized astral form or a spiritual form which is saturated with bliss energy. Just as they meditate and do not become aware of the subtle body as a distinct reality, and then they return to physical consciousness, they will do the same in the afterlife, except that it will be subtle body consciousness and no other perceptions.

There were cases of yogis who transited to a super-subtle or divine form while the physical body died. One must be advanced at meditation, to translate to a higher form. Usually a yogi waits until there is a loophole in time or a down-skip in the kundalini's hold on the physical body. When he catches that slot in existence, he influences kundalini to leave the body which dies.

Because there are distractions that ruin or at least retard practice, it is hardly likely that someone can do this in the modern setting. A yogi may not develop the required proficiency to make a sudden transit and escape from the routine of death of the physical form.

Mahasamadhi usually means that a proficient yogi assumes a trance state and attains a higher dimension at the time of death. *Maha* means great but in this case it means final. *Mahasamadhi* is the final trance state of a yogi. There is this opinion that *samadhi* is one practice of merging into the Supreme, but if you really want to know what *samadhi* is, read a reliable translation of the Yoga Sutras. Several types of *samadhi (samyama)* are listed in that text.

In India, disciples give the spiritual master the benefit of doubt about attaining a high trance state at death. In many cases this is the faith and expectations of the disciples and nothing else. Many spiritual masters do not enter into *samadhi* states at death, but instead merely go over completely into their subtle bodies on some level which is adjacent to this physical place. We can assume that at death a guru resumed or assumed a divine body but that would be wishful thinking for the most part.

Visualization and Reality (July 20, 2011)

In some experiences which relate to astral projection, lucid dreaming and transiting to other dimensions, there may be a thin line between imagination and subtle reality. This is why someone may be skeptical about psychic experiences. Some dismiss all of it as being unreal hallucinations.

In the Near East there used to be this idea that if a psychic, astrologer or seer made one mistake in a prediction, he should be discredited forever, but in the East, in India, people would still consult an astrologer if he made a wrong prediction on occasion.

I feel that we should accept the truth that psychic perception has flaws. We should research and figure the degree of error and use the flawed psyche.

Nobody will pluck his eyes, because he does not have perfect vision. We agree to use imperfect eyes because it is better to have a malfunctioning eye than no vision. One should use the subtle body but know its deviations.

If one meditates with great care and patience, one will gradually come to understand the deviations. Taking these into account one could adjust for errors in psychic judgment and perception. That is better than being a skeptic who aggressively dismisses psychic perception because it is not 100% accurate.

By being persistent in meditation, one comes to know the thin line between imagination and actual mystic perception. One will also understand the relationship between visualization and reality. Sometimes, visualization serves to promote psychic experience which is reality.

There are many people who have such a sensitive mind, that their visualizations cause them to transit to real subtle states. This happens even though the initial visualization is creative imagination only.

Buzzing Sounds and Lights in Meditation or Dream States

In some experiences when the astral body becomes super-energized a buzzing sound is heard. Sometimes there are loud thunder claps in the subtle body and even subtle lightning. If one is referenced to material existence, such experiences may cause fear.

When the astral body is energized to the level where it is filled with light, like sunlight, the person lives in a state of light and will perceive objects of that medium. He may see beings who use subtle bodies of light. In such a body one would rapidly transit to the sun and see buildings, trees, streets and people all made of light energy only.

Cosmic Energy

In the system of yoga there is cosmic kundalini (lifeForce), cosmic *buddhi* (intellect), and cosmic *ahankara* (sense of identity). Apart from these there is the supreme divine person.

Each spirit, you or me, has a sense of identity which is permanent. It cannot be eradicated. By it we are subjected to experiences as we transmigrate in various species, and yet, we cannot eliminate it. There is a flawless state of that sense of identity, but presently we do not experience that condition.

It is explained in the Puranas that when the MahaVishnu initiates the creations, trillions of limited spirits become aware of themselves in this place. These spirits become aware of themselves with psychological equipment, of which the sense of identity is one, along with an intellect and a life force.

It is similar to what happens when a baby births. Soon after a name is officially assigned. In some countries even a number is given. When these creations are initiated by the Supreme Being (MahaVishnu), there is also created a vast cosmic pool of intellects, and another pool of senses of identity and one for lifeForces.

Sometimes it happens that a person through meditation or by sheer divine grace without effort on his part, is connected to vast cosmic energy.

When this happens one first sees a light overhead or in the distance. It is a vast blinding cosmic apparition. Then one ray or two from that place strikes one either in the head or chest. When this happens, one is translated to a celestial or divine level.

There is also a bliss energy which enters one because it is the nature of those cosmic pools to be saturated with bliss. This experience may be for seconds, minutes or longer. Usually when the person resumes physical existence there is a residual effect which may last for minutes or even hours or days. Eventually it diminishes. One finds oneself with the usual human social consciousness.

Meditation Explained

What is called *samadhi* by Patanjali is rarely attained. This is because the social environment is hostile to deep meditation. Modern people are conditioned to concentrate for attainments and to relax and enjoy otherwise. This is not what Patanjali defined as *samyama samadhi* states.

Some persons acquired the idea that there is one type of *samadhi* but that is not factual. There are varied samadhis depending on the level of mind of the meditator.

Basically, the many-featured *samadhis* falls into two conditional stages, which are observational and neutral (non-observational). In the observational stage, the meditator notes what took place in the particular realm for consciousness. In the superior non-observational stage, he remains in the higher realm without the stress of being an observer. Even though the observatonal meditation is not as advanced as the non-observational stage, an advanced yogi who does observational samadhis is useful.

To understand this, we can consider that a man plans to go to another country. His relatives become aware of the plan and commit him to sending letters describing his experiences. The man consents. After arriving in that foreign land, he decides to send weekly letters. He sticks to that plan. His relatives are relieved. They are happy to get the information about the people in the foreign place.

Another man who also left that place, and promised to send letters to his relatives, became so involved in the new territory, that he had no time and did not remember his homeland. He sent nothing to the relatives. They remain worried and perplexed and wonder if he was deceased.

Obviously, the neglectful man is more absorbed in the new culture. The letter-sender who regularly objectifies himself to send reports, is in a sense out of touch and biased in reference to the new place.

Gurus who do the lower samadhis, the observational ones, are of much use to students. I for one, committed myself to take this body, just to do observational samadhis so that I could report of the experiences in real time. My literature may be of more value than even more advanced yogis, who experience non-observational states.

Observational transcendence is called *savikalpa samadhi*, which is to say with *(sa)* intent *(vikalpa)* transcendental state.

Non-observational *samadhi* is called *nirvikalpa samadhi*, which is without *(nir)* intent *(vikalpa)* transcendental state.

In the higher *samadhi* the yogi gives himself or herself over entirely to the experience with no notational energy interacting or checking the existential situation. But in the lower samadhi, the yogi goes in with an intention to get to the higher level and to observe the passage, energy operation, and descent from there.

Due to that observation, the yogi must of necessity be restricted but his report is of great interest and benefit to less-advanced persons, who may be inspired to practice after reading the descriptions.

But what is *samadhi*?

It is a relocation to a higher dimension. The transit process of getting to that higher place was termed as *samyama* by Patanjali, which is three linked stages which occur in sequence with or without jumps or digressions from one stage to another.

These three are:
- *dharana* (dharuh-naa)
- *dhyana* (dhee-an)
- *samadhi* (suh-mad-hee)

If one begins at *dharana* and does that efficiently, the state of mind will slide upwards into the next stage of *dhyana*. Or it may abruptly change to *dhyana* instead of shifting into that gradually.

One may then remain in dhyana and go no higher or one may even descend back to *dharana* without reaching the *samadhi* stage. But one may ascend to the *samadhi* stage and then complete the sequence which is labeled as samyama by Patanjali.

These three parts of the *samyama* sequence are the three higher stages of the eighth stepped yoga system explained by Patanjali. This also means that sometimes when a yogi begins at *dharana* and then progresses to *dhyana* and into *samadhi*, he or she may find the self suddenly down-shifted into *pratyahar* which is the stage below *dharana*.

Why does this happen? This occurs because the subtle body either has lower energies or it suddenly became saturated with lower energy. When this happens, the mind will downshift without warning. The yogi will find himself or herself in the level of *pratyahar* sensual energy withdrawal, trying to come to terms with the mind and to restrict it from random activities.

If one does no *pranayama* breath infusion which is the stage below the *pratyahar* sensual energy stage, what frequently happens is this:

One sits to meditate. According to the status of energy in the mind, one struggles to control the thought-image mechanism. Some yogis avoid that struggle by ignoring the thoughts and images. Others observe the breath rhythm in an effort to sidestep the thoughts and images. Some others observe thoughts in a detached mood stifling any emotions which may arise for interaction with the images. Some others use a vocalized or mentally sounded mantra in an effort to intimidate the unruly mind.

If one is successful, one will find that the mind spends more time in the thought-less image-less state, as if its thought-image producing part was disabled. If one remains in the thoughtless state for long periods, one will find the self in the *dharana* stage which is stage one in *samyama* even though it is the sixth stage of yoga.

What is *dharana*? It is the linking of the attention into a higher energy or dimension or person but doing so with effort.

The flaw of dharana is that it must be done with effort. The natural state of the mind is to link itself and focus itself into this physical world and the accessory astral levels which are the basis of this place. To change that tendency, one must make an effort.

Nothing moves or changes without energy being expended. That is what we face at every stage. That is the law of nature, which even the gods must contend with.

Before doing *dharana* which is to link the self to a higher plane of consciousness or a higher environment where people have divine, supernatural or super-subtle forms, one will experience the downtime of the mind.

What is this downtime? It is the stage of nothingness which occurs for a split second when the mind finished demolishing one idea and is about to construct another new related or unrelated one. Usually this occurs for a split second. It is done so fast, that one rarely observes it. It appears that the mind instantly switched to new ideas and images without a split-second blankness. If one views a video, one rarely notices the interval between the frames.

In the mind of the yogi, the interval may get longer and longer because in some meditative stages, the mind slows down and/or the yogi perception ability accelerates.

Before one can master *dharana* which is linkage with effort, one must master the downtime of the mind, such that its downtime, its blank instance, gets longer and longer, like seeing a video which is set to such a slow speed that one sees each frame as a still photo which slowly streams into view and then is not displayed, leaving a blank black screen for some seconds before the other frame comes into view.

Supernatural Perception

Yogis perform many meditative procedures to get supernatural experience. One such experience is the opening of the third eye. Usually in the head of a human being, with eyes closed, there will be darkness or darkness with speckled pin-points of color, but there is never clarity or clearness in the center of the eyebrows.

There is a chakra in the center of the eyebrows. When it opens one sees through it just as if one were seeing through a bay window. Sometimes the shape is oval or square or rectangular, and sometimes it is like a slit. When one looks through that opening one sees distant places in this dimension or one may see into other higher or lower dimensions.

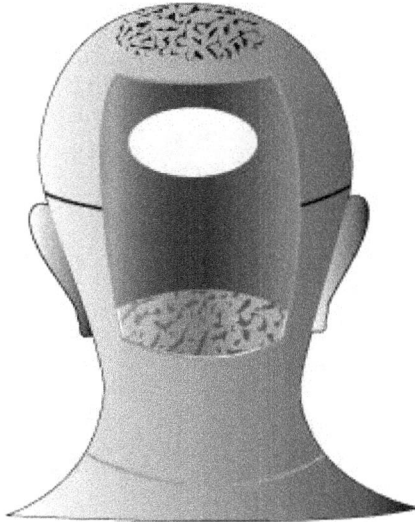

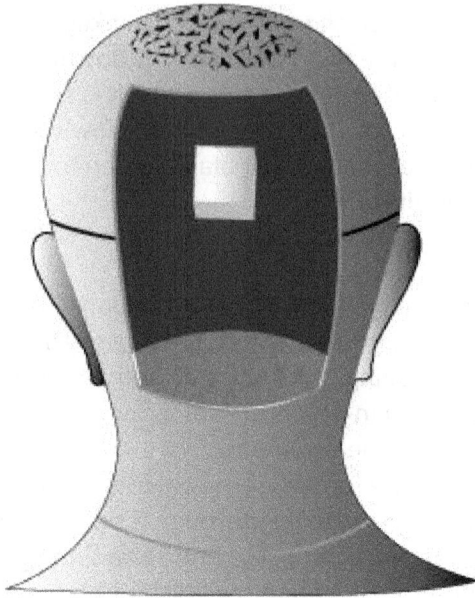

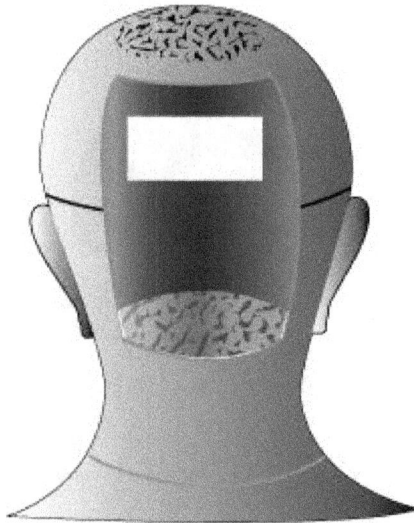

However, there is another psychic organ in the head of the subtle body. When one uses that in conjunction with the third eye chakra or by itself, one sees supernaturally in a special way.

The location of that psychic organ, which I call the intellect or imagination orb is in a position half way between the coreSelf and the third eye. It is usually oval shaped but when seen it may appear to be like a cream-colored jelly fish or like an oval like an egg. This organ is the psychic tool which is used to think or imagine in the mind. It functions as an eye. It works in conjunction with the third eye. It does analysis and is termed as the intellect. It processes and illustrates memories.

When it is accelerated in vibration, it affords supernatural or spiritual visions which are clear and which pertain to other dimensions which are near to or distant from this world.

Mission and Death (Buddha's Instruction)

A Buddha deity gave a procedure for grabbing kundalini and pulling it away from its root location. In this procedure, one must enter the spine and go downward in it, in actuality not in visualization or imagination. The coreSelf goes down through the sushumna central passage. When it gets to the base, it considers the condition of the kundalini at that place. If kundalini is not highly infused with energy, the core cannot do this practice because it will not have the power to hold kundalini.

The holding action is done by grabbing kundalini mystically from the outside of the spine. Kundalini is grabbed near its base rooting place. It is pulled up. It is held firmly by mystic power, since if one does not do so, it will immediately reattach itself to the base place. I found that kundalini in that configuration felt like a lamprey eel with its head facing downwards. It has a strong gravitational pull to the base place. One must exert mystic power to hold it away from that place. If one relaxes the hold, it immediately reattaches itself with compressing force as if it has a vacuum draw on that place.

If one can hold it for a while say five minutes, the bottom seals into a circular closed shape. The gravitational force disappears. The yogi is then free to take kundalini here or there as desired. He can turn it upwards and swim into the head with it.

This is one of the procedures which can be used when leaving a material body finally at death. If the yogi does this, he would not be compelled to look for another embryo immediately upon departure from the physical body.

In the *Mahabharata* there is a description of Balram, Krishna's brother, who when he left his physical body, was seen to be like a serpent which left through the mouth of that dying body. He went to higher dimensions. It may be that Balram used a similar procedure and made kundalini turnabout so that its downward facing direction was altered. It faced upwards, went through the trunk and then through the mouth of the dying physical body.

As a divine being, Balram would have no difficulty doing this but to accomplish this at the body's death, others would have to attain practice proficiency before death.

I am confronted with three objectives:

- Develop a process for extraction of kundalini which supersedes the normal process for leaving a physical body at its death.
- Write literature with details of the yoga process.
- Serve as a counterbalance in the developed countries.

The last objective is not my desire but I comply with it, as I requested by a Buddha deity.

The second objective is the reason why I took this present body.

The first objective is a reality which every yogi must deal with once he or she assumes an embryo. Once a yogi gets into a woman's womb and is delivered as a newborn child, irrespective of why he or she took that body, the reality is that the departure from it with control of where the subtle body goes and what it will do, must be accomplished afresh.

Taking a new body, has packaged with it, the task of carefully leaving that body in the end, otherwise the yogi will find himself or herself being recycled into another womb and into another life with mistaken identity.

Even though a yogi may be sent into this world by a greater yogi, or by a divine being like Krishna or Shiva, still the yogi has the task of liberating himself. Those divine people are the least concerned as to how the yogi will get out or as to if he will be compelled to take haphazard rebirths. They assume that he/she has the priority for liberation

There is a story about this in the Puranas. One celestial ruler named Indra, was condemned to be a pig on this earthly planet. When the time for death of that pig's body came, he used his mystic power to forestall death. His deity who was named Brahma became alarmed at his behavior and went to him astrally. Indra then explained that he had wives and children to care for. These were others in the swine family.

Seeing the condition of Indra's mind, Brahma arranged to have that pig body killed, in order to retrieve Indra for duties on the celestial places.

This story means that a yogi or a celestial being may become so conditioned to earthly existence as to resist going to higher dimensions during the assumption of a physical body and after in the astral world when that body dies. Each yogi should be aware of this and should honestly do some soul searching to see if that happened, where one is resistant to going to a higher plane and lost the celestial or divine point of reference.

One should not feel that one will be rescued by anyone. It is possible that one may be rescued but it is highly unlikely. For safety, one should do the austerities and mystic practice, so that when the time comes, one can escape promptly.

When I visited a Buddhist temple in South Korea during the month of May of 2011, a Buddha deity added the third objective.

He said this:

Stay in the developed countries. Your assistance is needed. Be a counterbalance. One yogi can offset a million materialistic souls. In this case the physical presence is required.

To the right of that Buddha deity, there was another Buddha deity who is *Bhaishavya* or the Medicine Buddha.

When I approached that deity, He looked down. He said this:

You are the one for this mission. In fact, what else should you do? I do not see an alternative. It is the only path open to you.

There was yet another Buddha Deity on the left side of the central Buddha who is *Shakymuni* or Gautama. This other Buddha Deity is called *Amitabha*. He is regarded as the Wisdom Buddha.

He was the only one to smile when I approached. It was a dry smile. He said this:

Why did you come here last? I am the only one with the gifts for you. The others intend to employ you. Why should a friend wait to see his friend, who considered visiting others as an urgency?

He then said,

I will give you the information for the other book. Good luck to you.

The book he mentioned is a book which was published. It described astral projection and the dimensions into which the astral body may enter. I completed one book for this Buddha already, which is the *sex you!* book. Since he did not comment about it, that is a signal that it is approved. Since Amitabha Buddha committed to giving information for those books, my lack of insight in any area was subsidized by him. Rishi Singh Gherwal also wanted those publications. He assisted with the compositions.

This is a resident temple of those deities:

This is the three Buddhas at another temple in South Korea:

In the center is the Buddha who founded Buddhism. He is Shakyamuni or Gautam.

To the right is *Bhaishavya*, the Medicine Buddha.

To the left, is *Amitabha*, Spiritual Wisdom Buddha.

Using Naad as a mantra *(Naad Nam Kriya)*

A Buddha deity inspired a method of using naad as a mantra. This is for situations in which a yogi finds himself mentally with a requirement for dependence and use of a mantra.

Traditionally in India, naad is not used as a mantra, but one can use the *Om* (A-U-M) sound for a time. When that absorption gets deep, one should release oneself from the practice and listen to the naad resonance.

However, I was told by a Buddha deity in Korea, that he used a naad nam kriya which is effective. This is the first time I heard of this method.

Naad is the sound which resonates causelessly producing a high-pitched frequency which is heard in the head near an ear.

Nama is a Sanskrit word. It is shortened in Hindi to *nam*. This word means name, nomenclature. According to that Buddha deity, after one hears naad in the head one can say its frequency mentally. If in hearing it, one finds that one's mind refuses to be fully absorbed in it, one should split the mind into two parts, the part that is attracted to naad frequency and the part which wants to do something else. The part which is contrary should be made to mentally create or express a sound which resembles the naad sound which is heard by the other part. This is mental. No sound is made by the physical vocal cords.

Amazingly this method works. I tried it after the deity informed me. Let us say for instance, that only 20% of one's attention remains spontaneously attentive to naad. Then let us say that another 20% remains deliberately focused on naad. That would mean that 40% of the attention would be invested in naad focus, listening, while 60% of the attention would be making efforts to go forward to the front part of the subtle head, with intentions of becoming occupied with unwanted images and sounds.

In that case instead of opposing that 60% or instead of accommodating it and having it destroy the effort for naad absorption, one could use the 60% to make a reinforcement of naad for repetition and focus. That 60% would keep repeating naad by mentally creating its sound and mentally making efforts to hear it and repeat what is heard. This is a reinforcing technique.

Naad as Frequency Resonance or Mantra

Naad frequency is a sound heard in the head. It is usually high pitched or is a blend of frequencies. Usually it is heard near an ear. It may be heard on the left or right side or in the top back of the head. This sound is similar to tinnitus which is considered to be a nuisance.

Naad sound may be heard when one is in a quiet place or by the ocean where there are no man-created sounds. This sound is heard during meditation and is a focus for yogis.

Naad *Nam* means when that sound is considered to be a mantra or is considered to be a holy name, where a person tries to make that sound mentally, not vocally.

In India *Om* (A-U-M) sound is used as the primary vocalization of the vocal cord. It is used mentally as well. But naad itself is only used mentally and never vocally. There is no need to say naad, because it is an inner sound. One needs to hear it only.

Sometimes *Om* is considered as *pranava* (pronunciation pruh-naav or pruh-naa-vuh) but as *pranava* it is the un-vocalized *Om* which is naad sound as described above.

The ancient procedure is that if you cannot hear naad, you should chant *Om* until you can hear naad, or chant *Om* for fifteen minutes, and then be quiet, and usually one will hear it. Chanting *Om* causes the distractions in the mind to disappear.

Everything has vibration. For instance, if we are in a building which has a generator, we can use the power from that machine to run an appliance. If the appliance is loud, we will not be aware of the sound of the generator. But if we turn off the appliance, we will hear the humming sound of the power supply. Thus, when all the mental sounds cease, one hears the vibration of existence.

Once you hear a sound you can repeat it. The repetition will not be what you heard but it will do. In the case of a mantra, you get it from a teacher. You repeat it. With naad, you do not get that from a teacher, you hear it.

Motivation for Mindfulness

Meditation is a bit like everything else, in that you do it because you must do it, or because you choose to. Many things we do in life are done merely because we must act for them. When someone tells us to do something, we usually do not like that because we feel we should be in control. But again, many things which we do from impulse are also forced on us by our emotions or moods.

Thus, when we stop and take a close look at the situation, we sometimes find that there is no purpose for living. We discover that we go from day to day aimlessly or being driven by trends which were introduced by others.

Traditionally, people learnt meditation in ashrams, either in India, China or Japan. What is an ashram? It was a boarding school. Just as today, in the modern societies, many children are forced to attend school, to learn how to speak and write the language, how to add and subtract, so some children attended ashrams to learn meditation.

But if a child is in an undeveloped country, or say in a tribe in the Amazon, that child may not be compelled to attend school. There is no government enforcing school attendance. Thus, the child grows without formal education in language and calculation.

Then a teacher or missionary comes there and teaches the child language and Math. But the child finds that he is not interested. When he is given home work, he does not do it. He does not feel motivated.

When Buddha set out to meditate, it was because he lost motivation for social life. He decided,

"I will not participate. It leads to a dead end. I saw the end of this, as death of the me, death of this body. Until I can deduce some sense in this, I will not participate."

With that he left his infant son, capable wife, concubines, status as a Prince, everything. He went into the night with determination to find something besides being born as a human infant, growing up, having sex, begetting children, being overtaken by ill health and then dying.

Think about it. Am I having sex because I wish it? Did I invent it? Did I give my body the urge?

Part 7

Past Lives Technique (July 16, 2011)

During meditation this morning I got a procedure from Buddha. This is a mystic technique which is a subtle or spiritual movement which may or may not have physical corresponding actions. For instance, to move the right thumb, one must execute a mental order or a willpower movement. but if the nerves to the thumb are damaged, the request will be ignored. In that case, there is a mental act but no corresponding physical one.

In yet another example, you may imagine moving your thumb and not execute a mental order. In that case, there is only an image in the mind with no corresponding mental nor physical act. These are three distinct actions. One should work in meditation to distinguish each act.

Skeptics feel that there can be no clear distinction in these acts but there can be and it does not have to be proven to anyone. The proof manifests in the yogi's development by progress in meditation.

In the meditation, Buddha gave an instruction for a procedure through which one can research past lives. This is not the only method for doing this.

This is a simple procedure as I will describe. Even though it is simple, one will have no success doing it if one did not master the art of stopping the mental imaging and sounding in the mind. Unless one practiced to stop the spontaneous ideation *(vrittis)* as instructed by Patanjali, one will have no success doing this, because one will not be in the dimension or vibration where this procedure is effective.

Here is the instruction:

- Get the mind space into a condition where there are no thoughts or images and no effort is required to keep the mind in that blank state.
- Listen for naad sound.
- Check to see that the self is attracted to naad and that its attention naturally holds to the naad with interest.
- Move to the back of the head.
- When you are sure that you are in the back and that you are still hearing naad and still aware of the entry point of naad, and are still moving backwards, look forward.

There should be shimmering light and a flash of an image or of many images. These will be sights from past lives.

Eating and Drinking

What one puts into the mouth for whatever reason does affect the type of consciousness one experiences in the body. Eating and drinking are a part of spiritual life. This is because the consciousness experienced in the body is subsidized by what one eats and drinks.

Consciousness as we experience it, is a composite energy, part of which is based on what is ingested into the body, not only what is drunk or eaten but what is breathe into the body.

If one is careless about what goes into the body, it may negatively affect one's aspirations for spiritual development. Sometimes people wonder why a yogi restricts diet. They feel that he deprives himself of enjoyment. One may consider that perhaps a yogi enjoys in some other world or in some other range of consciousness or in some other mental or emotional state, which is not available if the yogi were to have a normal diet.

In this world, we see that people smoke substances and drink coffee to achieve a particular type of consciousness. Some people drink liquor. Some take narcotics. These activities give access to a particular consciousness. The yogi endeavors for a certain level of consciousness. Why bother him when everyone else aggressively pursues the level they enjoy.

Sometimes people ask about developing more spiritual consciousness, to increase psychic perception, but if their eating and drinking is counterproductive to yoga, how would that be possible? If one wants to continue eating and drinking in the same way as before, one will get the advantage of that and will not get the advantage of increased psychic perception and arousal of kundalini.

One cannot have both worlds, the materialistic one and the spiritual one. It is one or the other. Just as to advance in the materialistic society one must deprive oneself of certain conveniences. One will have to adapt and change if one wants to advance in the psychic field.

Consciousness is in part a construct based on what we eat, drink, and ingest in other ways. To up the ante one must make adjustments. Instead of demanding higher perception while remaining with the same eating, drinking and breathing one should adjust the lifestyle to facilitate.

Evicted from the Body

In the infancy and youth of a body, one is ignorant of many processes and has many false assumptions. One does not pay attention to the potential ailments which will develop in the body. The body will age. Eventually one will be evicted from it and will not awaken as it. Still, one ignores this because of a preoccupation with enjoyment.

Hopes

Marriage is a human institution. It as a formal agreement as the human way of legitimizing something which nature enforced. Nature does not care about the registration of a marriage otherwise there would be no divorce ever.

Take for instance medical treatment. Humans spend millions of dollars for medical research. We send many youths to medical schools where they spend years studying how a body operates. Still, there is not one single case of a human being living say for one hundred and fifty years.

Some speak of a time in the future when a human body will live forever. However, presently there is not a single case out of millions of human beings, where medical science permits anyone, even the wealthiest person, to live for one hundred and fifty years. This means that to a certain extent nature does not care for our aspirations.

Look in another area, the mystic field. We have stories in the Bible for instance, about a person named Jesus, whom that book says resurrected his physical body by sheer mystic power. But within recent history, say the last three hundred years, there is not a single recorded case of this happening.

They were claims about yogis doing it in India, extending the life of their bodies and living on and on in such physical forms, but in India within the last 50 years, there is not a single case.

This means that nature is unwilling to support many of our hopes. Once you realize that and you know that you fight a losing battle, you will relax and not become tense with false expectations. If nature puts the pressure on someone for infidelity, that person will yield. The aspiration, spouse, or whatever cannot counter-force to prevent a breach.

This does not mean that one should fulfill every urge but it does mean that one should not hold oneself aloof as being someone who is above nature.

Bliss Body

This morning during kundalini exercises, kundalini rose from the lower torso in the form of 4-inch pads of beige-colored light energy. It was like a pad of ice crystals which were beige colored and which had a bliss energy content.

The first pad rose above the navel area. Then it disappeared. A second pad appeared and did the same thing. Some of the energy shot up into the neck. That felt like tiny needles of bliss force travelling upwards.

Rishi Singh Gherwal showed how yogis achieve the bubble bliss body, which looks like an inflated psyche and which is filled with higher level subtle energy. In that body the bliss force seems like tiny sand crystals, exuding bliss.

The development of this bubble bliss body, commences with the complete energization of the trunk of the subtle body below the throat. At first the neck area has a blockage which prevents the compressed bliss force from moving through the neck, but later as the practice proceeds this neck blockage is cleared. The energy reaches into the head. At that point one feels that one has a bloated bliss form which is filled with tiny bliss crystals.

Just as a human being gets a feeling that the physical body is made of flesh and bones, the yogi gets the feeling that there is nothing in the bliss body except tightly-compacted bliss.

Mission

Most human beings have no memory of past lives. Thus, they have no mission in that regard. They found themselves conscious as a human form.

Patanjali said that the purpose for the conjunction between material nature and the individual self is for providing objective experiences.

स्वस्वामिशक्त्योः स्वरूपोपलब्धिहेतुः संयोगः ॥२३॥
sva svāmiśaktyoḥ svarūpa upalabdhi hetuḥ saṁyogaḥ

sva – own nature, own psyche; svāmi – the master, the individual self;
saktyoḥ – of the potency of the two; svarūpa – essential form;
upalabdhi – obtaining experience; hetuḥ – cause, reason; saṁyogaḥ –
conjunction.

**There is a reason for the conjunction of the individual self and its
psychological energies. It is for obtaining the experience of its essential
form. (Yoga Sutras 2.23)**

तस्य हेतुरविद्या ॥२४॥
tasya hetuḥ avidyā

tasya – of it; hetuḥ – cause; avidyā – spiritual ignorance.

The cause of the conjunction is spiritual ignorance. (Yoga Sutras 2.24)

Like for instance if someone is born in New York that person will be
exposed to certain experiences. If at the same time someone is born in the
Sahara in a Bedouin family, that person will have a certain experience which
will be quite different and which will give him certain advantages which will
be useless if he relocates to New York.

What is the game plan? Some people feel that one should live in the *now*
in whatever happens in the environment. If we take that literally, it means
that if I find myself conscious as a lion cub, the *now* for me will be to kill
antelope. If I find myself as an antelope foal, the *now* for me will be to eat
grass.

This complies with Patanjali's statement that material nature is there to
provide experience. The term for such experience in Sanskrit is *bhoga*, which
means that which is enjoyed. But here the word enjoyed means experience.
It applies to both desirable and undesirable contact.

As a foal of an antelope, if I am separated from my mother, the
experience for me will be that of being chased and killed by a lion. That is
undesirable but it is still to be enjoyed in the sense of being experienced,
being endured.

Back in the human species, other circumstances take place. If I took birth
during Roman times, and lived in Northern Europe and was known as a
barbarian, I may be captured and made into a slave in Rome. That would be
an experience of White on White oppression. But if I lived in Africa during the

Colonial era, I may be captured and transported in a slave ship and taken to the West Indies, which would be White on Black oppression.

Conversely, if I was a white man who was a slave owner and who got rich by trading black human beings as slaves. That was an experience, too.

As soon as one is born there is a mission which is impressed on one. A kitten in an apartment has a mission because the wealthy woman who owns it, expects it to pass waste in a specific pan in the condominium, to greet her when she comes into the apartment and to sleep by her side when she does not have a companion.

If the kitten fails to use the pan for waste, the lady may call an animal shelter and have the kitten taken away. The kitten has a mission. If it fails to format itself, its mission is changed by fate in the form of a phone call by the owner.

The creation is full of mission and purpose. Most of it is short-ranged and has no spiritual content. Most of it involves evolutionary drives for eating, sleeping, mating and defending. That means nourishment, recuperation, reproduction and protection.

If one cannot discover the spiritual side to existence, it means that one can only serve the evolutionary drives which are compressed into the particular species of life one finds oneself to be at any particular time. But even in that case, there is mission.

Rotation of the Intellect

Meditation today began with a rolling feature of the intellect in the frontal part of the subtle head. As it rolled in slow motion, the coreSelf followed. There were no thoughts. An attempt to keep track of the activity was done in slow motion.

After three seconds, I noticed that the naad sound was on the right side near the ear. Just then I noticed that it was on the left side as well. Both sounds streamed but the sound on the left did not have the intensity as the right sound. I positioned myself on the left. The sound from that side was distant. From there I listened for both sounds but when I did so I was shifted into hearing the louder right sound. I shifted back into hearing the quieter left one.

Suddenly, I found myself rolling around the intellect in the frontal part of the subtle head. These rolls were in slow motion. The third eye was not in operation. The intellect itself was not in operation. The energy from the breath infusion caused the intellect to roll over and over in slow motion as the infused energy moved around it in a clockwise manner.

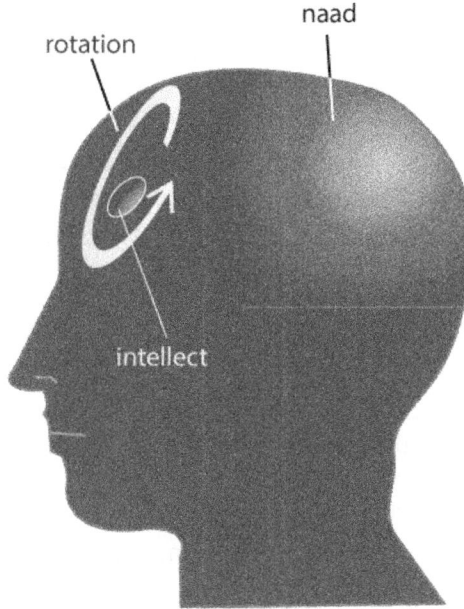

During this rolling action, I got a flash message from Rishi Singh Gherwal. I did not see him. At the time I was not existentially situated to translate the message. Soon after I shifted and read it. It said: "When this situation is demolished, it could be like this for centuries of time. How about existing like this for a universe's duration?"

Rishi Singh spoke of the pranic energy in which I rolled. Sometimes a universe terminates for a time. It decompresses. All entities in that situation are left without manifested existence, without form existence. People who come to meditation sometimes make jokes about a void or a non-manifested state, and about unity with everything. Do they know that a time will come when this universe will implode? They will have a void for billions of years?

Some people want to escape from diversity. They find identity and personhood to be troublesome. Little do they know that a time will come when existence will be suspended.

In Sanskrit there is a word for this which is *pralaya*. *Laya* means when something is stretched, relaxed out of itself, when something is broken down completely. The prefix *pra* means in total or well completed. When the universe is in *pralaya*, one may be in a non-existence, or in a formless condition. For billions of years, one may be aware or unaware of it.

Yogis like Rishi are aware of these epochs. They prepare themselves psychologically for such a break down in the manifested existence. If one is not prepared, and if one remains objectively aware when it happens, one will panic, except that there will be no way to stop it. Just as in the physical situation we must accept what happens politically, socially and climatically, one will have to endure that non-manifest energy state.

In meditation, we sometimes find ourselves in dimensions which have violent climates like lightning flashes from one planet to another, with so much electricity that it is unimaginable. The sounds which emanate from those vibrations are frightening. One shivers in one's boots. This happens in other dimensions. Sometimes a yogi is fortunate to enter such places.

Scenes Through the Third Eye

During the morning practice, after some breath infusion and twisting to the right and left, kundalini rose on the right and left side. It came up through the right center of the body and then on the left center. It hit the collar bone and then deflected through the bones in the arms and forearms.

When it rose to the collar bone, it did so in a spiral pattern with two laser-like charges firing through the spiral's energy.

As soon as I sat to meditate, naad sound became evident. I went into it. As I was in the back-right side, I got an energy pulse from the frontal part of the head. That came into the psyche from a person in South America. I was in South Korea which is half way around the planet. Still the person's thought reached me.

This was from a lady, who thought that I should be positioned in my next life so that I could have a relationship with her.

Such thoughts serve to remind a yogi that if he is not careful, he will take a haphazard rebirth on the basis of a whimsical and perhaps costly desire energy which came from someone and which he responded to carelessly. I did not give attention to the energy pulse which contained this desire of the lady.

After that energy pulse was dismissed, I stayed in naad energy. Suddenly I looked forward. Scenes from another dimension passed rapidly just outside the third eye. It was at a speed as if I sat on a train and looked through a window and saw the scenery of the landscape passing by. After about ten seconds, it turned into night in that dimension. I saw shadowy shapes.

Visitor during Kundalini Arousal

During the meditation, a lady who is now deceased, came. She was a practicing yogi while she had the last body. She also came during the kundalini exercises yesterday. She did not say anything. She silently observed the meditation. Because of using only a subtle body and not having a physical one to de-energize her subtle form, her subtle perception increased considerably as compared to when she was alive as a human.

She has an interest in kundalini yoga and came to see how the kundalini is aroused when it is charged by breath infusion.

For a yogi, it is not a good idea to have anyone present on the astral side during practice. If the person is a yogi/yogini then it is permitted.

If someone who is sexually-attracted comes during kundalini infusion, that person will be attracted to the infused kundalini and will cause it to take a sexual route, which will in effect cancel kundalini's interest in rising upwards into the brain.

Some astral persons who come to a yogi who infused kundalini, see the energy flashing through and out of the subtle body. They are attracted to it. Some take bits of the energy, just as one may take a cream and rub it on the body. They experience a bliss energy from it.

Distinction Between Third Eye and Intellect

Third eye and buddhi intellect orb are two psychic facilities in two different locations. The third eye cannot be used unless one first peers through the intellect orb but the intellect can be used without looking through the third eye.

An example could be a binocular. One cannot see through it unless one peers through the physical eyes but one can use the physical eyes without using the instrument.

The third eye is usually located at the brow chakra which is usually between the eyebrows on the skin or membrane of the subtle body.

The intellect has a position somewhere between the center of the head and the brow chakra.

default locations of core-self and

psychic adjuncts in head of subtle body.

kundalini which is in subtle trunk

is not represented

sense of   coreSelf
identity   intellect

third eye

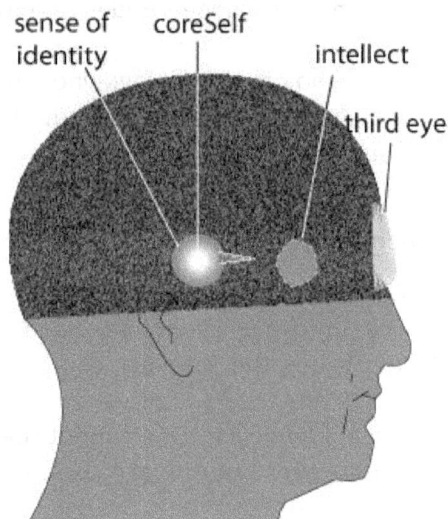

While the third eye is relatively easy to see, the intellect orb is almost impossible to see. But the third eye is only easy to see in terms of its brow chakra configuration.

Have you ever seen your eye? Actually, unless you have a mirror, usually you do not see the eye even though you see other objects easily through the eye. Peering through the ocular mechanism is easy but seeing the parts of it, is not that easy.

In modern times we have mirrors but say about 1000 years ago, hardly anyone saw their eyes on a regular basis, even though seeing the eyes of another person was common.

Here are some hints:

Forget about seeing the third eye, instead see the brow chakras which is where the third eye vision occurs.

Forget about seeing the intellect orb, instead see the illustrations and ideas of the orb and use those to determine its location. Once you know its default location then with full confidence always know that it is located at that place.

Brow chakra is not the third eye but it is part of the third eye configuration. Hence knowing about the chakra and experiencing it is important for anyone who wants to use the third eye.

Another hint:

Do not attempt to make the third eye function. Instead, relax, have a slight focus on it during meditation. Wait for it is open.

Yet, another hint:

Third eye becomes accessible and visible as soon as one is no longer focused into physical existence. It depends on how much confidence one can transfer to the subtle existence. The natural stress we put on physical existence is itself a deterrent for use of the third eye.

To identify which psychic adjunct one uses, identify the location of the event. Mark the location of the thoughts and ideas in the mindscape. That place is the intellect.

One important distinction is that the third eye happens in the configuration of the brow chakra but it is not the brow chakra. Many feel that they use the third eye when they see the brow chakra. This is a false conclusion.

Suppose I see the cylindrical edges of a telescope does that mean that I use the telescope and see a mark on the moon?

Naad: Right/Left

When I sat to meditate, there were two naad sounds, one of the top left and one of the top right. I tried to contact but I found myself shifted towards the one on the right. When I was shifted, I lost touch with the one on the left.

I got an intuition to move to the top left. After moving there, I heard both sounds. I saw color. The one to the top right had a brown hue. The one on the left had a grey and then red hue.

These are subjective colors which means that they may or may not be the objective colors of those zones. Subjective sight is produced by looking through energy. It is energyVision, pranaVision.

If one is in an aircraft above an ocean, the water will appear to be aqua marine blue. But if one dives into the same water, one will see the water as being clear. The clear appearance may be compared to subjective sight since the view occurs in the medium being observed and the viewer is not objectified to the medium. pranaVision enables one to make subjective observations. In the physical world, people belittle and mistrust subjective perception. However, in yoga practice it is a valid perception.

When through intuition I shifted to the left naad sound, I became conscious of both the right and left naad sounds. They were different frequencies. They touched but did not mix.

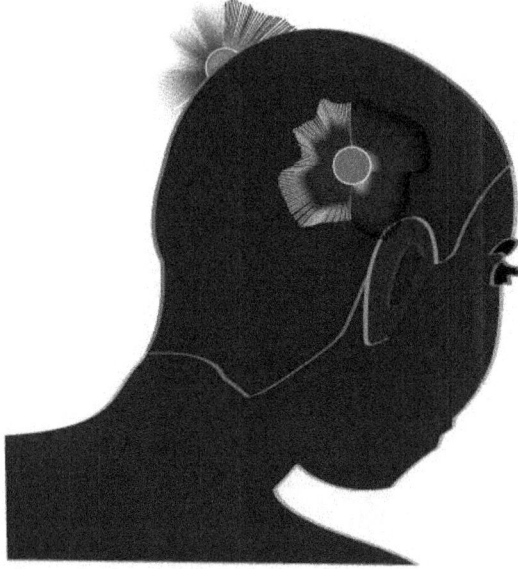

naad sound on right and left

In advanced meditation, there may be a blending of several naad sounds. This is mentioned in Krishna's instructions to Uddhava:

प्राणस्य शोधयेन् मार्गं
पूर-कुम्भक-रेचकैः ।
विपर्ययेणापि शनैर्
अभ्यसेन् निर्जितेन्द्रियः ॥९.३३॥

prāṇasya śodhayen mārgaṁ
pūra-kumbhaka-recakaiḥ
viparyayeṇāpi śanair
abhyasen nirjitendriyaḥ (9.33)

prāṇasya — of the vitalizing energy; śodhayen = śodhayet — should purify; mārgam — the passage, route; pūra – inhalation; kumbhaka – retension; recakaiḥ — with exhalation; viparyayenapi = viparyayena — by the reverse order + api — also; śanair = śanaiḥ — by graduating; abhyasen = abhyaset — should practice; nirjitendriya = nirjita — having controlled + indriyah — the sensual energy.

One should purify the passage of the vitalizing energy by inhalation, retension and exhalation, and by graduation in the reverse order, having the sensual energy controlled. (Uddhava Gita 9.33)

हृद्य अविच्छिनम् ओकार
घण्टा-नाद बिसोर्ण-वत् ।
प्राणेनोदीर्य तत्राथ
पुनः संवेशयेत् स्वरम् ॥९.३४॥

hṛdy avicchinam oṁkāraṁ
ghaṇṭā-nādam bisorṇa-vat
prāṇenodīrya tatrātha
punaḥ saṁveśayet svaram (9.34)

hṛdy = hṛdi — in the heart chakra; avicchinnam — continuous without breakage; oṁkāram — Om sound; ghaṇṭā — bell; nādam — sound; bisorṇa-vat = bisa – fibre + ūrṇa – lotus + vat — like; prāṇenodīrya = prāṇena — by the vitalizing energy + udīrya — raising; tatrātha = tatra — there + atha — thus; punaḥ — again; saṁveśayet — one should blend with; svaram — of musical notes, tones.

In the heart chakra, the Om sound which is like the continuous peal of a bell, resonates continually, like a fibre in a lotus stalk. Raising it by using the vitalizing energy, one should blend that sound with the musical tones. (Uddhava Gita 9.34)

एवं प्रणव-संयुक्तं
प्राणम् एव समभ्यसेत् ।
दश-कृत्वस् त्रि-षवणं
मासाद् अर्वाग् जितानिलः ॥९.३५॥

evaṁ praṇava-saṁyuktaṁ
prāṇam eva samabhyaset
daśa-kṛtvas tri-ṣavaṇaṁ
māsād arvāg jitānilaḥ (9.35)

evam — thus; praṇava — Om inner sound; saṁyuktam — premixed; prāṇam — vitalizing energy; eva — indeed; samabhyaset — should direct; daśa – ten; kṛtvas = kṛtvaḥ — procedures; tri-ṣavaṇam — three

times; māsād = māsāt — month; arvāg = arvāk — after; jitānilaḥ = jita
— conquer + anilah — the life air.

**Thus, one should carefully direct the pre-mixed Om sound and the
vitalizing energy, ten times, thrice per day. (Uddhava Gita 9.35)**

I did not hear a blend of the sounds. After fifteen minutes, I found myself
in the naad on the right side. I checked but the sound on the left side was
absent.

This means that the sound was there but I was desynchronized from it.
Up on the top of the head there was a large space which was filled with an
energy which seems to be an energy of absence, a place which in that
dimension was vacated of subtle objects.

Buddha as a Special Being (July 9, 2011)

In the book, *In the Buddha's Words* by Bhikkhu Bodhi, Gautama Buddha
explained his unique place in human history. This was in a conversation he
had with monks about the distinction between himself and all others who
would take the path he pioneered.

Is this for real or is this his ego talking? I repeatedly asked persons of the
Buddhist system to take Buddha the person into account.

Without veneration for him for the path he divulged, it not possible to
use that path to its fullest perfection. This is because the full method will not
open itself nor be discovered in that way.

Read this passage from the book. This is from pages 413-414 (ISBN:
0861714911).

Excerpt:

Gautam Buddha said:

*"Monks, through disenchantment with form, feeling, perception,
volitional formations, and consciousness, through their fading away and
cessation, the Tathagata (Tut-haa-guh-tuh), the Perfectly Enlightened
one, is liberated by nonclinging, he is called a Perfectly Enlightened One.
Through disenchantment with form, feeling, perception, volitional
formations and consciousness, through their fading away and cessation,
a monk liberated by wisdom is liberated by nonclinging, he is called
liberated by wisdom."*

*"Therein monks, what is the distinction, the disparity, the difference
between the Tathagata, the Arahant, the Perfectly Enlightened One, and
a monk liberated by wisdom?"*

"Venerable sir, our teachings are rooted in the Blessed One, guided by the Blessed One, take recourse in the Blessed One. It would be good if the Blessed One would clear up the meaning of this statement. Having heard it from him, the monks will remember it."

"Then listen and attend closely monks, I will speak."

"Yes, venerable sir," the monks replied. The Blessed one said this:

"The Tathagata, monks, the Arahant, the Perfectly Enlightened one, is the originator of the path unarisen before, the producer of the path unproduced before, the declarer of the path undeclared before. He is the knower of the path, the discoverer of the path, the one skilled in the path. And his disciples now dwell following that path and become possessed of it afterward.

"This, monks, is the distinction, the disparity, the difference between the Tathagata, the Arahant, the Perfectly Enlightened One, and a monk liberated by wisdom."

Time Limit

A yogi must always keep in mind that there is a time limit. This is providence. No one has an unlimited span of time to achieve anything. Even the resources in the universe are limited even though it is not possible for any limited being to exhaust these. We find that providence puts us in slots where we cannot realize the unlimitedness of certain things. For instance, in the case of electric energy which now powers practically every home in the world, we are finding that there is a limit to how much we can produce. There is an unlimited amount of electricity in the cosmos, but we are not in a position to exploit it. We have a sun which for earthly needs, has an unlimited supply of energy. It emits an unlimited supply moment after moment. Still we cannot use it except for its natural distribution of daylight to our planet.

One tiny nuclear explosion in the sun can supply a big city like New York with electric power for years, but still we cannot exploit it. Knowing that this unlimited supply is there, does not give us the power to exploit it.

Time is infinite but still the body I use currently will die for the most after its existence for about 100 years. A bug has about two weeks or months to live. Then its body deteriorates and it must transmigrate using a subtle form. Time does not allow it to continue as that lifeform.

When one is transferred to another zone at death, one may not have authority or standing in that place. One's easy life here and the philosophical basis here which was connected to the sense of security one has in the social world here, is finished, more or less, when time shifts one into an other domain.

For that matter one does not know what level of consciousness one will be on, or if one would be objectively aware with insight or memory of the previous life. A yogi must therefore squeeze as much time as he or she can for meditation practice, so that while using the physical body he or she may gain insight about the hereafter.

Meditation Questions

Advanced meditation comes after years of practice but the motive for practice can limit the progress made. Meditation is not one process for everyone. To really meditate, one needs a tailored recommendation from an advanced teacher, who knows the student, knows the student's motive, and advises the student with those considerations.

There is a standard process which was expounded by Patanjali in the *Yoga Sutras*. There are methods designed by other masters over the ages.

Meditation is for researching, controlling and making extra-physical use of the mind.

In meditation one should discover the psychic components of consciousness and transcend what is physical about the self.

Some important questions which meditation should clarify are:
- What is the self?
- What is the mind?
- How are thoughts and images produced in the mind?
- Can the self exist apart from the physical body?
- What is emotion?
- Are there psychic organs in the mind, just as there are physical organs in the body?
- Does a psychic organ produce thoughts and images?
- Can the self live outside of the mental space which it is housed in or is it entirely dependent on that space, the way a gland like the pineal is dependent on the rest of the brain?
- Does the self stay in a particular location in the mind, the way the pituitary gland has a set location in the brain?
- Can the mind exist outside the brain?
- Can the mind leave the brain space and reenter it without death of the physical system?

Subconscious Mind / Causal Body Penetration

There is a yoga practice which can be used to enter the subconscious mind which holds memories which are inaccessible to the conscious mind.

One can also use this process to enter the causal body, which is not a body but which is part of a space in the cosmic energy which one is assigned to.

Just as on this planet there is land, and a piece of that land may be called a continent, a piece of which may be called a country, a piece of which may be called a county, a piece of which may be called a property, so there is a causal energy which is inhabited by trillions of living entities, individual spirits.

To enter the subconscious mind or the causal body, one should in meditation take care to reach a plane where thoughts and images cease occurring in the mind. If one has to observe or oppose thoughts, one cannot do this.

As soon as one finds that one is in a mental place or space, where there are no thoughts in the frontal part of the subtle head, one should try to go downwards through the neck as if one went through a funnel.

Usually one will find that one cannot do this, as if there is a resistance that prevents one. Until the resistance to the downward movement changes, one should persist in the effort and meditate practicing this for some time.

Please take caution to consider that this should be an actual psychic movement not an imagined nor a visualized activity. One should feel that the iSelf moved downward.

When one enters the neck, one is in the subconscious region. When one goes lower and enters the chest region, one is in the causal body. Since there is no sensual faculty like eyes, ears or nostrils there, this may seem to be no achievement. The only thing one finds there is compact energy. That is compressed subtle information. In the subconscious there are compressed memories from many past lives. In the causal body, the transcendental impetus that drives the numerous lives and numerous bodies we take is there as well.

These energies can be translated into the conscious mind so that a person can see what they would manifest as, in real time in a life experience.

If one practices this meditation regularly, there will come a time, when one will find that after coming up from the neck or chest, one sees images and scenes, even scenes of past events as well as what will occur in the future. In other words, the informational energy which one carries back into the conscious mind, will convert into real circumstances. One will see past lives and future events.

Naad Advanced Meditation (July 6, 2011)

Those who practice kriya meditation or the Patanjali system of meditation should seriously use naad sound as the mantra and main centering device. This sound is automatically there. It does not require vocalization for its usage.

Rishi Singh Gherwal directed that I give an instruction. He said that there are many mantras. They are given in a misleading way. Yogis should not waste time using the majority of mantras, except for a few like *Om namo Shivaya*, *Om mani padme hum, hansa, Om* (by itself), *Om namo bhagavate vasudevaya, gayatri* mantra, and tantric guru-imparted mantras like *Om Hrim*. Ultimately no mantra should be used and only naad sound should be used as the shelter.

Rishi is of the view that if one studies Patanjali Yoga Sutras and understands with Krishna's Universal Form, all problems will be solved. To understand the Universal Form, one should study the *Bhagavad Gita*.

He said this with emphasis,

Since the material world is pivoted away from the spiritual level of existence, one cannot expect to transcend it by focusing on it. Therefore, naad is important because it comes from the spiritual domain. It is not created by the human vocal organs or the human low-level mind.

If one fails to take help from the Supreme Being, one will never be liberated because it just happens to be the case that without getting his assistance one does not have the strength to lift oneself out of the mundane energy. It is a practical matter, where you do what is necessary to complete the objective.

For this help must be taken from Krishna. A limited self does not have the power to free itself from these gross and subtle energies which surround it on all sides."

In reciting a mantra verbally or within the mind mentally, one must be attentive to the recitation. The most powerful mantra for this purpose is the age-old standard mantra which is om. *There are many other mantras but ultimately for meditation,* om *is the ultimate sound.*

The problem with chanting is that it requires attentive energy. When using naad no attentive energy is given for recitation because it is produced causeless by the clash between the material existence and the spiritual one.

However, beyond om *there is the naad sound which is the final word in mantras. It is free. It does not require mental or aural endeavor. Once contact is made with it, it is there for the taking.*

Naad was mentioned by Patanjali and also by Krishna to Uddhava. It is not mentioned in the Bhagavad Gita. The instructions to Uddhava are higher instructions for isolated yogis.

At first one should remain in the coreSelf's default position and listen to naad. When that becomes a habit, one should move the core from its default position. Move it into the naad which is usually on the back left or right side near the ear.

Usually naad is a sharp frequency sound which is like a blend of notes. It rings continually. It is always there even though one is not always focused on it.

Once a yogi gets used to it and can find it easily when he sits to meditate, and once the coreSelf gets used to it, accepts it and prefers to focus into it than to focus on images and thoughts, he should move the core from its default location. In the beginning there will be resistance. The core may refuse, but one should exert to relocate it.

Eventually the resistance will decrease. One will move it into naad sound, in the back part of the head, mostly on the right or left side near the ear.

Keep doing this for some time, until the core no longer has resistance to relocation and stays there in meditation without resuming its default position.

Once you attain that the next stage is to let the coreSelf remain in its default position but also note that while it is there it does not adhere to that place as before. It will stay there but with willingness to move.

At that stage one should remain in the default position and listen to naad. If one is existentially situated at the right mental place, one will find that naad comes to the coreSelf. Before when the core was in its default position, it focused on naad, but now naad sound is attracted to the core.

This is the stage where one can meditate until this becomes an effortless process. In this state the mind should produce no images or thoughts. The breath should not be observed. The only thing being observed is naad sound. Once you settle into this practice, focus forward into the intellect or into the brow chakra.

Kirpal Singh

There is an interesting instruction from Sri Kirpal Singh in the book *The Anurag Sagar Kabir (The Eternal Traveller)* from Page 25 to 32. It is a very advanced instruction. It shows something which Kirpal Guruji stressed:

Shabd or Word – the primal Sound Current – is the only Guru for the entire world and Surat – individual consciousness – is the only disciple, as the latter cannot do without the former. In fact, there is the principle of Unity, for God is One, though He has manifested Himself variously.

The Sound Current – Naam or Word, Shabd – as It is described in that scripture is first basically audible always from the right side. In further state when some Spiritual Progress has been made, you can listen to It as coming from above.

If those people really accepted the Sound coming from the right and listened to it, they would realize after some time that It is getting louder and clearer and has a raising effect. Nevertheless, these people also need – if they want to progress – eventually the Holy Initiation because without it no Inner Progress can be achieved. Only through initiation one can progress starting at the point which one had reached during his past life.

Value of Social Merits

One miscalculation of religious inclined people and even people who do not believe in religion but who believe in doing good, is that their social contributions to the family and nation are worth spiritual returns after death.

Even people who do not believe in God, try to bargain with others, with religious leaders, after death, for a spiritual reward on the basis of whatever good they did in this world while using the last material body. When they realize that social efforts cannot be exchanged for spiritual benefits, they detest religion and belief in deity.

Last night in the astral world, I was approached by a lady who raised a family and who still uses a physical body. She realized that her physical body was on the verge of death. Since most people never face that reality, this is insightful for her. However, she wanted to show the socially beneficial acts she did for her children. She wanted spiritual realization and revelation on the basis of her family work. Knowing that I placed a value on family cultivation, she felt that I would endorse the idea that she could get spiritual benefits from domestic service. At no time in the past did I assure her that she could.

Social work is social work. If it pays off, it will do so in a physical social situation in the future. Even though for sure, it will come about, since material nature logged the efforts and will sometime in the future create a circumstance in which the equations can be worked out, there is no telling when and where that future will be. Whatever is done for the family by the relative or for the nation by the civil servant, can be cashed sometime in the future, even though it may be in the next life or in a million years, according to the layout of the time and circumstance. But there will be no spiritual reimbursements for social affairs. A social account will be settled in the social way in a similar type of circumstance like the one in which it was generated.

One can ask the question as to why I advised anyone to commit social or national service, when I know that it has zero spiritual returns. The answer is that we cannot live in this world for free. We must deposit social services, national work and sometimes even global service in the form of willing and unwilling services to one and all. So long as we will require physical forms, that must happen. It is sensible to willingly do social services even though their spiritual worth is nil.

More importantly, if one has no choice but to keep taking rebirth because one cannot figure a way out of the reincarnation recycle system of nature, it is in one's interest to voluntarily and willingly commit the services since one will have to deal with the same set of recycled souls in new bodies over and over. One would do well to ease resentments and prejudices which naturally develop in the course of history.

The plain truth is that most of us, say about 99.9% must take rebirth, regardless of whether we desire to or not. The freewill, the need for self-expression and freedom from dominance cannot transcend the process of transmigration. The flow of many lives is antecedent to our volition. Transmigration has no respect for freewill. It has no plans to respect it in the future. Taking that into consideration, one should do the needful to lube the friction of these cyclic births and deaths, at least until one finds the key to unlock this great enigma and can transcend nature's secretive all-restricting transmigration game.

Prepping the Mind before Resting (July 4, 2011)

Over the years, teaching meditation, I introduced methods for setting the mind before resting. This relates to meditation, astral projection and lucid dreaming. If the mind is set properly before resting. that will help with meditation after rising. It will also help with conscious astral projection and clear lucid dreaming.

Patanjali listed sleep as one of the mento-emotional disturbances which affect meditation and which deter enlightenment. Sleep is a necessity for the physical and subtle bodies. There is no way to eliminate it. But we must work for its efficient usage. Sleep is an action of the kundalini life force. It involves an unconscious state of the intellect. The problem with sleep is that it is not controlled by the coreSelf. Hence to understand it the core has to be observant and must develop psychic sensitivity.

The basic method for setting the mind before resting consist of having the physical body in a reclined position and then checking through the mind's contents. This is not a method for advanced detached meditators but it is a common method if you are socially involved, as most people are. It does not matter if I think that I am advanced or enlightened. What matters is how involved I am in social affairs. If I am involved, it will be necessary to check the contents of the mind before resting. If I fail to do this it will negatively impact the next meditation session.

The mind is a container. Within it there are thoughts and images. These energies lurk in the mind and attract the coreSelf which is usually helpless in this regard. Before resting, sort and catalog the contents of the mind into three distinct values:

- What should be done before resting?
- What should be done at some other time after resting?
- What should never be done?

An example of something that should be done before resting, is urinating. Instead of going to bed with liquid in the bladder, one should discharge it from the body. If one fails to do so it will negatively impact the resting session.

An example of something that should be done after resting, is calling your employer to inform him that one has a dental appointment.

An example of what should never be done is the idea in the mind that one should perform a criminal act.

As simple as these examples are and as common place as they may seem, if these are not sorted before resting, they will impact sleeping and negatively affect the next meditation session. Just as one is about to rest, one should routinely check the mind contents and sort it as explained. However, this is not the advanced procedure.

The advanced procedure is this.

- mentally express appreciation to the yoga teachers, especially to the ones who currently assist by their advisories and inspirations.
- check the mind's condition.
- put the mind in order if anything is amiss
- meditate on naad sound

In the advanced procedure one may notice that at the time of resting the mind has a tendency to go downward into the body through the neck. The mind feels heavy as if it has weight, psychological weight. It feels as if it is so heavy that it should and must fall through the neck. The meditator should patiently shift it to the naad sound in the back part of the subtle head. This may be done repeatedly since the default condition of the mind at this time, is to fall downwards into the trunk of the body.

One may find that as soon as one does not hold the mind to naad sound, it is falls towards the neck. One should patiently absorb it in the naad sound. One should do this until slumber ensues.

The burden for reprocessing the mind falls on the individual meditator. If there is no effort, the default habits of the mind will continue indefinitely. Self-effort must be made for individual mind control.

Karma Yoga

The application of spiritual realization to social life is not an easy skill to master. Social life is karma. Spiritual realization is acquired through yoga. If the two are combined it is karma yoga. But even for yogis, karma yoga is not an endowment. Most people do not know it but besides being an archer, Arjuna was a proficient yogi. His austerities were so effective that in the Himalayas he attracted the attention of Shiva. That is described in the *Mahabharata*.

Let us consider his case. He was born in a political family. He was educated in private schools and had select professors as royal families afford. He mastered trance consciousness. He left his body for days on end while he travelled in the celestial world. Still, he did not know about karma yoga, about how to apply yoga proficiency to social life.

In the *Bhagavad Gita*, Krishna explained that karma yoga, was his (Krishna's) yoga, that he (Krishna) had the monopoly to teach it. This means that karma yoga is so difficult to master that God is the teacher of it.

I have the instinct of karma yoga, of the application of yoga to cultural life. I have it as a propensity. That gave me an advantage where I could efficiently service the social obligations to ancestors of my body and also proceed with spiritual progression. But it was not until Babaji Mahayogin dictated the commentary of *Kriya Yoga Bhagavad Gita* into my consciousness, that I really took a hard look at the practice of karma yoga, and realized its importance in the life of a yogi.

If one does not understand karma yoga, one will act in confusion. One will be more and more implicated with social debts. But really why does a person who exhibits great spiritual realization, become socially-deficient and cannot get his act together in the simple matter of settling with ancestors by giving them bodies. Let me show you how I could have made very similar mistakes. When this body was about 17 years of age, it made a boast to some friends that it would never marry, never be tied down by a family.

However, I was lucky because some of the ancestors of my body were very intelligent ladies. In the astral world they appealed to me, not to do that. Based on their good will, I decided to form a family and do the needful but I was determined not to make social life the priority. That means that a yogi may do it but he should expand it no more than necessary. He should not allow it to mute spiritual practice.

When my body was seventeen years of age, Swami Shivananda advised me in the astral world. He said, "Better to hurry up. Take a wife. Beget children to please the ancestors. All the while, do yoga. Later, when the children become adults, you will be a free man to maximize the real reason for which you took this body. Do not try to cheat the ancestors because Krishna and I will not approve that behavior."

Fortunately, I had help from both sides, from relatives who were deceased and from spiritual masters. At seventeen I had no objective idea about details in the *Bhagavad Gita*. I did not have the idea about karma yoga which Babaji later explained in detail, Still, because I had some good luck, there was a positive outcome. It is not in every life that one has such good luck. Providence may smile in one life and then present obstructions in the next.

In relation to why advanced people do not see the light, it has to do with bad luck. This life is much more than any individual, which means that without support from providence, guess what?

Neither the Supreme Being nor nature will always support an individual for all time. That will not happen. If one does not get the proper support, one cannot achieve the objective. Understanding how to apply yoga realization to social concerns is a special skill, otherwise Krishna would not stress its importance to Arjuna.

Analytical Orb Submits to Naad

Usually when listening to naad, the intellect is not involved. During naad absorption the coreSelf loses tract of the intellect. That is good for the yogi. If for one reason or another, the intellect gets out of commission, thoughts will cease entirely. That is compliant with Patanjali's request that there be no routine mental operations during meditation.

There is however an advanced stage of naad practice where the intellect moves from its default position and relocates near to naad or in naad sound. Usually the orb is located midway between the coreSelf and the middle of the eyebrows

That is its default position. If, however the self customizes itself to naad, the intellect becomes detached from its default location. It finds that the intellect moves back either near to naad or in naad. It does so in complete silence without images or thoughts and without any type of attracting force which may pull the coreSelf into its images and other expressions.

The default position of the self is to look forward in the brain towards the intellect but if one practices naad meditation frequently, a time will come when the self takes up a new default habit which is to be attentive to naad and to ignore to the intellect.

Naad Sound Caves

There are many variations in naad practice, but the common factor is three-fold. Either one listens to naad from a distance or one listens and becomes emerged in naad or one does not focus on listening to its sound. One can listen to naad from a distance and not be avoiding its resonance, or one can be emerged in naad and not listen to its sound specifically but be absorbed in its transcendental energy.

This morning during meditation, it took about five minutes before hearing naad. Even though the subtle body was properly infused, still there were a few thoughts which demanded attention. I checked the ideas and decided that they had no importance. However, since the persons who sent those ideas considered them to be important, the ideas had the power to hold my attention and to stick in the mind even though the mental energy was highly infused.

However, these thoughts were like shadows. They quickly disappeared. Then I heard naad and realized that I was not absorbed in it. Naad was on the surface of the right back portion of the head. When I tried to enter it, I could not. It emanated a repulsion energy, such that I could not enter it. I also found that as the coreSelf I was shifted to a position outside the subtle head. I stayed in that position since it seems to be a natural place from which to hear naad. Then I noticed that naad caved on itself, over and over and over, like waves crashing against a beach at regular intervals.

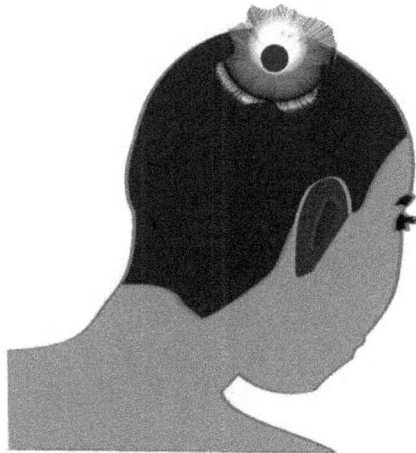

The sound of naad was a bit different. After some time, for about fifteen minutes, I looked forward and noticed some glow of light in the frontal part of the subtle head.

Part 8

A Yogi's Spine Out-of-Place

The spinal column is a useful part of yoga practice. The two parts of the body namely the head and the spinal column have value in the effort to understand consciousness and its operations in a body.

Anyone who is serious about enlightenment should take care of the spinal column. Even when sitting, one should make sure that the spine is properly supported and if there is spinal discomfort, one should attend it and do the needful to eliminate it.

One risk is to have surgery on the spine. That is like asking for a death sentence but in some cases, like in auto accidents and in other types of spinal injury it may be unavoidable.

In getting a spinal injection recently, I was involved in the risk of something going wrong. As a yogi, the risk of losing use of the spine is a nightmare. When the anesthesia was applied, there was no sensible feeling from the waist down. There was feeling but it was more like everything from the waist down was a gel in thick plastic bag. That was the interpretation formed by the intellect in the head of the subtle body.

By the way that is a case of one of the vrittis which Patanjali called wrong perception. The intellect derived incorrect sensual information from the kundalini. Since the intellect is reliant on that informer for news of events in the body, the intellect had no alternative but to express a report which was a wrong perception. The coreSelf for its part, is reliant on the intellect. Hence when the intellect supplies incorrect information, the core must make decisions from that.

It gives some idea about the value of the nerves which spread from the spine. Kundalini below the waste was as if it was non-existent, and above the waist it was aware of everything except with a hollow feeling that something was amiss elsewhere in the body.

I was stuck at computers now for the last 5 years in the effort to get books published. For four times, I had back problems because of sitting badly on a chair.

For yoga, one cannot afford to have a displaced spine because sitting up to meditate would be a problem. Even lying down to meditate may be a problem and raising kundalini would be surely be problematic.

One may be rich or poor, but if one practices meditation, a spine is essential regardless of the financial position. Money did not fix my back, only quick action, self-adjustment, did. If I went to a physician, he may have said surgery. If I permitted that, my spine may be fixed or damaged further.

Chiropractors are good but much of what they do is guess work since they are not the person feeling what the back does. Usually the person is in much pain and discomfort as to be unable to analyze the misalignment.

I cannot overstress that persons who are serious about meditation, should always be aware of the condition of the spinal column when sitting, when lifting and when doing anything through which the back can become misaligned.

Do not take your spine for granted. Attend to it. Make adjustments as soon as you sense that your sitting posture has a negative effect. When a vertebrate shift occurs, one may not know of it at the moment. It may take a day or a week before one notices that something is affected but if one analyzes the situation, one can quickly make whatever little adjustment is required. Always be skeptical of a surgeon who suggests cutting the spinal fibers or bones. That may result in a permanent disability.

When one sits on a chair. It is important that the lower back be braced. The same applies when sitting to meditate. Use a cushion to make sure that the lower back is supported.

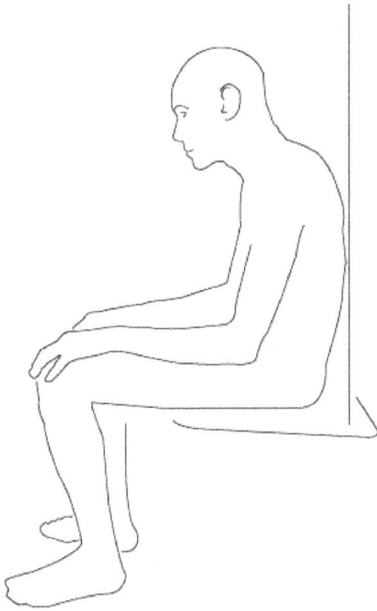

unfavorable sitting posture
chest collapsed inward
neck thrown forward

preferred sitting posture
chest lifted for spinal balance

cushion support
needed here

Spinal Injury during Childhood

During childhood when one is in the care of parents, anything can happen. Puppy love is the endowment of nature into the subtle form of the parents but it is not enough to give real knowledge about how to care for the body. The parents themselves are usually pleasure-starved and pleasure-craved. They must tend to their needs before they can take time for the long-range interest of the bodies and social behaviors of the children.

There is also the tendency of the parents to use the children as a pleasure source. That blind-sides them from acting in the interest of the children.

Anytime one takes a body one runs the risk of having the form become deformed or damaged in some way during childhood. A common mishap is tooth decay, something that is totally in the hands of the parents since they provide eatables for their children. Nowadays of course most parents in the developed countries are not in charge of their children's diet, but the schools and the commercial companies are.

Other aspects like muscle control, bone growth and body immunity have to do with luck and chance. In childhood, a polio epidemic struck the area my body resided in. By chance I did not acquire it.

When one assumes the next embryo, one will not be in a position to cover all the bases. There are many variables which comprise fate.

When all is said and done, one should do the best one can and discover if the defect applied by fate was due mostly to a habit one had. For instance, most of my jaw teeth are either filled or missing entirely. That was due to childhood conditions. The first thing is to forget the lack of duty of parents and tend to one's part in it. Even if you give someone perfect parents if that person has bad habits, problems will arise anyway.

What was my part in it? Thus, I acted to wean myself from sugar addiction and also to struggle with parts of it which were my contribution or which were due to my susceptibility to pleasurable but destructive social influences and trends.

In the family in which I took this body, I noticed during childhood how some adults who had diabetes and who were suffering terribly were unable to abandon sugar craving. From that I understood that human beings cannot necessarily take themselves away from suicidal habits.

There is also another thing which I learnt over the years. If you train a child in a good way, the child may depart from that and adopt destructive habits. This is because in the nature of the individual there may not be a power to support the preferred behavior.

In the *Bhagavad Gita*, this is brought to our attention when Krishna asked to Arjuna about the purpose of repressing habits?

Some people use that statement to support the idea that it is no use in trying to influence anyone to change a habit. Actually, that is not what Krishna meant. He implied that unless there was some complete therapy applied beforehand if a habit is repressed, it will resurface for sure.

The main thing is to supervise the psyche and to be responsible for its behavior but one cannot do that in infancy and childhood. The risk is there, that parents and other seniors may not know what to do for one's welfare. Even with parents who are aware and who act in one's long ranged interest, there is the overriding aspect of fate which supersedes everything. We should do the best under the circumstances.

No one will gain anything by riling against fate or by thinking that fate is disordered. It is really irrelevant if one likes fate or not, or if fate makes sense or not, or if fate is personally interested in one's interest or not. There is no coming to terms with fate, except for the opportunities it does or does not provide.

CoreSelf / Sense-of-Identity

In some meditations, the coreSelf can remain in its default position and simultaneously keeps contact with naad. This is not recommended because when the coreSelf is in its default position, it presses an interest energy towards the frontal part of the brain. When it is in that mode, it is unlikely that it will remain absorbed in naad.

Ultimately the yoga practice which is called *pratyahar* is completed when the coreSelf masters the retraction of its interest energy into itself.

That last statement however is wrong because what actually happens is that the coreSelf falls under the influence of the sense of identity which surrounds it and that sense of identity is the thing which sends out the interest energy.

It so happens however that usually the coreSelf cannot distinguish itself from the sense of identity. Thus, we have to say that the core emits the interest-ray even though it does not directly do so. It experiences itself as one with the sense of identity since it cannot distinguish itself from the identity force.

This discussion began with focus on naad contact, while the coreSelf is in the default position. In the advanced stages one can make contact and maintain contact with naad while staying at the default position at the center of one's consciousness. This happens because the self becomes released from a possession energy which usually restricts it.

Patanjali hinted this by two definitions of *kaivalya*, the first being when the coreSelf is distinguished from the flawed perceiving mechanism and the second is when the core is reunified with the purified perceiving mechanism.

One should not try to do the advanced practices but should instead be patient to gain proficiency in the elementary stages and then advancement will follow naturally.

If when one is at the default position, one finds that there is no interest energy emitted, then one can listen for naad from that position. If there is an interest energy emitting, one should relocate the coreSelf into the naad sound which is towards the back of the head.

In and Out of Naad

When doing naad meditation, there is a preliminary and advanced stage. The preliminary one is when one listens to naad from a distance. The advanced stage is when one enters naad and either listens during that entry or simply remains in it without listening.

These are distinct stages. One should not generalize nor confuse one with the other. Clarity is important. Merging and loss of distinction is not desirable.

There is a default position of the coreSelf. This self usually remains in the existential center of the subtle head. It is surrounded by a sense of identity which it does not have the power to remove. It can detach itself from that sense of identity's interactions with the intellect but it cannot remove nor destroy the sense of identity.

One must recognize this default position because when the self is located there it is limited as to what one can do in meditation. Due to the inability to move from the default position, the self can listen to naad but only from a distance. It cannot enter naad but if it shifts from that position, if it can relocate itself, the possibility of entering naad becomes evident.

Suppose you hear a whistling sound from a distance. Someone informs that it comes from the wind that passes through a tunnel which is ten miles away. You may develop some curiosity about the tunnel. You may develop a desire to see it. Suppose you are in a prison and have no means of escape, your desire cannot be realized. You will have to be satisfied with listening to the sound only.

Now if you are released from prison, you could walk to the tunnel even though it would take some time to do so. You would see the tunnel and hear that sound as well. Once you see that tunnel and hear that sound, you may develop the desire to enter the tunnel.

If you made entry, three possibilities could become a reality for you.

- see the tunnel
- enter the tunnel and hear the sound simultaneously
- be in the tunnel and not listen to the sound

The complete naad practice is to be in the tunnel, to perceive a spread of energy in the tunnel and to hear the sound as well.

One can never perceive the complete spread of naad energy, because one's consciousness will never have that infinite reach but still one could perceive a vast segment of it. That is *samadhi* absorption practice.

The Mind

What is the mind? That is an important question in any spiritual conversation. It is important that each of us agree that the definitions may be different. Once we agree on a definition, we can begin a sensible non-argumentative conversation. In the *Bhagavad Gita*, Krishna has two definitions for the mind. One is that the mind is the thing which is called *buddhi* in Sanskrit, which to us is the analytical function of the mind. Krishna also defines the mind as being the whole chamber of psychological energies which are in the head. In this second definition, the word *manas (manah)* is used in the Sanskrit language

In my books I stick to one definition only. That is the second one of Krishna *(manah)* which is the chamber of psychological energies which is the head of the subtle body. To be clear about this, I state that in this chamber there are components.

- coreSelf
- sense of identity
- intellect
- sense functions
- flash memory

No one should think that he or she has to accept my definition. You can have your own, just be clear about it.

Yoga Siddha Body Development

Rishi Singh Gherwal instructed yesterday that I should mention that for a yogi who desires to get a yoga siddha body, that form must developed out of the same subtle form being used in dreams. He said that if the siddha form is not developed before passing from the physical body, it is hardly likely that one would develop it hereafter.

To develop such a body, he tutored this:

One should forego the natural way the subtle body processes and stores energy. One must develop a desire for another way of using the energies. The main thrust is for removal of the sexual direction in which these bodies usually go which is to use gender for reproduction and pleasure purposes.

As it is, the system is that the energies ingested by these bodies are processed in the physical and subtle forms with the intentions of reproduction. The subtle body does not need to reproduce but in so far as it feels that a gross body is a necessity, it stresses reproduction and causes itself to be focused on that.

For reproduction, very refined concentrated energy is required. When this hormone energy interacts, there is pleasure. Thus, in the act of reproduction, there is development of addiction to pleasure.

For a yoga siddha body, the yogi must discover or realize how the energy in the system is accumulated, stored and distributed. If such a system is hostile to yoga success, the yogi should find a way to make it agreeable to yoga achievements.

Generally speaking, the energy is taken in by eating and breathing on the physical plane. After breath and food are processed, energy is derived. That is distributed and stored in the physical body and in the psychological and emotional contents. This stored energy is accumulated as sexual energy or hormones.

In a direct way a yogi should track this system to come to the conclusion that as designed by nature, the ultimate mission of eating and breathing is reproduction through sexual interplay. This system is already formatted. No one can change nature's intentions. At this time, no one can create forms by another method. This is the biological method.

If out of the subtle body one is to develop a yoga siddha body, one must change the design of this system so that the energy's main concern is not sexual reproduction. To achieve this a yogi should inFocus on his or her own form. No yogi will change the system universally, but by the grace of supernatural nature, a yogi may change his or her individual form. This can be done with great effort because nature will resist the change.

To move quickly from one old diseased or badly-damaged form into a parental energy where kundalini can create for itself a new form, it is must be desperate for sexual access for reproduction. When a yogi realizes that this attitude of kundalini is based on fear of death, fear of not having a facility to transfer into, the yogi can make a decision to monitor that attitude of kundalini.

If one needs another body, one must take advantage of the reproductive urges of kundalini. Therefore, why should a yogi try to escape from being dominated by this attitude? Obviously, the answer is that the yogi finds that such a facility is no longer required by him.

When a yogi reaches a level where he or she does not require perishable bodies, and when that desire is inbred, when the experiences to be gained using physical bodies are no longer part of the requirement for fulfillments, that yogi can take actions to divert the accumulated energies away from reproduction.

A yoga siddha form is a subtle body which is resistant to physical rebirth and which has an innate tendency to complete the austerities which are necessary for liberation or for translation to a spiritual dimension.

The destination of a yoga siddha form is the astral realm which is above the Swargaloka heavenly places. In terms of association siddhaloka is an astral territory where great yogins reserve subtle realms for their advanced disciples who have resistance to rebirth and strong tendency to keep practicing the yoga austerities to proficiency.

A yoga siddha form can revert back if the yogi is careless or if he is sent to teach on lower planes of existence. Careless means if he somehow or the other hears or perceives in any way people who are in the lower astral regions or on the physical level of existence operate. If he fails to keep his attention upwards, he may become aware of the condition of people in lower astral or physical place. That awareness could easily cause descent.

Ray of Interest-Energy in Meditation

In the exercises this morning, I infused much breath into the system. Subsequently, there was a high charge of energy. The mind shifted into a higher level of consciousness, making meditation easy and causing the psyche to immediately do what Patanjali termed as *samyama*, which is *dharana* progressing into *dhyana* and progressing into *samadhi*.

Dharana is when you focus on a higher level of consciousness either to shift focus into that higher plane or to shift into something or someone on that higher plane. Sometimes one is linked to a divine being on a higher level. It may not be random energy. In most meditations, one may only make contact with energy and never encounter anyone existing on those planes.

Dhyana is when one shifts into a higher level spontaneously, with no effort on one's part. *Samadhi* is when *dhyana* is more than momentarily. It lasts for a time.

It is important not to think that you reached the highest level, because that is hardly likely. Keep the mind open for something higher than what you experienced before. Awareness has several levels. Do not assume that you are on the highest or purest level. Admit that you were on a higher plane but leave some room for further revelation and elevation.

When I first sat to meditate after infusing the subtle body with breath energy and after focusing on infusing the subtle head, I noticed naad sound which was high in the back of the head. It was there. It was not there simultaneously. I went into it.

Because the breath infusion energy shifted it from its thought-producing mode, there were no thoughts or images appearing in the intellect. I checked that condition then I continued to move into the naad resonance. I noticed that there was a slight focus forward into the visual beam of energy which usually leaves the intellect. I retracted that.

However, the beam was persistent and reasserted itself. I then looked back at it. I noticed that the sense of initiative which surrounds (envelopes) the coreSelf had issued an interest energy in a ray form which struck the intellect. I retracted that and kept moving backwards into naad.

The sense of identity was in a mood for issuing another ray of energy to strike the intellect. I kept it in confinement and remained in naad.

intellect emits visual beam feeler
to acquire information from senses

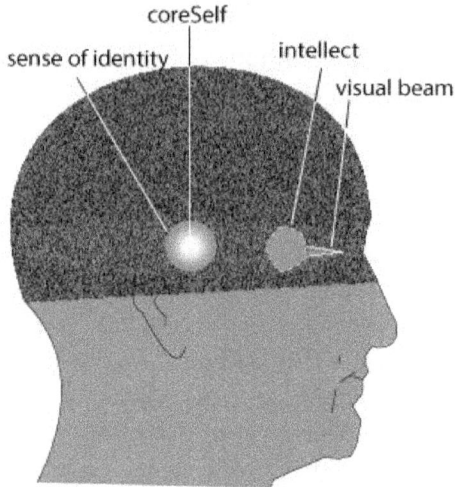

sense of identity emits ray of interest-energy
to detect images, ideas and thoughts
in intellect

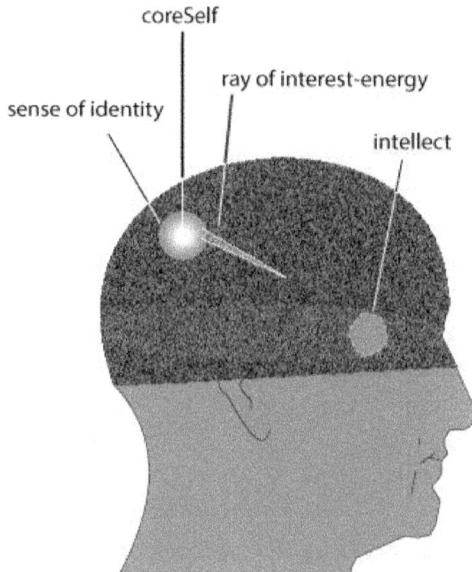

A Not-so-Good Meditation Session

Because of a superficial wound, I was unable to do a full session. In fact, for weeks to come I will not do the asana postures which I usually perform in a session. I will do some breathing. I knew that my system was starved of the usual supercharge of fresh air which I usually put into it but I will have to live with this until the wound heals.

After some breathing, I sat to meditate. The first thing I noticed is that there was not such a high charge of energy in the subtle body. The head of it was not on a very high level of consciousness even though it was not on the normal waking level which nature endows everyone with.

There were a few thoughts but they did not have a force of attraction. I looked at them, the way a businessman would look at papers which were put on his desk by a secretary. I glanced through those ideas. None of them had significance but some were projecting an aura of importance nevertheless. I noted that, how certain ideas carry with them a power of importance even though they have absolutely no value in one's life and even though they may in fact detract from a quality life.

Even if they have no value, ideas which are reinforced by their creators have a sense of importance. They project themselves as the priority. I checked for naad which was elevated on the right back side of the head. I decided to enter naad. When I did so there was a reinforcing energy to help with that practice. It came from Krishna's instruction to Uddhava to practice listening to naad, and another reinforcing energy came from Rishi Singh Gherwal who left an instruction energy in my psyche which insisted that naad should be the mantra which I adhere to.

Naad was different as compared to when I do a full session of postures and breathing practice. I noticed that. Pranayama does accelerate meditation. It is not a waste of time. Before meditation, do it if you can. Take help from yoga gurus. Give up the idea that you are God and that you can do this by yourself. Take help from yoga gurus.

After being in naad for ten minutes, I looked forward and noticed a light-yellow shimmering energy at the third eye. It was not stable. It changed this way and that way and then vanished.

I resumed focus on naad. After ten minutes, I checked forward. The same yellow shimmering energy was there. It acted in the same way. The intellect, the thought-image-producing subtle organ, was silent. This was desirable.

To do this practice I could not assume a lotus posture. I squatted, sitting on the heels since due to the superficial surgery that is the only posture I could assume.

Someone asked about the inability to be consistent in practice. The answer is that it is reduced to accountability. What we do is usually based on how we are motivated and the pressure applied by peers and authorities.

Do not fool yourself into thinking that because you do spiritual practice, you are free from motivation. Be honest. What is the motivation? If that is lacking, you will not practice? Who will be pleased if you practice?

Survival of the Human Species

To me the human race as a whole is an evolving lifeform, like a fungus which grows, but on the individual cellular level of that fungus there is diversity, fragmentation, individualization and just plain selfishness.

Despite that, the system functions as a whole, just as when you have a pain, say in your big toe. As a child, I ran in Georgetown, Guyana. I did so bare-footed. Sometimes my eye would miscalculate and my big toe would collide into a hard object. Immediately the body would be alerted. There would be pain. Sometimes tears would pour from the eyes. The same eyes which miscalculated would then express empathy for the toe which smashed into the hard object.

In another circumstance, sometimes during the mango season, I would eat at least twelve mangoes at a time. Then a few days after, the skin would break with sores and itchy spots, or somewhere in the body an abscess would erupt. The eyes would be yellow. There would be a bilious condition in the intestinal track. A fever would be felt.

The tongue would be silent, because it was afraid that the rest of the body would curse it. That is how I see the human race, as one organism which survives but it wants to extract enjoyment from what it perceives.

The question is deep as to whether it is good or bad for this one species to survive. This adds another factor which is the whole life form on the planet, human and all others including rudimentary life forms like amoeba and paramecium. From that angle, it is important for homo sapiens to survive, because our species is the culmination of the other genus. Our set is the graduation class. If you cannot get to the graduation, the course of evolution does not complete. Each spirit, or coreSelf, using any of the various life forms moves on the evolutionary conveyor belt, the top of which is the human species.

The idea is to step off once you get to the top and enter into a divine species in a totally different dimension. The way the evolutionary escalator is designed, there is no facility for stepping off unless one gets to the top but it has a facility for moving downwards and then moving upwards again at some other time.

If the human species is absent, one will assume a species like a dog, ape, lion, horse, cow, dolphin or parrot and will remain there forever or go to a lower species. One will never get the hint about stepping up to the divine existence.

There is a text from India called the *Brahma Sutras.* It begins like this:

- *athato brahma jijnasa*

This suggests that now that one reached the human threshold, one should inquire into *brahma,* into the divine existence. *Jijnasa* means to dig, search, and research something.

In a sense though, the question is loaded because the human race, even if it does not commit wholesale suicide, will be destroyed in time anyway. Astronomers stated that the sun will in time, increase in temperature and explode, such that this planet will be fried crisp. Eventually even the solar system will fail. In the Indian books it says that the sun will at one time in the future increase by a factor of twelve. Everything will fry. Some mythology and science agree on this future. Hence it means that the extinction of the human race is unavoidable.

Since homo-sapiens will become extinct either by its own doing or by climatic force, what is undesirable about that extinction? The answer is that so long as all desires for human life are extinct or go into dormancy at the time of the extinction, there will be no regret or feeling of lack of fulfillment but if anyone continues existing with such desires and is unable to fulfill them through the use of human system, that person or persons will feel the frustration.

It hangs on desire and our ability to snuff that out, tolerate it without fulfilling it or feel frustration if it is not fulfilled. Patanjali listed hope and desire energies as being eternal. If that is true then one should learn how to put desire into dormancy or how to tolerate it if it cannot be fulfilled at any given time. If one cannot master that, frustration and the related psychosis will inevitably set in.

Social Life of a Yogi

This morning Rishi Singh discussed the social life of a yogi and the acceptance of the outlay of reality scattered by time. He remarked:

A yogi should cooperate with time and allow it to manage everything except his yoga practice. For yoga practice the yogi may have to squeeze it into the daily schedule. When time eases, when the social obligations decrease for a time, the yogi should accelerate the practice and know that nature may again cause reduction of practice, when it presents social obligations again. Social service should be rendered with a positive attitude, with no resentment or sulking. No matter how great one is or how great ideas one nurtures, the body may need help from others in its elderly years or if it is damaged or diseased early on.

The uselessness of physical existence does not in any way eliminate it. A yogi's obligations for services received from others in the present or in past lives, do not cancel. One must reimburse for the services on the schedule which is laid out by Time. One will never be the master of that fate. There is such a master in the form of Krishna's Vishvarupa, his Universal Form.

Saying that Krishna is not the master of time and that we are makes no sense, no more than a prisoner who is sentenced gives the argument that he is a human being and the judge is a human being. Therefore, the judge cannot have punitive authority. It is a good argument but in real terms it has no value. It is better to assume that a Supreme Being controls this. Whosoever that person is, he/she is the architect of time.

It is not that one has to reimburse every past obligation. That is not the point. Yogis who are liberated no longer deal with the issue of the supervisory time but so long as one is not liberated one would be sensible to be prompt in reciprocating with time, otherwise even one's attempts at spiritual disciplines will be thwarted. It just happens to be a fact that time has this situation under rigid control.

Whatever is due for others because of past services rendered, will be acquired by them either willingly or by force. No matter what one's philosophy is and no matter if one feels that personality is an aberration or illusion, one will still have to pay voluntarily or as inconvenienced by the pressures put on by Time.

Paranormal Powers

One thing is certain. The use of psychic ability for purposes other than self-purification is not approved in yoga. However, for ulterior motives and for military conquest, there was extensive use of it in the time of the *Mahabharata*.

The big difference between defense of the body and defense of the soul is that, in defense of the body you have to be concerned with other entities, while with defense of the soul, your only concern is the components in your individual psyche. There are enemies in the psyche itself. One either has to defeat them or be defeated by them.

What happens is that as one advances, the paranormal powers increase but if one uses it to be a superman in the physical world, the spiritual progress decreases as the physical footing increases. Eventually if one misuses the paranormal powers, nature and society will react in an unfavorable way.

The proper procedure is that as you advance and your paranormal powers increase you use them to put the psyche in order and to get closer and closer to divine status. What happens is that many people are not trusting of direction from others. Due to that when they advance in meditation, they are left to their own devices which means to the influence of their kundalinis, analytical mental operations and sensual preferences. That causes confusion and flawed actions. It is important to have a yoga guru and to adhere to his demands for good behavior.

When we were kids, we did certain good things because adults insisted. As soon as they were absent, we diverted. That proves that by nature we were mischievous. Since that is the case, as a yogi one should use that experience by tying oneself to a worthy elevated good behaved guru, a person with whom one is not encouraged in anti-social acts which nature may react to unfavorably.

There is a story about a disciple who was given a rooster by a guru. The disciple was told to go out of sight and kill the bird in a lonesome place. The student went into a forest and killed the animal. Another disciple was sent with another rooster. The guru told him the same thing but after a few days he returned with the rooster. When asked why the bird was not killed, he explained that he could find no place where either the sun, moon, elements, atmosphere and insects did not observe everything.

There are two kinds of people, the supersensitive ones like the second disciple who could not kill the bird and the insensitive ones like the one who wasted no time disposing the animal. It depends on what kind of person you are. If you are supersensitive you may attain perfection without a guru's constant supervision. But if you are an insensitive person, you should constantly check with the yoga guru.

Sometimes when one sees the future effects and know that they are unfavorable, one is still compelled for a suicidal act. That is when the opinion of a guru helps.

Say for example, I see that an act will cause negative reaction in some other life. Because of compulsion, I still feel to do that act. Then because of being accountable to a yoga guru, I may resist the urge to act in that detrimental way.

Yogesh advised about paranormal powers. He said,

Do not use the power unless it helps you to go higher in meditation practice. Do not exhibit the power to others.

I was sick recently. Rishi Singh Gherwal came about three hours before I took a partial anesthesia and during the time when part of my body was paralyzed by the drug. To get that association, one must be a loyal and respectful student. Suppose I pass from this body suddenly, then will I, all by myself, reach the divine levels of existence?

One should use one's intelligence and act in one's long ranged interest and not do anything stupid which causes one to become spiritually stunted.

There is nothing in this world that we did by ourselves and yet we have these fantasy ideas that we do not have to take help from anybody for spiritual progress and that we do not have spiritual seniors and that we are God and we are absolute. The scope of this is ridiculous.

Rishi on Patanjali's Instruction

One consideration in meditation practice is to know what another teacher did and to see clearly one's action which is different to that instructor. Because of a strong sense of insecurity, a meditator may try to write his or her practice into the process of another teacher.

This morning I had a visit from Rishi Singh Gherwal but it was a remote visit. This means when a yogi comes to a student from a remote place but does not come to the student. One senses a projection of the teacher's presence. One hears a small voice speaking.

The senior yogi gave advice on what to do if one manages to master the procedure stipulated by Patanjali in the second sutra. This sutra says this:

yogah chittavritti nirodhah

Which is to say that yoga is essentially the termination of the mental and emotional fluctuations in the psyche.

To be clear and so as not to let anyone preempt him and give another meaning for what he stressed, Patanjali said that there were five vrittis. He listed them as

- accurate perception
- inaccurate perception
- imagination
- sleep
- memory

When these aspects are curtailed and when they stop operating in meditation, one reached the fundamental level required for transcendence.

Rishi said this:

Suppose someone does pranayama *breath infusion and attains the stage required for Patanjali practice, then what?*

Comb through Patanjali to get details? What did he say about the next stage? Remember that we discuss Patanjali, not what I said or what you said or what another teacher said. We examine the method of Patanjali.

In the meantime, until one can find the next step in his sutras, do this:

Gather the mental and emotional energy. Keep it gathered like you would a concentrated energy. I give that as the next stage. I did not say that Patanjali gave that. There is no need to be dishonest with Patanjali.

Check his sutras. Know his next stage. In the meantime, use my instruction.

After doing thorough breath infusion, which results in interiorization, introspection, Patanjali instructs one to do dharana, *which is the first of that three sequential highest states* (samyama).

The stage after dharana *is* dhyana. *If* dhyana *is completed the meditator may move higher into* samadhi *absorption of whatever principle or reality he or she was focused on.*

There is only one thing that may upset samyama *which is memory. Memory is dormant in the psyche but it may present an impression which attracts the yogi from the objective. When that happens, he may not realize that influence. Patanjali gave an alert about this when he explained that the mental and emotional energy* (chittavritti) *may make itself the motivation for a meditation, and then the yogi will obviously be taken on a wild goose chase and will lose track of the objective.*

The way to beat this deviation is to practice regularly and be vigilant to observe the alterations in consciousness. Another important effort is to complete the first stage of samyama *with great patience. That is* dharana *which is the deliberate focus on the objective. If the yogi is careless with* dharana *and does not do it proficiently, or if he is lax with it and did not master it, he will not have the momentum to keep the desired focus when* dharana *develops into* dhyana. *He will find himself in a lost zone of consciousness during the session.*

Let me review the three stages of samyama:

- dharana: *using all gathered energy of the self and focusing that energy on something or someone which is transcendental.*

- dhyana: *using all energy of the self and having a natural effortless focus on something or someone which is transcendental.*

- samadhi: *using all energy of the self and having a natural effortless but continuous focus on something or someone which is transcendental.*

Some say that samadhi *is an egoless state. I say that in my experience it is not so. It is a state in which the ego is present but it not asserted or applied.*

Memory Thoughts in Meditation

During meditation some long-lost memories arose. These were sneaky powerful memories which had a compelling force for viewing. These were formed originally with a *must-see* force such that when they would be expanded in the mind, I would be compelled to view them.

Question is. How is it that a memory from say forty years ago, can surface as a compulsion energy, such that even a yogi must view it?

It is cute to see thoughts and memories in the mind and to not observe if they are compelling or not, because one can keep on with a practice with the nice idea that one is advanced. But if one gages whether the thoughts are compelling or not or gages the degree of one's resistance, one will really become advanced. Not all thoughts have the same compelling influence.

Extroversion during Introversion (June 26, 2011)

This morning while doing exercises, kundalini attacked the lower torso, the inner area where the lower and higher intestines are housed. It felt like compressed pearly drops of energy bristling with bliss force. At one time I was caught off-guard when kundalini came up into the head. This is not good. When doing kundalini yoga, one should be attentive to energy developments. Any slight movement or supercharge of kundalini should be noted.

The main reason for not tracking kundalini's micro-movements is the natural inability to introspect. Most people have no idea that the human psyche is against introspection. It is hard to admit that. Many people feel that spiritual glory is natural. They claim that it is God-given or nature-given.

However, I state emphatically that introspection is unnatural. It is so unnatural that even when one meditates, there is extroversion within the psyche.

In meditation, there is an external environment in the mind. If during meditation one is involved in that external environment, one is not introspecting internally. When doing kundalini yoga, if one finds that one is occupied with thoughts, one is not attentive. One is not introspecting even though one is in the mind.

Normal Instinct

The problem with the coreSelf is that it is conditioned by the analytical process in the mind and by the sensual preferences of the psyche.

But the core does not understand how it is conditioned. This ignorance causes it to make decisions which deprives it of having the upper hand. So long as the core is influenced by the sensual energies and the rapid analytical functions of the mind, it will be reluctant to have an interest in arousing kundalini through the spine.

In the astral world, I notice that most people whom I meet who still use physical bodies, remain interested in sexual life, no matter what. Most of these persons have sex in the back of their minds and it is not that this is something which they deliberately do.

It is instinctual. Such persons have no interest in making the endeavor to raise kundalini. They do not see the need for it. They are awarded a natural way to do that which is sexual expression and enjoyment. They feel absolutely no need to endeavor in a practice like kundalini yoga.

Many people inquire about kundalini yoga and then the interest disappears. The psyche is unwilling to do anything with kundalini which nature did not encourage as being natural.

Thought Speed

During the exercises, kundalini rose frequently. In one experience it rose through the trunk of the body evenly. It went to the front of the throat and disappeared. In the throat there was a vortex which drew kundalini into it. Kundalini disappeared on the other side of the vortex.

This felt like trillions of little pearl drops of menthol bliss energy compacted and moving upward smoothly until it narrowed into becoming a streak of light and then disappearing into a vortex.

When I sat to meditate, I did so after much infusement of breath energy into the head. At first, I was aware of naad sound by the right ear. Then I lost track of it for some time. There was a thought but it moved in slow motion, so that instead of flashing for just a second, it lasted for three minutes. I realized that I peered at its formation. Then I refocused on naad. This happened five times.

As a Student in the Hare Krishna Ashram

Last night I was in association with two persons who were sannyasis of repute in the Hare Krishna Movement. Both individuals came to ruin. One misused political power in the spiritual society. The other was blighted through female association.

Sannyasis take a vow to forgo female sexual association. If they are found to indulge in intimate relationships with women, their status as monks is imperiled.

Both persons said that I should surely lecture and write. The second one offered me the seat of the lecturer in the hall in which we discussed some topics about presenting the teachings of the *Bhagavad Gita*.

Their idea was that the *Bhagavad Gita* can be taught in a series of booklets, with each of the ideas in the *Gita* presented in very simply easy-to-read terms.

I listened to their ideas. More or less, these persons are hashing over their failures to maintain themselves as monks. Due to mistakes, their purpose for taking their present bodies was foiled. Now they are desperate to get their disciples to help them to fulfill the purpose. They fail in the effort to get disciples to write books, give lectures and keep on the course of fulfilling a spiritual mission for giving information from *Bhagavad Gita*.

For my own part, I will get some information published. I am pressed for time. There is little chance that I can help anyone in what he or she was supposed to do.

Time is such that one can hardly take care of the mission one took a body to fulfill. Hence, there is little chance that one could work to assist others.

One sannyasi's idea was to make at least 18 books or more out of *Bhagavad Gita*. Eighteen is the number of chapters of the text. His view was that one should sort the various topics and write on each in a simply way.

The other's idea was to sit with disciples and determine what they need to know from the Gita, then get those ideas in books and then train disciples to go directly to the Gita, research it and find solutions to their problems. He was convinced that every human problem had a solution in the Gita.

These are good ideas but from the view of yoga practice, students should search for psychological techniques for reforming the individual self. Thus, the information in the *Gita* which refers to that is utilized. One should learn how to use the information to reform and change the psyche.

It is funny in a way that one swami asked me to get involved in his writing mission. When I sat at his feet, as one was compelled to at his ashram, I had to wait a week, or two or three even, to get him to review two or three pages of writing. At that time, he was the swami senior. To get near to him, to get him to look at anything, one had to bow low and follow his system.

He was busy with other matters like building golden temples for his guru and supervising hundreds of disciples. He had no time for writing.

I remember that when I first went to his ashram, he was interested in the fact that his guru instructed me years before to write a *Bhagavad Gita* for children. When I presented the manuscript to him, he looked at it and smiled and said that some of it was not authorized.

As it was in such situations, I agreed. With his permission I began publishing a few small magazines. I printed them with a ditto machine. Other persons in the ashram were astonished. Some even said that the magazines were contraband and were not authorized, even though unknown to them I submitted the literature to him for approval. He reviewed it at leisure. He marked it up. He called me a few days after and make comments, criticizing anything that was not consistent with what he was taught by his guru.

His procedure was one of full submission, both superficially and in real terms. Some others in the ashram were astonished how I published even within a month after arriving there but I used to have private talks with him and I knew how to be a student.

As a student one should be submissive. It is not a game. One should be genuinely submissive if one is to learn from another person. The sannyasi was flawed in many ways but that did not prevent me from learning from him. I had to learn of the standards of the lineage. He was not the kind of person to teach anything to anyone who was insubmissive.

In his dealings with his teacher, he was an ideal student. In turn if one wanted to learn from him, one had to be sincere.

I went to him early in the morning around 7 am. I would bow, sit and wait. On some occasions, he simply ignored me. On some other occasions he would be glad to see me. At other times, I was like a needless bothersome insect. As a student one should overlook neglect and maintain the reliance on the teacher.

Within a short time, due to being a student, I got the message from him about what it was to be a writer in the disciplic succession which came through his guru.

Once when I decided to leave the ashram, I did not inform him. However, as fate would have it, he sent a message for me to visit him. When I arrived, I sat and waited. After a time, he came. He stood over me and said that he wanted me to take a preaching center in another city.

It was like this,

"We need a leader there, a swami. You are done with married life (grihasta). Go there and supervise the preaching."

I looked at him. I was appalled. I still had infants. I was still responsible for the two women who were the mothers of those children. Because his guru's method was to herd children into a boarding school system which was called gurukula, he did not figure those factors into the equation. And as for spouses, they were engaged in devotional service which was any activity conducted by the society. Soon after that within three weeks I left the ashram.

Some months after this swami's legal difficulties began with his having to serve a jail term in the US Federal system.

Preaching to people is not my mission. My mission is simply to get myself out of this natural world and to leave behind a record of how I did it. Otherwise I have no concern with anything here.

I wrote three commentaries on *Bhagavad Gita*. Recently Swami Rama and Rishi Singh Gherwal requested that I translate the Anu *Gita* which is an instruction given to Arjuna after the *Bhagavad Gita* was explained. I am not concerned with writing books to give lectures or to section the *Bhagavad Gita* into parts. I publish books but the problem is how to put the principles described into practice.

Index

About the Author

Michael Beloved (Yogi *Madhvāchārya)* took his current body in 1951 in Guyana. In 1965, while living in Trinidad, he instinctively began doing yoga postures and tried to make sense of the supernatural side of life.

Later in 1970, in the Philippines, he approached a Martial Arts Master named Arthur Beverford. He explained to the teacher that he was seeking a yoga instructor. Mr. Beverford identified himself as an advanced disciple of *Śrī* Rishi Singh Gherwal, an Ashtanga Yoga master.

Beverford taught the traditional Ashtanga Yoga with stress on postures, attentive breathing and brow chakra centering meditation. In 1972, Michael entered the Denver, Colorado Ashram of *kundalini* yoga Master *Śrī* Harbhajan Singh. There he took instruction in bhastrika pranayama and its application to yoga postures. He was supervised mostly by Yogi Bhajan's disciple named Prem Kaur.

In 1979 Michael formally entered the disciplic succession of the Brahmā - Madhava-Gaudiya Sampradaya through *Swāmī* Kirtanananda, who was a prominent sannyasi disciple of the Great Vaishnava Authority *Śrī Swāmī* Bhaktivedanta Prabhupada, the exponent of devotion to Sri Krishna.

However, yoga has a mystic side to it, thus Michael took training and teaching empowerment from several spiritual masters of different aspects of spiritual development. This is consistent with *Śrī* Krishna's advice to Arjuna in the *Bhagavad Gītā*:

Most of the instructions Michael received were given in the astral world. On that side of existence, his most prominent teachers were *Śrī Swāmī* Shivananda of Rishikesh, Yogiraj *Swāmī* Vishnudevananda, *Śrī Bābāji Mahasaya* - the master of the masters of *Kriyā* Yoga, *Śrīla* Yogeshwarananda of Gangotri - the master of the masters of *Rāj* Yoga (spiritual clarity), and Siddha *Swāmī* Nityananda the Brahmā Yoga authority.

The course for kundalini yoga using pranayama breath-infusion was detailed by Michael in the book *Kundalini Hatha Yoga Pradipika*. This current book was composed from meditation and breath-infusion notes which were originally shared in staple bound booklets as Yoga Journals.

Michael's preliminary books relating to this topic are *Meditation Pictorial*, *Meditation Expertise*, and *Meditation ~ Sense Faculty* (co-author). Every technique (kriya) mentioned was tested by him during pranayama breath-infusion and *samyama* deep meditation practice.

This is a result of over forty years of meditation practice with astute subtle observations intending to share the methods and experiences. The information is published freely with no intention of forming an institution or hogtying anyone as a disciple.

Publications

English Series

Bhagavad Gita English

Anu Gita English

Markandeya Samasya English

Yoga Sutras English

Hatha Yoga Pradipika English

Uddhava Gita English

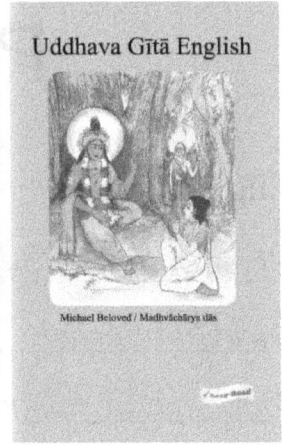

These are in 21st Century English, very precise and exacting. Many Sanskrit words which were considered untranslatable into a Western language are rendered in precise, expressive and modern English.

Three of these books are instructions from Krishna. **In Bhagavad Gita English** and **Anu Gita English**, the instructions were for Arjuna. In the **Uddhava Gita English,** it was for Uddhava. Bhagavad Gita and Anu Gita are extracted from the Mahabharata. Uddhava Gita was extracted from the 11th Canto of the Srimad Bhagavatam (Bhagavata Purana). One of these books, the **Markandeya Samasya English** is about Krishna, as described by Yogi Markandeya, who survived the cosmic collapse and reached a divine child in whose transcendental body, the collapsed world was existing.

Two of this series are the syllabus about yoga practice. The Yoga Sutras of Patañjali is elaboration about ashtanga yoga. Hatha Yoga Pradipika English, is the detailed information about asana postures, pranayama breath-infusion, energy compression, naad sound resonance and advanced meditation. The Sanskrit author is Swatmarama Mahayogin.

My suggestion is that you read **Bhagavad Gita English**, the **Anu Gita English, the Markandeya Samasya English,** the **Yoga Sutras English,** the **Hatha Yoga Pradipika** and lastly the **Uddhava Gita English**, which is complicated and detailed.

For each of these books we have at least one commentary, which is published separately. Thus one's particular interest can be researched further in the commentaries.

The smallest of these commentaries and perhaps the simplest is the one for the Anu Gita. We published its commentary as the Anu Gita Explained. The Bhagavad Gita explanations were published in three distinct targeted commentaries. The first is Bhagavad Gita Explained, which sheds lights on how people in the time of Krishna and Arjuna regarded the information and applied it. Bhagavad Gita is an exposition of the application of yoga practice to cultural activities, which is known in the Sanskrit language as karma yoga.

Interestingly, Bhagavad Gita was spoken on a battlefield just before one of the greatest battles in the ancient world. A warrior, Arjuna, lost his wits and had no idea that he could apply his training in yoga to political dealings. Krishna, his charioteer, lectured on the spur of the moment to give Arjuna the skill of using yoga proficiency in cultural dealings including how to deal with corrupt officials on a battlefield.

The second Gita commentary is the Kriya Yoga Bhagavad Gita. This clears the air about Krishna's information on the science of kriya yoga, showing that its techniques are clearly described for anyone who takes the time to read Bhagavad Gita. Kriya yoga concerns the battlefield which is the psyche of the living being. The internal war and the mental and emotional forces which are hostile to self-realization are dealt with in the kriya yoga practice.

The third commentary is the Brahma Yoga Bhagavad Gita. This shows what Krishna had to say outright and what he hinted about which concerns the brahma yoga practice, a mystic process for those who mastered kriya yoga.

There is one commentary for the **Markandeya Samasya English**. The title of that publication is Krishna Cosmic Body.

There are two commentaries to the Yoga Sutras. One is the Yoga Sutras of Patañjali and the other is the Meditation Expertise. These give detailed explanations of ashtanga Yoga.

The commentary of Hatha Yoga Pradipika is titled Kundalini Hatha Yoga Pradipika.

For the Uddhava Gita, we published the Uddhava Gita Explained. This is a large book and requires concentration and study for integration of the information. Of the books which deal with transcendental topics, my opinion is that the discourse between Krishna and Uddhava has the complete information about the realities in existence. This book is the one which removes massive existential ignorance.

Meditation Series

Meditation Pictorial

Meditation Expertise

CoreSelf Discovery

Meditation Sense Faculty

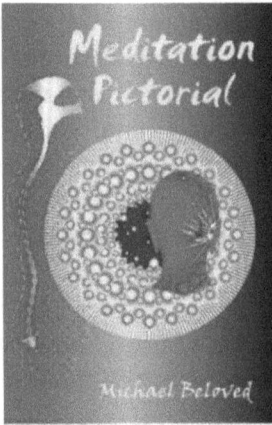

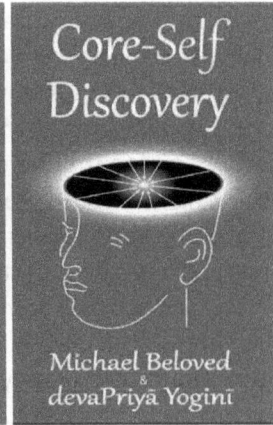

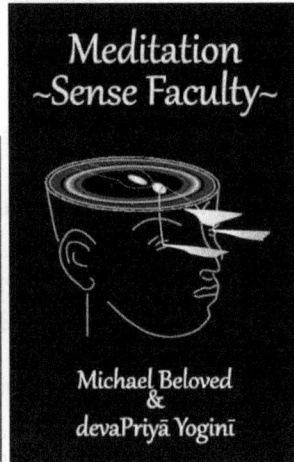

The specialty of these books is the mind diagrams which profusely illustrate what is written. This shows exactly what one has to do mentally to develop and then sustain a meditation practice.

In the **Meditation Pictorial,** one is shown how to develop psychic insight, a feature without which meditation is imagination and visualization, without any mystic experience per se.

In the **Meditation Expertise,** one is shown how to corral one's practice to bring it in line with the classic syllabus of yoga which Patañjali lays out as the ashtanga yoga eight-staged practice.

In **CoreSelf Discovery,** (co-authored with *devaPriya Yogini*) one is taken though the course of pratyahar sensual energy withdrawal which is the 5th stage of yoga in the Patañjali ashtanga eight-process complete system of yoga practice. These events lead to the discovery of a coreSelf which is surrounded by psychic organs in the head of the subtle body. This product has a DVD component.

Meditation ~ Sense Faculty (co-authored with *devaPriya Yogini*) is a detailed tutorial with profuse diagrams showing what actions to take in the subtle body to investigate the senses faculties. The meditator must first establish the location and function of the observing self. That self must be screened from the thoughts and ideas which usually hypnotize it.

These books are profusely illustrated with mind diagrams showing the components of psychic consciousness and the inner design of the subtle body.

Explained Series

Bhagavad Gita Explained

Uddhava Gita Explained

Anu Gita Explained

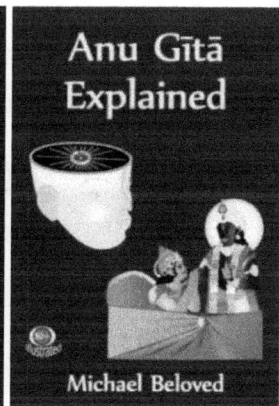

The specialty of these books is that they are free of missionary intentions, cult tactics and philosophical distortion. Instead of using these books to add credence to a philosophy, meditation process, belief or plea for followers, I spread the information out so that a reader can look through this literature and freely take or leave anything as desired.

When Krishna stressed himself as God, I stated that. When Krishna laid no claims for supremacy, I showed that. The reader is left to form an independent opinion about the validity of the information and the credibility of Krishna.

There is a difference in the discourse with Arjuna in the Bhagavad Gita and the one with Uddhava in the Uddhava Gita. In fact these two books may appear to contradict each other. In the Bhagavad Gita, Krishna pressured Arjuna to complete social duties. In the Uddhava Gita, Krishna insisted that Uddhava should abandon the same.

The Anu Gita is not as popular as the Bhagavad Gita but it is the conclusion of that text. Anu means what is to follow, what proceeds. In this discourse, an anxious Arjuna request that Krishna should repeat the Bhagavad Gita and again show His supernatural and divine forms.

However Krishna refuses to do so and chastises Arjuna for being a disappointment in forgetting what was revealed. Krishna then cited a celestial yogi, a near-perfected being, who explained the process of transmigration in vivid detail.

Commentaries

Yoga Sutras of Patañjali

Meditation Expertise

Krishna Cosmic Body

Anu Gita Explained

Bhagavad Gita Explained

Kriya Yoga Bhagavad Gita

Brahma Yoga Bhagavad Gita

Uddhava Gita Explained

Kundalini Hatha Yoga Pradipika

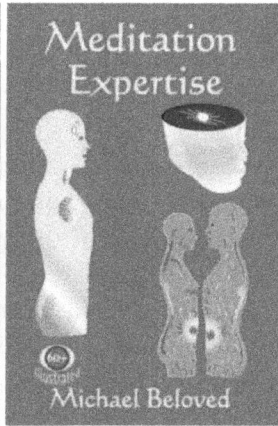

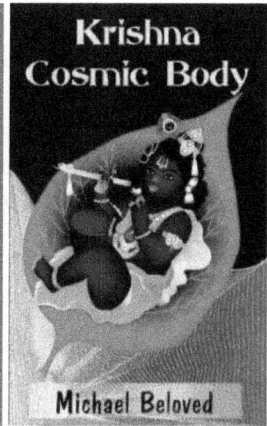

Yoga Sutras of Patañjali is the globally acclaimed text book of yoga. This has detailed expositions of yoga techniques. Many kriya techniques are vividly described in the commentary.

Meditation Expertise is an analysis and application of the Yoga Sutras. This book is loaded with illustrations and has detailed explanations of secretive advanced meditation techniques which are called kriyas in the Sanskrit language.

Krishna Cosmic Body is a narrative commentary on the Markandeya Samasya portion of the Aranyaka Parva of the Mahabharata. This is the detailed description of the dissolution of the world, as experienced by the great yogin Markandeya who transcended the cosmic deity, Brahma, and reached Brahma's source who is the divine infant, Krishna.

Anu Gita Explained is a detailed explanation of how we endure many material bodies in the course of transmigrating through various life-forms. This is a discourse between Krishna and Arjuna. Arjuna requested of Krishna a display of the Universal Form and a repeat narration of the Bhagavad Gita but Krishna declined and explained what a siddha perfected being told the Yadu family about the sequence of existences one endures and the systematic flow of those lives at the convenience of material nature.

Bhagavad Gita Explained shows what was said in the Gita without religious overtones and sectarian biases.

Kriya Yoga Bhagavad Gita shows the instructions for those who are doing kriya yoga.

Brahma Yoga Bhagavad Gita shows the instructions for those who are doing brahma yoga.

Uddhava Gita Explained shows the instructions to Uddhava which are more advanced than the ones given to Arjuna.

Bhagavad Gita is an instruction for applying the expertise of yoga in the cultural field. This is why the process taught to Arjuna is called karma yoga which means karma + yoga or cultural activities done with yogic insight.

Uddhava Gita is an instruction for apply the expertise of yoga to attaining spiritual status. This is why it explains jnana yoga and bhakti yoga in detail. Jnana yoga is using mystic skill for knowing the spiritual part of existence. Bhakti yoga is for developing affectionate relationships with divine beings.

Karma yoga is for negotiating the social concerns in the material world. It is inferior to bhakti yoga which concerns negotiating the social concerns in the spiritual world.

This world has a social environment. The spiritual world has one too.

Currently, Uddhava Gita is the most advanced and informative spiritual book on the planet. There is nothing anywhere which is superior to it or which goes into so much detail as it. It verified that historically Krishna is the most advanced human being to ever have left literary instructions on this planet.

Even Patañjali Yoga Sutras which I translated and gave an application for in my book, **Meditation Expertise**, does not go as far as the Uddhava Gita.

Some of the information of these two books is identical but while the Yoga Sutras are concerned with the personal spiritual emancipation (kaivalyam) of the individual spirits, the Uddhava Gita explains that and also explains the situations in the spiritual universes.

Bhagavad Gita is from the *Mahabharata* which is the history of the Pandavas. Arjuna, the student of the Gita, is one of the Pandavas brothers. He was in a social hassle and did not know how to apply yoga expertise to solve it. On the battlefield, Krishna gave him a crash-course on yogic social interactions.

Uddhava Gita is from the *Srimad Bhagavatam (Bhagavata Purana),* which is a history of the incarnations of Krishna. Uddhava was a relative of Krishna. He was concerned about the situation of the deaths of many of his relatives but Krishna diverted Uddhava's attention to the practice of yoga for the purpose of successfully migrating to the spiritual environment.

Kundalini Hatha Yoga Pradipika is the commentary for the Hatha Yoga Pradipika of Swatmarama Mahayogin. This is the detailed process about asana posture, pranayama breath-infusion, complex compressions of energy, naad sound resonance intonement and advanced meditation practice.

This is the singular book with all the techniques of how to reform and redesign the subtle body so that it does not have the tendency for physical life forms and for it to attain the status of a siddha.

These books are based on the author's experiences in meditation, yoga practice and participation in spiritual groups:

Specialty

Spiritual Master

sex you!

Sleep Paralysis

Astral Projection

Masturbation Psychic Details

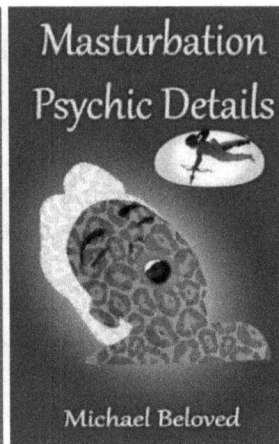

In **Spiritual Master**, Michael draws from experience with gurus or with their senior students. His contact with astral gurus is rated. He walks you through the avenue of gurus showing what you should do and what you should not do, so as to gain proficiency in whatever area of spirituality the guru has proficiency.

sex you! is a masterpiece about the adventures of an individual spirit's passage through the parents' psyches. The conversion of a departed soul into a sexual urge is described. The transit from the afterlife to residency in the emotions of the parents is detailed. This is about sex and you. Learn about how much of you comprises the romantic energy of one's would-be parents!

Sleep Paralysis clears misconceptions so that one can see what sleep paralysis is and what frightening astral experience occurs while the paralysis is being experienced. This disempowerment has great value in giving you confidence that you can and do exist even if one is unable to operate the physical body. The implication is that one can exist apart from and will survive the loss of the material form.

Astral Projection details experiences Michael had even in childhood, where he assumed incorrectly that everyone was astrally conversant. He discusses the lifeForce psychic mechanism which operates the sleep-wake cycle of the physical form, and which budgets energy into the separated astral form which determines if the individual will have dream recall or no objective awareness during the projections. Astral travel happens on every occasion when the physical body sleeps. What is missing in awareness is the observer status while the astral body is separated.

Masturbation Psychic Details is a surprise presentation which relates what happens on the psychic plane during a masturbation event. This does not tackle moral issues or even addictions but shows the involvement of memory and the sure but hidden subconscious mind which operates many features of the psyche irrespective of the desire or approval of the self-conscious personality.

inVision Series

Yoga inVision 1

Yoga inVision 2

Yoga inVision 3

Yoga inVision 4

Yoga inVision 5

Yoga inVision 6

Yoga inVision 7

Yoga inVision 8

Yoga inVision 1
Michael Beloved

Yoga inVision 2
Michael Beloved

Yoga inVision 3
Michael Beloved

Yoga inVision 4
Michael Beloved

Yoga inVision 5
Michael Beloved

Yoga inVision 6
Michael Beloved

Yoga inVision 7
Michael Beloved

Yoga inVision 8
Michael Beloved

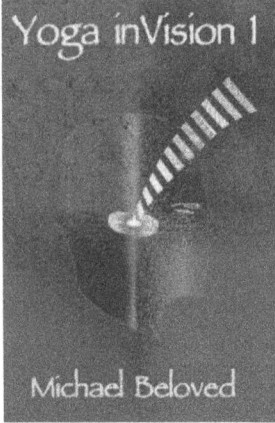

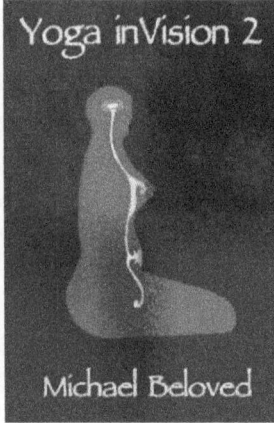

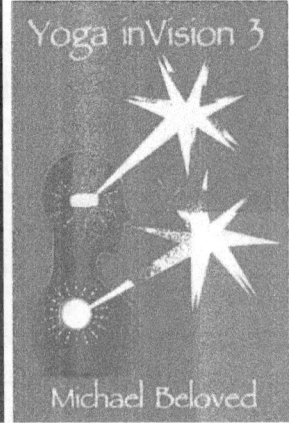

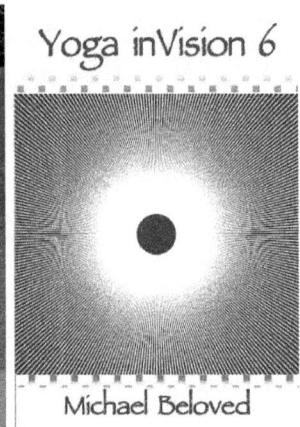

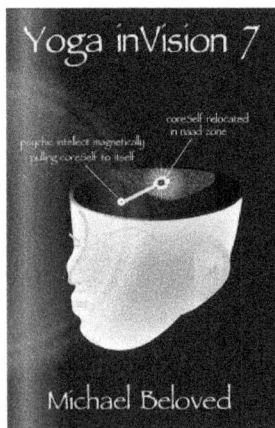

Yoga inVision 1, the first in this series, describes the breath-infusion and meditation practices during the years of 1998 and 1999. There are unique, once in a lifetime as well as recurring insights which are elaborated. inFocus during breath-infusion and the meditation which follows is an adventure for any yogi. This gives what happened to this particular ascetic.

Yoga inVision 2 reports on the author's experiences from 1999 to 2001. Each day the experience is unique, illustrating the vibrancy of practice. Many rare once-in-a-lifetime perceptions are described.

Yoga inVision 3 reports on the author's experiences from 2001 to 2003.
Yoga inVision 4 reports on the author's experiences from 2006 to 2009.
Yoga inVision 5 reports on the author's experiences from 2006 to 2008.
Yoga inVision 6 reports on the author's experiences in 2010.
Yoga inVision 7 reports on the author's experiences in 2011.
Yoga inVision 8 reports on the author's experiences in 2011.

Online Resources

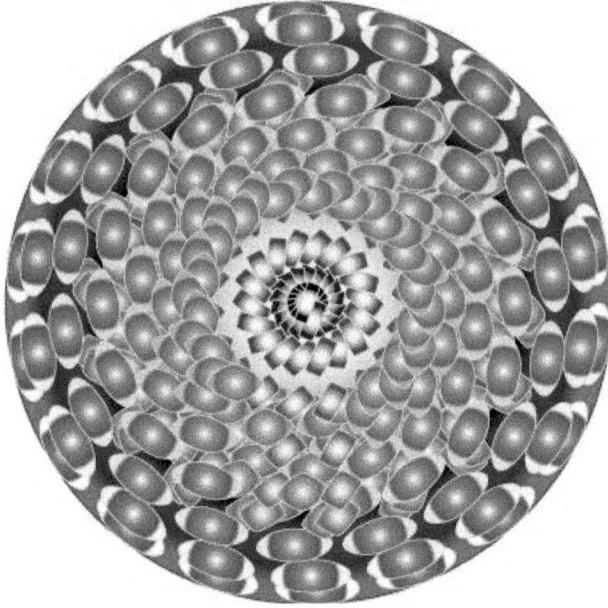

Email: michaelbelovedbooks@gmail.com
axisnexus@gmail.com

Website: michaelbeloved.com

Forum: inselfyoga.com

Posters: zazzle.com/inself

www.ingramcontent.com/pod-product-compliance
Lightning Source LLC
Chambersburg PA
CBHW072341090426

42741CB00012B/2878